The Dark Matter of Children's 'Fantastika' Literature

Bloomsbury Perspectives on Children's Literature

Bloomsbury Perspectives on Children's Literature seeks to expand the range and quality of research in children's literature through publishing innovative monographs by leading and rising scholars in the field. With an emphasis on cross and interdisciplinary studies, this series takes literary approaches as a starting point, drawing on the particular capacity for children's literature to open out into other disciplines.

Titles in the Series:

Adulthood in Children's Literature, Vanessa Joosen
The Courage to Imagine: The Child Hero in Children's Literature, Roni Natov
Ethics in British Children's Literature: Unexamined Life, Lisa Sainsbury
Fashioning Alice: The Career of Lewis Carroll's Icon, 1860-1901, Kiera Vaclavik
From Tongue to Text: A New Reading of Children's Poetry, Debbie Pullinger
Literature's Children: The Critical Child and the Art of Idealisation, Louise Joy
Rereading Childhood Books: A Poetics, Alison Waller
Irish Children's Literature and the Poetics of Memory, Rebecca Long
Metaphysics of Children's Literature, Lisa Sainsbury
British Children's Literature and Material Culture, Jane Suzanne Carroll
Space, Place and Children's Reading Development, Margaret Mackey
British Activist Authors Addressing Children of Colour by Karen Sands-O'Connor

Forthcoming Titles:

British Children's Literature in Japanese Culture: Wonderlands and Looking-Glasses, Catherine Butler
Marketing Chinese Children's Books, Frances Weightman

The Dark Matter of Children's 'Fantastika' Literature

Speculative Entanglements

Chloé Germaine

BLOOMSBURY ACADEMIC
LONDON • NEW YORK • OXFORD • NEW DELHI • SYDNEY

BLOOMSBURY ACADEMIC
Bloomsbury Publishing Plc
50 Bedford Square, London, WC1B 3DP, UK
1385 Broadway, New York, NY 10018, USA
29 Earlsfort Terrace, Dublin 2, Ireland

BLOOMSBURY, BLOOMSBURY ACADEMIC and the Diana logo are trademarks of Bloomsbury Publishing Plc

First published in Great Britain 2023
Paperback edition published in 2025

Cover design: Eleanor Rose
Cover image © ansoz/ Shutterstock

A catalogue record for this book is available from the British Library.

A catalog record for this book is available from the Library of Congress.

Library of Congress Cataloging-in-Publication Data

Names: Germaine, Chloé, author.
Title: The dark matter of children's 'fantastika' literature : speculative entanglements / Chloe´ Germaine.
Description: London ; New York : Bloomsbury Academic, 2023. | Series: Bloomsbury perspectives on children's literature | Includes bibliographical references and index.
Identifiers: LCCN 2023017691 | ISBN 9781350167018 (hardback) | ISBN 9781350417274 (paperback) | ISBN 9781350167025 (pdf) | ISBN 9781350167032 (epub)
Subjects: LCSH: Fantasy fiction, English–History and criticism. | Speculative fiction, English–History and criticism. | Young adult fiction, English–History and criticism. | Children's stories, English–History and criticism. | English fiction–21st century–History and criticism. | Fantasy fiction, American–History and criticism. | Speculative fiction, American–History and criticism. | Young adult fiction, American–History and criticism. | Children's stories, American–History and criticism. | American fiction–21st century–History and criticism. | LCGFT: Literary criticism.
Classification: LCC PR830.F3 D37 2023 | DDC 823/.0876099282–dc23/eng/20230622
LC record available at https://lccn.loc.gov/2023017691

ISBN: HB: 978-1-3501-6701-8
PB: 978-1-3504-1727-4
ePDF: 978-1-3501-6702-5
eBook: 978-1-3501-6703-2

Series: Bloomsbury Perspectives on Children's Literature

Typeset by Deanta Global Publishing Services, Chennai, India

To find out more about our authors and books visit www.bloomsbury.com and sign up for our newsletters.

For PFW
we're in this together now

Contents

Acknowledgements

I wrote this book during a difficult time, and I am grateful for the generosity and friendship of many people without which I would have given up the whole endeavour. I hope I've included everyone here. I owe a debt to Jonathan Newell for the genesis of this book and for our discussions of philosophy and literature that date back to 2015. The book would not exist without our late-night chats in far-flung places. Thank you for them and for your friendship, which continues to be very important to me. Thank you to Nick Mizer, Brian Onishi, and Nathan Bell of the ecoweird reading group. I am also grateful to academic communities who support research around key themes important to this book. These include the International Gothic Association, the *Gothic Nature* journal and online community, the British Society for Literature and Science, the YA Studies Association, and the *Fantastika* journal and conference. I am indebted to the work of Chuckie Palmer-Patel and Kerry Dodd in fostering research community around the literatures of Fantastika. Thank you to my PhD students at Manchester Metropolitan University, especially Leone Betts, Fredrik Blanc, Ezeiyoke Chukwunonso, Nicole Dittmer, Charlotte Gislam, Connie Hamilton, and Jack Warren. Conversations with you helped to shape the ideas in this book. I am grateful to various people for the opportunity to share my work in progress in supportive venues. Many thanks to the University of Glasgow's School of Critical Studies for the opportunity to talk about my work on minds and machines and giving me generous feedback. Thanks also to the organizers of at GifCon, the YASA conference, the BSLS annual conference, and various IGA conferences over the years for providing a supportive space for sharing research. Thank you to Clive Bloom for editing *The Palgrave Handbook of Contemporary Gothic* (2020), in which I was able to develop my concept of occult materialism, to Michelle Smith and Kristine Moruzi for editing *Young Adult Gothic Fiction: Monstrous Selves/Monstrous Others* (2021) and for their helpful feedback on my application of ontoethics to YA literature, to Justin Edwards and Rebecca Duncan for editing the *Edinburgh Companion to Global Gothic* (forthcoming) and for feedback on my ideas about uncanniness, intimacy, and ecology. Many thanks to the Faculty of Arts and Humanities at Manchester Metropolitan University for granting a sabbatical to support the completion of this book at the end of 2021, and to my colleagues in the Manchester Centre for Youth Studies, especially Benjamin Bowman and Hannah Smithson, for their generous support during the past few years. There are several individuals whose academic work and friendship have shaped this book and supported the writing of it. My gratitude especially, to Sara Wasson, Paul Wake, Dale Townshend, James Louis Smith, Jon Newell, Caitlin Nunn, Kevan Manwaring, Laura Kremmel, Daniel Kasper, Sarah Ilott, Matt Foley, Stephen Curtis, Ginette Carpenter, Benjamin Bowman, and Emily Alder, and loads of other brilliant people who inspire and influence me. Thank you to my friends, especially Dale, Meg, Mike, Laura, Louise, Mark, Steve, Sam, Helena, Baz, James, Gina, Kevan, and Craig. Particular thanks to Jon Buckley for his support during our marriage and to mum and dad for being awesome in a crisis. Immense love and thanks to Paul Wake, to whom this book is dedicated. You encouraged me to finish even when things got tough. And to my son, Lucas: I'm always so proud of you. Your enthusiasm for books and ideas and the environment is inspiring.

Introduction

The ontoethics of entanglement in Fantastika fiction

The dark matter of Fantastika

Fantastika is an umbrella term that encompasses multiple modes and genres of fantastic and speculative fiction, all of which, in different ways, explore precarious entanglements of human, animal, and plant life. Throughout this book I claim that the narratives of Fantastika are concerned with the ethics of ecological interrelationships. Here, the word 'ecology' evokes the everyday idea of a natural environment as well as the more specific meaning of webs of interdependent processes that persist across domains of life, from the biological to the social. In this latter sense, 'ecology' is a term that suggests the fundamentally entangled nature of all systems, rendering the distinction between the natural and the cultural at best permeable, if not an outright fabrication. I examine the entangled ecologies of Fantastika, especially those marked by relationships of parasitism, exploitation, vulnerability, and violence, considering these relationships as ontological and ethical matters. In so doing I deploy the term Fantastika in a distinct way to other critics who have used it to describe the genres of fantastic fiction (see, e.g., Clute 2016a; Palmer-Patel and Dodd 2016). My claim is that the literatures of Fantastika offer unique responses to, and mediations of, the condition of ecological belonging, a condition that is simultaneously real and speculative, material and imaginative. Evoking the idea of matter in both senses of the word (materiality, or physical stuff, and meaning, or values), I follow the 'material turn' in philosophy and critical thought that has occurred over the past two decades in my exploration of this claim. 'Dark matter' is thus a phrase I use to describe the physical, bodily, environmental, and otherwise material manifestations of ethical problems in Fantastika. Of course, dark matter also refers to a topic of study in physics and cosmology – to the idea that as much as 95 percent of the matter and energy that comprise the universe is invisible and undetectable. My evocation of this sense of 'dark matter' is likewise deliberate and points to the loosening of epistemological certainty and to the tentative explorations that are necessary in fiction, philosophy, and science. Throughout the book I move between these domains to explore the eco-ethical dark matters that concern Fantastika written for young audiences.

To introduce the idea of dark matter, I begin with three brief examples. The first comes from Hayao Miyazaki's comic, *Nausicäa of the Valley of the Wind* (1982), which predates the animated film of the same name. In the opening panels, dark matter manifests in images of the collapsing landscapes on a dying planet. A lone girl, who turns out to be heir to a precarious kingdom at the edge of the toxic zone, explores a vast forest, a mask over her face to protect from the spores that suffuse the atmosphere. Later she learns that the huge trees of the forest, an expansive fungal network, and colonies of highly intelligent insects, work together to process the fallout of a long-dead human 'civilisation'. Meanwhile, the surviving humans engage in destructive warfare. The heroine, Nausicäa, becomes a mediator between human and more-than-human worlds as she struggles to save her home and those with whom she shares it. Violence and division also characterize the Nigerian American author Tochi Onyebuchi's contemporary young adult (YA) fantasy, *Beasts Made of Night* (2017). In this novel, young Taj is forced to serve corrupt mages and 'eat' the 'sins' of the wealthy elite. These sins materialize as physical monsters regurgitated from within the body of the sinner. Here dark matters are metaphors made flesh, and what ensues is a violent bodily contest that leaves indelible tattoos on Taj's skin, each representing a sin, or creature, he has killed and eaten. Sin-eaters live short, impoverished lives, or go mad, while those whose sins are eaten retain their power over a divided city. As is typical of YA novels, Taj is figured as a hero poised to fight this oppressive system despite his lowly status. Materialist magic and economic degradation also feature in Alex Pheby's British gothic fantasy written for adults, *Mordew* (2020). In the opening pages a starving boy, Nathan, plunges his hands into the 'living mud' that engulfs the slums of the city, desperate to catch a 'deadlife' creature to sell to the tanner for a few coins. Mordew is infused with the sickly light of the 'Master's' magic, which leeches power from the land and its people. As the book progresses, Nathan's own 'spark', which allows him to transform and enliven dead matter, brings him into conflict with this Master, as they struggle for control. These different examples of Fantastika are, despite hailing from distinct periods, genres, and cultural contexts, indicative of a thematic engagement with dark matter and the ethics of the natural-cultural ecologies that entangle humans and more-than-humans in fantastic settings.

Although only one of these books was written for a young audience, each centres on the character of a young person who is represented as being uniquely situated within, vulnerable to, and yet able to transform a damaged world. They demonstrate that in the dark matter of Fantastika young people often carry the weight of responsibility for repairing, saving, or else transforming their worlds. This book addresses such burdens attributed to young people in the dark imaginaries of Fantastika by focusing on texts written for young audiences, including readers identified as older children, a group typically characterized by writers and publishers as beginning at age eight or nine, and young adults, a category that tends to be identified on book jackets as beginning around age twelve. These categories, socially constructed and applied to young audiences by adult gatekeepers, are useful insofar as they allow me to interrogate figurations of young people as they are imagined by adults who feel they are writing about ethical matters that pertain specifically to young people who might be already conscious of them, as opposed to younger children who are typically addressed as being in need of both literary and moral education. In my inclusion of works for older children alongside those for young adults, I follow Alice Curry in deliberately conflating the two categories since, as she argues, both mark essentialist and constructivist values imposed on children in contemporary discourses on childhood (2013: 6). Although the examples I offer earlier suggest that the themes, aesthetics, and ethics I call 'dark matter' extend well beyond writing for young audiences, I contend that Fantastika that explicitly addresses those audiences is alert to, and so able to reflect upon, the material-discursive positioning of young people in entanglements that render them vulnerable, and yet lay heavy responsibilities upon them. Again, this accords with Curry's identification of older children and young adults as identities constructed as borderline, facing 'imminent entry' into systems of adult responsibility, a positioning from which a critique of both essentialist and constructivist values might take place (2013: 6). Historically, a paradoxical construction of childhood has tended to dominate in one form or another: older children are constructed as simultaneously the site of adult desire and expectation, on the one hand, while being silenced or otherwise marginalized from enacting social power in their day-to-day lives on the other.

The contemporary climate crisis provides a particularly fraught context for this paradoxical figuration of young people; it is also a situation that makes reflection on the marginalization of young people from political and social power even more urgent. As I have suggested elsewhere, in relation to gothic literature, reflexiveness tends to be a feature of contemporary writing for young audiences (Germaine Buckley 2018: 15). In that analysis, I demonstrated how such reflexiveness on the figuration of young people in fictional texts produced a generous and nomadic model of subjectivity in contrast to the tragic and pathological models that have tended to dominate in psychoanalytic and literary accounts of childhood and maturation. Continuing to resist these conceptions of young subjectivity, I am less optimistic in the present study than in my previous work because the texts I examine take on a real-world urgency in the contexts of a rapidly worsening global and ecological crisis.

Young people, real-world crisis, and fictional figurations

The lack of meaningful action on the global climate crisis most severely affects the futures of young people. Children calling on governments to act through protests and school strikes recognise this. The watershed moment for youth-led action was 2018, which saw the growth of the Fridays for Future movement through which young people have fostered global solidarity (Pickard, Bowman and Arya 2020). The positive framing of this youth-led action, in sympathetic media coverage for example, often represents young people as climate heroes poised to save the world, but, as Bowman and Germaine point out, this misses the point of the strikes: young people are not interested in saving the world, not in its current form at least, and their action contests their representation as guarantees of continuity from the past into the future (2021: 19). In addition to fraught representations of young people in relation to the climate crisis, young people continue to be marginalized from the political power and institutions where they are calling for change to happen (Thew et al. 2020). As many young people recognize, their global movement means very little if governments and those who wield economic power continue business as usual. In this context, positioning young people as climate heroes and burdening them with the task of sustaining, or saving, society for the future, a society that marginalizes them, further objectifies young people, and constitutes a failure to listen to what they are saying and to take seriously the futures of climate change they wish to bring about. It is in this context that I suggest that the figurations of young people in the dark matters of Fantastika might become a site for much-needed reflection on the ways in which adults respond to young people in terms of the representations we construct and proliferate, as well as the ways in which we might better act as allies in the context of young people's concerns about the future in the real world.

Although it is a discursive site in which adult writers (re)imagine and (re) mediate cultural ideas of childhood and youth, a space in which children are constructed, literature written for young people is a productive means of encountering and thinking through real-world problems such as how young people might exert agency in the face of complex and intersecting ecological and social crises. Though the child is a vital material-semiotic figure in contemporary environmentalism, the issue of their agency is a fraught one. Rebekah Sheldon notes that environmental discourse paradoxically deploys 'a child in need of saving' alongside a 'child who saves', exploring the ways in which the child has become a resource 'freighted with expectations and anxieties about the future' (2016: 2, 3). In her study of contemporary climate fiction written for adults, Adeline Johns-Putra (2019) detects a tendency for narratives to capitulate to a moral framework of posterity that insists on the need to preserve the world for future generations. This moral framework around climate change relies on a normative ethics of parental care that silences children. The situation in youth literature provides a useful counterpoint to this fraught construction of children in adult-led environmental movements and literatures, eschewing the notion of the child as an object of care and tending to focus on the 'child who saves' via heroic young protagonists. Such imaginative constructions of youth agency are replete with problems and contradictions, of course, but they also contain possibilities that tend to be foreclosed in representations of young people that occur in adult fiction. Curry's ecofeminist reading of YA dystopia novels identifies a 'major preoccupation' with the potential for 'agency within largely disempowering social systems and the hopeful association of much YA fiction with individual empowerment through negotiation of the protagonists' interrelationships with the outside world' (2013: 5). Curry suggests that dystopias written for young audiences imagine their protagonists as empowered and agentic, as capable of saving or transforming the world. Although this is more generous to young people than the paradoxical and limiting representations that exist elsewhere, the individualistic model of agency on which the child's empowerment rests remains problematic for ecological thought.

Addressing this hopeful, yet individualistic, figuration of youth agency in a context of young people's real-world action on the climate crisis, I assemble a theoretical apparatus informed by the material turn in philosophy. Through this, I read contemporary Fantastika written for young audiences in order to complicate the too-easy attribution of 'agency' to young people on the one hand, and their construction as objects of care on the other. Moreover, I follow the lead demonstrated in young people's own action on climate change by questioning whether the notion of individual agency is helpful at all, even possible, given the complex and a-symmetrical natural-cultural networks in which we are enmeshed. As Bowman and Germaine discuss, young activists are vocal about the injustices and inequalities that comprise the climate crisis and recognize the need to establish solidarity, to speak for one another, and negotiate collectives (2021: 17–18). Individual heroes cannot solve climate change no matter how much media coverage they might receive. This book, then, reads contemporary Fantastika written for young audiences in the light of the real-world climate crisis, examining the difficult discursive-material entanglements that comprise the collective worlds in which young people must live, as well as those worlds which may yet come into being as the future of climate change. These are the urgent dark matters with which my analysis is ultimately concerned.

Enchanted matters: Fantastika and the material turn

Motivated by my concern with the urgent matter of the climate crisis and my claim about the eco-ethical dimensions of Fantastika, I read the mode with and through the material turn in contemporary philosophy. The material turn is a critical discourse that originates in work by Manuel de Landa (1995) and Rosi Braidotti (2002) and seeks to dismantle transcendental and humanist modes of thought, themselves an outgrowth of philosophical dualism, which these thinkers claim haunts cultural theory in the West. Braidotti's elaboration of neo-materialism is most significant for the present book since my reading of Fantastika grows out of my previous work on nomadism, which, via Braidotti, identifies Deleuze and Guattari's notion of 'becoming' as key to the subjectivities explored and imagined in children's gothic (Germaine Buckley 2018: 6–13). The material turn recasts nomadic becoming as *materialization*. Where my previous work explored nomadism in relation to the subjectivity of young humans, here I consider materialization as a more-than-human process that encompasses the formation of spacetime itself, the (re)production of organic and biotic systems, and the ground from which all manner of subjectivities emerge. In other words, becoming is no longer considered a solely human matter. Writing more recently, Braidotti describes her view as a 'neo-materialist vital system' in which 'all human and nonhuman entities are nomadic subjects-in-process, in perpetual motion, immanent to the vitality of self-ordering matter' (2018: 36). As Braidotti's evocation of the 'nonhuman' suggests, neo-materialism is an extension of posthumanism. Braidotti's articulation of posthumanism emphasizes the freedom and self-determination of matter itself. She claims that 'this understanding of matter animates the composition of posthuman subjects of knowledge – embedded, embodied and yet flowing in a web of relations with humans and nonhuman others' (2018: 34). In this way, Braidotti's neo-materialism seeks to solve the apparent paradox of posthumanism: the simultaneous disappearance and over exposure of the human. This paradox is not simply a theoretical conundrum; it has taken on material urgency in the contemporary climate crisis, which has been unequivocally caused by human actions yet has unleashed events and processes occurring at a scale and level of complexity that utterly rupture the fallacy of human transcendence from 'nature' and our exceptionalism.

The material turn encompasses a variety of approaches, all of which share a rejection of philosophical dualism. Serenella Iovino and Serpil Opperman summarize the material turn as comprising myriad new 'ways to analyse language, and reality, human and nonhuman life, mind and matter, without falling into dichotomous patterns of thinking' (2014: 2). For many scholars, such dichotomous patterns trace back to the European Enlightenment and the Scientific Revolution, which inaugurate a dualist philosophical tradition. As Tim Ingold argues, these historical moments seed the beginnings of epistemological and disciplinary divides that persist in the present, and which separate the humanities from the natural sciences (2000: 1). This disciplinary divide derives from 'a single, underlying fault upon which the entire edifice of Western thought and science has been built – namely that which separates the "two worlds" of humanity and nature' (Ingold 2000: 1). Bruno Latour describes this fault as the 'Great Divide', an operation whereby the so-called moderns first separated humans from nonhumans ('nature'), before separating 'us', that is, Westerners, from 'them', that is, the rest of the world, especially indigenous peoples who were subject to colonization (Latour 1993: 11–12). Despite his stated aim to move beyond the colonial divide inaugurated by modernity, however, Latour's theorization relies on and so perpetuates the idea of animism as primitivism (Lillywhite 2018: 102). In this way, Latour echoes a problematic misreading of animism. Thus, although I make use of Latour's concept of the Great Divide throughout this book to help understand how Western thought sought to de-animate 'nature', and find useful his description of our coming to awareness of an animated earth in a time of climate crisis (2017: 70), I also turn, in Chapter 2, to new animists and indigenous thinkers for more nuanced accounts of animism. What is important here, though, is that the fault lines and divides identified by writers such as Latour and Ingold not only create disciplinary divides, which the material turn in the humanities seeks to complicate through engagement with hard sciences, but that they undergird both European colonialism and capitalism, two global systems responsible for the contemporary climate crisis. Diana Coole and Samantha Frost argue, for example, that the dominance of dualism in the West has 'provided the basis for modern ideas of nature as quantifiable and measurable' (2010: 7). This idea sanctions the extraction and exploitation of the material, or 'natural', world. Thus, the contemporary climate and ecological crises are a result of dualist thought.

The new materialisms challenge patterns of thought that would render matter mute substance for human extraction. Such patterns of thought include versions of poststructuralism as well as classical dualism. Thus, new materialists seek to complicate modes of 'constructivism', such as the 'linguistic' turn of the late twentieth century, which hold that immaterial idealities, especially human language, consciousness, subjectivity agency, mind, soul, and so on, are 'fundamentally different from matter and valorised as superior' (Coole and Frost 2010: 2). Where Cartesian dualism renders matter brute *thereness*, the radical constructivism of the cultural and linguistic turns privileges (human) language, discourse, culture and values over matter and material processes (Coole and Frost 2010: 3). The response of the new materialisms is not to reject the lessons of constructivism outright, however, but to insist that the world is not *only* a construction. Latour's work on Actor Network Theory prefigures this idea, suggesting that the very notion of a social order is impossible to define without nonhuman actants. He states: 'Yes, *society is constructed, but not socially constructed*' (1999: 198; emphasis in the original). The new materialisms build on this idea with the complementary argument that matter is not simply moulded into shape by human thought, language, society, and culture, but that it asserts its own 'immanent vitality' (Coole and Frost 2010: 8). This emphasizes an 'emergent, generative' materiality, suggesting that matter materializes rather than simply is (Coole and Frost 2010: 8).

Because I read Fantastika as an eco-ethical mode of fiction, I identify within its corpus imaginative corollaries to the ways in which the new materialisms have theorized the vitality of matter, but especially its penchant for imagining enchanted, animate worlds. An important touchstone throughout the book is Jane Bennett's work on the generative, agentic, and enchanting capacities of matter (2001, 2010). For Bennett, paying attention to materiality challenges a narrative of disenchantment that pervades the contemporary world and discourages affective attachment to it (2001: 3). Such an attachment is, says Bennett, necessary for cultivating 'ethical generosity' towards more than humans and humans alike (2001: 3). In later work, Bennett elaborates upon the idea of enchantment via her concept of vibrant materialism, a philosophy that 'affirms a figure of matter as an active principle, and a universe of lively materiality that is always in various states of congealment and diffusion' (2010: 93). New materialist philosopher Karen Barad echoes this idea with her description of materiality as a 'desiring dynamism, a reiterative reconfiguring, energised and energising, enlivened and enlivening' (Tuin, Dolphjin, and Barad 2010: 15). Barad and Bennett's vibrant matter already finds expression in our culture, of course, despite the various disenchantment stories told by Western philosophy and science. Enchanted and animate worlds manifest in childhood play as well as in the imaginative arts, and persist, despite social prohibitions, into adulthood. Fantastika written for young audiences provides an apt companion for Bennett and Barad's theories, then, since it lends imaginative vibrancy and ethical significance to the animate things that emerge through young people's encounters with the world. As I will suggest, Fantastika echoes the affirmative project of the new materialisms because it eschews a state of affairs wherein agency is ascribed to only one half of a binary, or one portion of the world. Its fictional worlds suggest, in contrast, that the entire world is 'saturated with powers of agency and intentionality' (Ingold 2000: 14). In this sense, Fantastika exemplifies Haraway's insistence that 'sf' (speculative fabulation) is about 'worlding and storytelling', a means of 'passing patterns back and forth, giving and receiving' in multispecies worlds (2016: 13, 12). As the texts discussed in this book suggest, too, Fantastika echoes the call of materialists that 'storytelling is not just a property of human language, but one of the many consequences of being thrown in a world that is by itself, fully articulated and active' (Latour 2014: 13). Fantastika, then, gives imaginative voice to the vitality of matter, aiming to (re)enchant through its evocations of speculative encounters with animate landscapes, between species, and with other modes of consciousness than the human.

In this summary of the material turn I have used the words 'West' and 'Western' to describe patterns of thought that underwrite the dismaying social, political, and ecological realities of the present, but this convenient shorthand needs to be complicated. Western philosophy is not a monolithic tradition and many of the new materialisms draw on resources and voices from within it, including Spinozist monism and Bergsonian vitalism, which run counter to Cartesian dualism. As Ingold argues, 'Western' thought is as rich, multifocal and contest riven as any other tradition (2000: 6). In his examination of a range of twentieth- and twentieth-century art, Jeffrey L. Kosky suggests that Western artists 'have grown disenchanted with modern disenchantment and are seeking a new story to tell about it', providing in their work 'places where we might encounter mystery and wonder, hopes for redemption and revelation, transcendence and creation' (2013: xiii–xiv). Fantastika is an important mode in this rebuttal of the disenchantment story since it emerges and develops as a response to the Enlightenment. The history of Fantastika also complicates any simple divide between a so-called 'Western' tradition and cosmologies from other parts of the globe. For example, despite the strong tradition of disenchanting thought in the West, animism, which is a word originally used by colonialists to impute a 'primitive' belief in spirits to indigenous tribes (Tylor 1873), has continually found expression in Western mythologies and narrative traditions. Finally, I acknowledge, too, that deploying the idea of the 'West' sustains the binary logic of the Great Divide. An alternative is to consider the so-called West as the 'Minority World', following Shahidul Alam's (2008) expression of 'the majority world' of the Global South as a challenge to the dominance of Western perspectives. Whatever the terminology, any challenge to binary thinking, such as that developed by the new materialisms, ought to complicate a simple dichotomy between the West and the Rest, not least because this dichotomy has been the cause of violence, exploitation, and oppression for centuries. Again, I find Fantastika a productive site for complicating a monolithic idea of the West, as its cosmologies and imagined worlds tend to be syncretic and hybridized, generating dialogue between seemingly disparate modes of thought and belief, including science, religion, myth, and magic. It is also a site in which the violence of such divides can be exposed, and alternatives considered.

Indeterminacy, probability, ghosts: Materiality and quantum physics

An animist world populated by vibrant matter may seem as far away from modern science as it is possible to get, but the new materialisms combine such a view with a rigorous engagement with the so-called hard sciences, as well as drawing on critiques of science from feminist science and technology studies. One domain of science that has been generative for the new materialisms, and important in the present book, is quantum physics, the theories and experimental data of which have provided their own challenge to classical modes of thought. Where new materialists upend the philosophical legacy of Descartes, quantum physics punctures the Newtonian conception of the universe. The Newtonian, or classical, universe is a container in which separate objects with individual and determinate properties interact with one another via a linear model of cause and effect. Science writer John Gribbin describes this as 'local realism' and suggests that it is a view of the world that has underwritten science – as well as our everyday assumptions about the world – since the time of Isaac Newton. The epistemology of local realism suggests that humans draw objective conclusions about the real things of the world through independent observation (Gribbin 1984: 222). Local realism is thus indebted to Descartes as much as Newton in its conception of the thereness of *res extensa* – matter – and the independence from this of *res cogitans* – the human mind.

As I will suggest throughout this book, the local realist view of the world has consistently been challenged through fantastic and speculative fiction, but this is not the only mode to challenge the Newtonian and Cartesian view of reality. Quantum physics disproves the existence of separable, distinct objects with individual properties, independently observable by an external mind, in favour of the view that reality is radically relational. As physicist and science writer Carlo Rovelli explains, quantum physics reveals that there is 'no reality except in the relations between systems' (2017: 115). Barad, whose work draws closely on the so-called Copenhagen Interpretation of quantum physics, describes reality in a similar way, as 'things-in-phenomena', the word 'phenomena' denoting 'entangled material agencies' (2007: 140, 66). She insists that there is no distinction between objects and the agencies of observation inherent in the world, as is the case in Cartesian thought (2007: 119). As the quantum physicist Niels Bohr suggests, 'we are a part of the nature we seek to understand' (qtd in Barad 2007: 184). *Dark Matter* finds in Fantastika imaginative expressions of this relational view of reality and the embeddedness of humans, and of their idealities, within an entangled mesh of materiality. The present book is also inspired by the 'spooky' legacy of quantum physics in popular thought, relating this to the speculations of Fantastika, since both defy the disenchantment stories of modern science. As Gribbin's language intimates throughout his discussion of quantum physics, giving up the objectivity promised by Newton and Descartes plunges us into uncertainty: 'persist in asking for a physical picture of what is going on', he says of quantum theories, and 'you will find all physical pictures dissolving into a world of ghosts' (1984: 174). Exploration of just such a world of ghosts has been a key feature of Fantastika, making it an apt imaginative companion to quantum physics for the present investigation.

Alongside Barad's philosophy, other scientific theories emphasizing matter's self-organizing and indeterminate properties have been important to the development of the new materialisms, including theories of information and developments in evolutionary biology. As Coole and Frost note, these different approaches to materiality recognize matter as 'constantly forming and reforming in unexpected ways' (2010: 10). This account of materiality follows the conclusions of quantum physics, applying its view of the world at the scale of chemical compounds, the growth of cells, and the development of organisms. As Carlo Rovelli explains, the absence of determinism appears to be intrinsic to the biochemical processes of nature (2017: 104). Such scientific theories, as they are elaborated by the new materialisms, emphasize indeterminacy in their suggestion of the dynamic, fluid, and temporally complex congealing of matter in contrast to the classical view of fixed laws and linear causality. Matter comes into being, evolves, and transforms through moments of chance rather than through a process of mechanistic determinism. As Coole and Frost show, many new materialists thus conceive of matter as force, energy, or intensity rather than as a substance (2010: 12–13). For new materialists keen to explore the ethical and political implications of contemporary scientific discoveries, the indeterminacy of materiality suggests the possibility of bringing forth new worlds that are discontinuous with a present state of affairs. As Barad notes, the liveliness of matter suggests that possibilities themselves do not sit still: they are continually reconfigured and reconfiguring in the ongoing process of materialization (2007: 177). For Coole and Frost, this idea of an indeterminate reality replete with possibility has much in common with older strains of materialism, such as Althusser's 'aleatory materialism', which emphasizes contingency, risk, chance, and other such non-deterministic principles (2010: 35). Matter emerges from within provisional phenomena, through chance encounters, containing possibilities that are fluid rather than fixed. Such a conception of materiality suggests the possibility for the transformation of present social and political conditions. Following this claim, the idea of the 'encounter' is developed through the present book. Encounters occur, following Haraway's discussion, between human and nonhuman actors and actants; they are 'interactions that materialize worlds in some forms rather than others' (Haraway 1997: 67). Each chapter of this book thus pays attention to which forms emerge and which are foreclosed, in the speculative encounters imagined in Fantastika.

From what is to what if: Extramaterialism and ethics

My reading of Fantastika for young audiences follows the new materialisms in emphasizing the indeterminacy, possibility, and the potential for change inherent in the processes of materialization, in what some describe as the 'worlding' of the world (Barad 2007: 160; Haraway 2008; Haraway 2016: 10, 13). Worlding includes various processes of materialization, or encounters, between actants, including quantum physical, biochemical, organic, evolutionary, and so on, but also material-discursive processes, including communication, imagination, speculation, and storytelling. The latter are particularly important because the concept of worlding insists on the possibility of a future that is not necessarily determined, nor foreclosed, by present conditions. Worlding is a material-discursive intra-action that partakes of the virtual as well as the actual. This is the case of whether the communications involved are the chemical electrical signals shared through a mycelial network that prepare trees in forest ecosystems to defend against threats posed by changing climate conditions, or whether they are stories told by humans to other humans to find ways out of present political predicaments, such as those we call 'climate fiction'. In both cases, multispecies collectives respond to possible futures. As Haraway points out, 'SF', which she defines as 'science fiction' and 'speculative fabulation', and which I hold to encompass the literatures of Fantastika, is 'the patterning of possible worlds and possible times, material-semiotic worlds, gone, here, and yet to come' (2016: 31). It is significant that speculation plays such a role in Haraway's philosophy given that she identifies herself as a 'thoroughgoing materialist' (2016: 42). Indeed, a key feature of the new materialisms is the insistence that ideality is imbricated within and through the material. This should not be understood as a (re)capitulation to the logic of dualism but, as Elizabeth Grosz suggests, as an *extra*materialism, or the 'subsistence of the ideal in the material' (2017: 5). Any materialism that rejects anything other than the physical capitulates to dualist thought. As Freya Mathews points out, reductive materialism and most forms of idealism are both 'just flip sides of dualism itself' (2003: 26). For Mathews, who is a panpsychist, 'the true converse of mind-matter dualism is neither materialism nor idealism but a position that posits some form of non-duality or mind-matter unity, implicating mentality in the definition of matter and materiality in the definition of mind' (2003: 27). Mathews's focus is on the mind-body problem of dualism but new materialists, as I have discussed, consider other iterations of such a division by precisely imputing an immaterial, incorporeal, or speculative dimension to matter itself.

The inherence of ideality in the material, or the immaterial conditions of materialization, and the material conditions that constrain and form the emergence of as yet immaterial possibilities, are explicit topics of discussion in the science that informs the new materialisms. Quantum physics implies an extramaterialism in its refusal to give a physical picture of reality and in its proposition of the cloud of possibilities in which electrons, for example, exist. The quantum description of reality holds that the 'virtual' (which might be, say, all possible paths to be taken by an electron) just *is* the material without implying the separate existence of the 'ideal' and the 'material' (Rovelli 2017: 114). Elsewhere in quantum physics, Chris Fuchs describes his own interpretation of the experimental data – known as QBism – in terms that support the non-dualistic principles of the new materialisms. He states that the world is neither built of stuff on the outside, as strict materialists would have it, nor is it only made of stuff on the inside, as in idealism, but that the 'stuff of the world is in the character of what each of us encounters every living moment – stuff that is neither inside nor outside but prior to the very notion of a cut between the two at all' (Gefter and Fuchs 2015: n.p.).

Such a cut, or division, between the material and ideal is also eschewed in new theories about the role of information in the processes of life. As Paul Davies argues, information (such as that stored in DNA) does not have an autonomous existence; it is instantiated in materiality (2019: 47). In the interdisciplinary study of biosemiotics, too, extramaterialism is an explicit principle. Biosemiotics is the 'study of the myriad forms of communication and signification observable both within and between living systems', from DNA to human semiosis (Favareau 2010: v). Terrence Deacon's work in this area locates what he calls 'ententionality', a modality of the extramaterial that includes teleology, purpose, meaning, interpretation, information, and adaptation, as inherent in diverse physical-chemical processes and material substrates, rather than as concepts that sit outside nature (2011: 47). Deacon shows how 'dynamical processes can become organised around and with respect to possibilities not realised' (2011: 33). The (im)material dynamics of form also emerge in Eduardo Kohn's *How Forests Think* (2013), in which he develops a more-than-human anthropology. For Kohn, form is, 'like the basic intentionality of the pig and the palpable materiality of its meat, [. . .] something real' (2013: 160). Form emerges from the constraints on possibility that exist in the physical world; it moves through organic and inorganic phenomena, and it conditions 'thought', which is shared across human and more-than-human beings. Without extramaterialism, then, whether this is expressed as the cloud of possibility in which electrons exist, the ententionality imbricated in chemical processes, or the dynamics of form as it emerges from physical world, nature is, to borrow Deacon's word, 'incomplete'.

The conditional possibilities of the extramaterial dimension of the world are what Fantastika, along with other modalities of 'SF', explores, but the exercise is neither merely metaphysical nor ontological: it is ethical. The consequence of extramaterialism is a shift from metaphysics as ontology (an investigation of what is) to ontogeny, which is the exploration of 'growth and formation'

(Ingold 2021: 8). The disciplines given as examples here focus on growth and formation across the organic and the social, as do the literatures of Fantastika in their exploration of the creation of possible worlds. Grosz describes this 'way of thinking about not just how the world is but how it could be, how it is open to change, and, above all, the becomings it may undergo' as ontoethics (2017: 1). A relational ontology that holds that reality comprises things-in-phenomena, and an extramaterialism that emphasizes the imbrication of possibility in such phenomena, suggests, then, that the entanglements that comprise the world and its becoming are ethical in nature. As Ingold states, 'things are far from closed to one another, each wrapped up in its own ultimately impenetrable world of being [. . .] they are fundamentally open, and all participate in one individual world of becoming' (2021: 8). Ontoethics implies an entangled world in which responsibility is 'a burden all must carry' (Ingold 2021: 8). The idea of entanglement as an ontoethical principle will be elaborated in detail below, but it is important to state here that it is implicit in the very notion of *extra*materialism, not least because the contingency of the relations that comprise materiality demand ethical attention. If worlding might bring about worlds different to that suggested by present conditions, then all who participate are responsible for what emerges. Writing for young audiences is a particularly productive space for exploring these ideas, as Lisa Sainsbury suggests, finding in British children's literature an engagement in ethical discourse at the level of philosophical enquiry despite a dearth of education in British schools in either ethics or moral philosophy (2013: 9). Though children's literature, particularly in the nineteenth and early twentieth centuries, has typically been seen as moralizing and didactic, Sainsbury suggests that it, in fact, encourages ethical enquiry and 'courageous thinking' (2013: 9). I show how this propensity functions alongside the speculative bent of Fantastika to demonstrate ontoethical engagement.

The great outdoors: Materialism and speculation

Speculation is also an important concept in another contemporary philosophical trend that informs this book. To elaborate on the ontoethics of Fantastika, I draw on the so-called 'speculative turn', prompted by Quentin Meillassoux's *After Finitude* (2008), a text that critiques what it describes as 'correlationism' in continental philosophy. Correlationism is, according to Meillassoux, the 'idea according to which we only ever have access to the correlation between thinking and being, and never to either term considered apart from each other'

(2008: 5). Following Meillassoux, the speculative turn aims at getting outside the confines of the correlationist circle of human thought to the possibility of articulating the world-in-itself, or things-in-themselves, beyond their givenness. Alternatively described as speculative realism and speculative materialism, the speculative turn is a loose designation that encompasses diverse thinkers and approaches not all of which agree. However, the 'common enemy' for these diverse approaches is the dominance of post-Kantian metaphysics in modern thought, including phenomenology, hermeneutics, and deconstruction (Dukić and Morin 2017: 3). The latter is described by Levi Bryant, Nick Srnicek, and Graham Harman as the 'tiresome' linguistic turn, echoing discussion of the same in new materialist discourse (2011: 1). The response of speculative realism to correlationism, and its resulting focus on human thought and language, is 'to revive questions about realism, materialism, science, representation and objectivity' (Brassier 2014: 417). There is some crossover here with the new materialisms, though the focus of critique is slightly different. Just as the new materialisms challenge constructivism for according too much agency to language, discourse, culture, and other idealisms, so do speculative realists wish to move beyond a focus on 'text, discourses, social practices, and human finitude [. . .] toward reality itself' (Bryant, Srnicek and Harman 2011: 3). Many thinkers associated with speculative realism draw on fiction as a resource, especially modes of the dark fantastic such as horror and the weird, to articulate reality beyond human though, a domain that Meillassoux names 'the Great Outdoors' (2008: 7).

From the point of view of speculative realism, the need for speculation is a result of the rejection of correlationism, which confines itself to questions of human access, subjectivity, and finitude. In imposing such constraints, post-Kantian metaphysics neglects, runs the argument, the real world, including the present crises of ecological catastrophe and the infiltration of technology into the everyday world (Dukić and Morin 2017: 6). This neglect is a result of the anthropocentrism of correlationism, of its reduction of everything that exists to its being encountered by humans, and the resulting separation of science from the humanities, according to which the study of things in themselves is left to the supposedly objective methods of empirical science (Dukić and Morin 2017: 7). For some speculative realists, the word 'speculation' has a specific meaning in this context, referring to the use of reason to gain access to the Absolute (Meillassoux 2008: 34; Bryant, Srnicek and Harman 2011: 3). Elsewhere, as in the object-oriented ontology of Graham Harman, 'speculation' has a more everyday meaning, and suggests the need to partake in imaginative techniques, such as those found in the literatures of Fantastika, to find ways of 'disengaging objects from subjects' (Sparrow 2014: 62). Both definitions of 'speculation' suggest it as a method for countering the anthropocentrism of metaphysics in Western philosophy, a way of asking *what are things in themselves when they are not being thought by humans?* Though this use of speculation is different to the task of imagining a world that might be otherwise than its present condition, it is nonetheless an important aspect to the ethical function of dark matters in Fantastika and offers another way of exploring what Bennett describes as the vibrancy of materiality beyond its instrumental use to humans.

This discussion of the need for speculation as a mode of engaging with materiality implies, then, an ethical, even political, agenda, but it is also the case that the speculative realists have been accused of neglecting the ethical implications of their theories. Austin Lillywhite, for example, claims there is a 'concern that speculative realism exhibits a counterproductive, reactionary response' to the problems it identifies (2017: 16). Focusing on Meillassoux and Harman in particular, both of whom are interested in the autonomous existence of things in themselves, Lillywhite objects to the 'anti-relational' thrust of the speculative turn, which 'reveals a neo-positivist conception of reality: an atomistic, fundamentally non-relational, non-contextual ontology combined with a muscular, exhaustively absolute objective science that is uncontaminated by political investments' (2017: 16). This could not be more different to the new materialisms, which, as Coole and Frost state, are explicit about the imbrication of the metaphysical and the political, and which seek to reveal how ontological questions are entangled with questions of identity, history, and collective life (2010: 5). For Christopher Breu, the new materialisms, rather than speculative realism, contribute to fostering better understanding of the politics of the present, particularly the 'material extraction of values from bodies and the commons' and 'the slow violence of global ecological disaster' that characterize neoliberalism in the West (2016: 16). It is difficult to see how some of the speculative realisms might respond to this context, particularly those that aim at totalizing, systemic descriptions of reality characterized by autonomous objects rather than by entanglements and relationships.

Though I proceed with caution with respect to speculative realism, then, I nonetheless find it a useful resource for the present exploration of the ethics of Fantastika. Chapter 1 considers Meillassoux's provocations to philosophy through a reading of the 'occult' landscapes of children's fantasy, which reveal their autonomy from human subjectivity. In this chapter I also consider the work of Eugene Thacker, who interrogates the intersection of horror literature and philosophy, identifying 'blind spots' of the latter through innovative readings of a variety of fictional texts (2011: 10). This use of 'speculation' is something I put into practice in my readings of children's fantasies, particularly their evocations of darkness and their appeal to the strategies of both the gothic and the weird. At the same time, I put theories hailing from speculative realism in dialogue with approaches from the new materialisms to better consider the ethical and political ramifications of the dark matters presented in the fiction. This includes, for example, bringing Jane Bennett and Bruno Latour into conversation with Thacker to further elaborate on the agentic nature of the landscapes of children's fantasy. Here I also challenge some of the premises of speculative realism, showing that their foundational claims regarding what they describe as 'correlationism' are already established in other discourses. In so doing, I bring diverse approaches to the problem of thinking reality-in-itself. Elsewhere in the book I draw on works that promote what has been called object-oriented ontology, specifically the work of Tim Morton, but I put these approaches in dialogue with philosophies that have been rejected by the speculative realists, including phenomenology. As Dukić and Morin suggest, despite the censure it has attracted, this latter branch of philosophy seems apt for tracing the familiarity and strangeness of reality with which speculative realists are so concerned (2017: 11). In Chapter 4, which explores ecoweird fiction, I draw on phenomenology to elaborate on this paradox, using the terms 'intimacy' and 'estrangement' to interrogate how weird fiction imagines being human in a more-than-human ecology.

The material turn in childhood studies and children's literature criticism

So far in this introduction I have outlined a synthesis of critical tools through which to read Fantastika, the application of which is new in the study of children's and YA literature. Nonetheless, it is also the case that children's literature critics are already interested in the dialogue between the humanities and science, and in centring ethical and ecological concerns in their work. Thus, my work also draws on and contributes to developing themes and methodologies that already exist in the study of childhood and children's literature, and that might be said to partake of the 'material turn', even if this engagement is not always explicit. As childhood studies and children's literature criticism have developed in the twenty-first century, they have turned to critical frameworks such as posthumanism, ecocriticism, animal studies, and, more recently, plant studies. These approaches signal that critics are moving away from a constructivist view of childhood, a shift that Alan Prout advocated as early as 2005, arguing that although children are a social phenomenon, childhood is 'made up from a wider variety of material discursive, cultural natural, technological, human and non-human resources' (2005: 2).

Children's literature criticism has increasingly recognized this material-discursive heterogeneity, typically exploring it through an engagement with posthumanism. Here Victoria Flanagan and Zoe Jacques have been influential. Reviewing posthuman approaches to YA literature for the *Edinburgh Companion to Children's Literature*, Flanagan interrogates the category of the 'human' through a reading of the 'cyborg' subjects that appear in children's fiction (2017). Her claim that there is a tendency, in YA literature particularly, to align readers with nonhuman characters in order to 'interrogate conventional assumptions about "humanity"' is considered in Chapter 3 of the present book, which also considers cyborg and robot characters in the context of disrupting Cartesian conceptions of mind-body dualism (Flanagan 2017: 31). Jacques's work on posthumanism looks beyond cyborgs to make the wider claim that children's literature offers 'potentially radical destabilisations of being which can be read in light of post-humanism's interest in ontological mutability' (2015: 5). Jacques's work also influences the approach in the present book because of her emphasis on the ecological dimension of posthumanism, and her inclusion of animals and the environment in children's literature as pertinent to the project of posthumanism. She holds that children's fiction is a 'resource for understanding cultures of the human and nonhuman' (2015: 6). Jacques goes on to develop this argument through a reading of animal studies and children's fiction, analysing the ways in which children's literature challenges the 'ontological divide' inaugurated by Descartes writing on the differences between animals and humans (Jacques 2017: 43). The present book draws on this elaboration of posthumanism with respect to children's literature in Chapter 3, which analyses Peter Brown's novel *The Wild Robot* (2016) in which 'artificial' and animal life become entangled.

As well as engaging with posthumanism and animal studies, children's literature criticism follows the material turn through critical plant studies, considering the representation of vegetal life in children's literature. Lydia Kokkola, for example, suggests that children's texts depict an active vegetal world and so have a role to play in the radical, but necessary, reconsideration of human-nature politics (2017: 279). Sainsbury also draws on critical plant studies to interrogate the metaphysics of children's literature, identifying texts that conjure a 'rhizomorphic system' of plants and other modes of life, a system that refuses 'to limit the metaphysical boundaries' of biotic communities (2021: 99, 109). *Dark Matter* builds on these insights, considering the ways in which Fantastika for young audiences draws human characters into complex material assemblages of more-than-human life, inclusive of plants. Vegetal–human collectives are discussed in the final chapter, which examines their figurative use in climate fiction. This chapter is also indebted to the feminist ecocritical readings of YA literature developed by Curry, discussed earlier. Her work for the *Edinburgh Companion*, suggests that YA literature makes clear the ways in which the human is 'enmeshed in the material world' at different scales (2017: 71). Her 'scaled' reading of contemporary texts explores the potential for children and YA literature to model radical environmental change (2017: 72). Here Curry builds on her reading of dystopia narratives and their construction of young people in relation to degrading environments and the possibility of social transformation (2013). In the final chapter, I expand this investigation by considering how the proliferation of plant and fungal life in devastated environments both supports and complicates such narratives of youth agency, entangling children in more-than-human processes of materialization.

These approaches to children's literature are ecological in the sense of considering the interrelationship between bodies, environments, and stories, and each suggests that the study of children's and YA literature is already responding to the provocations of the material turn. Furthermore, the diversity of new readings of, and new critical tools for examining, children's literature suggests it as a particularly productive site for (re)examining and challenging normative ideas about (more than) human being and agency. Indeed, the proliferation of diverse engagements with the materialisms of children's literature lend weight to Sainsbury's claim that children's books 'respond to some of the ultimate questions of reality' in a unique way, and that they develop 'metaphysical structures' that provide young readers with a sense of the nature of reality and what it means to be in the world (2021: 7). For *Dark Matter*, the metaphysical structure identified as key to Fantastika for young audiences is entanglement, a concept that brings together some of the disparate concerns discussed in this section (posthumanism, ecology, plant studies, and so on) within an explicitly relational ontology derived from quantum physics that insists upon the ethical and political implications of metaphysical speculation in imaginative fiction.

Entanglement as ontological principle

The core concept that drives the book's concern with ethics in Fantastika is 'entanglement'. As discussed, this idea originates in twentieth-century quantum physics and has been applied to the work of cultural critique by Barad (2007). According to Barad, entanglement is a provocation to a key principle of Western metaphysics: the belief that the world is populated with individuals, or individual things, each with their own set of determinate properties (2007: 19). Eschewing such a picture of reality, entanglement functions not merely as a synonym for interconnectedness or interdependency, nor any kind of relationship that assumes the *a priori* existence of individuals or objects. Barad explains that the experimental data of quantum physics shows that there are no pre-existing objects and subjects, but that these emerge from 'intra-actions', a coinage she develops because the term 'interaction' implies a separability the science rejects (2007: ix). The entanglements that comprise reality emerge and evolve through intra-actions, which are ongoing processes of contingent and shifting materialization. Barad's account of quantum physics and entanglement describes the imbrication of ontology, epistemology and ethics in all human, and more-than-human, engagements with the world. Entanglement is thus key to what Barad calls 'ethico-onto-epistemology' (2007: 90). It not only describes what the world is made of, but conditions how we know (where knowing is inclusive of a broad range of modes of engagement that go beyond human cognition) and implies ethics as constitutive of the relationships that are the world. Leaving aside the epistemological concerns at the forefront of Barad's work, I develop the concept of entanglement through the work of Grosz and Ingold and present it here as an ontoethical principle.

Understanding entanglement as an ontoethical principle that comprises reality from the bottom-up and conditions the ethical relations that are the world requires a little discussion of quantum physics. Barad draws on Niels Bohr's synthesis of various theories of quantum physics that had emerged by the late 1920s: the Copenhagen Interpretation. This combines his own idea of particle-wave complementarity with the theory of probability waves and the uncertainty principle.[1] The result of Bohr's synthesis of these theories is an insistence on non-locality, which describes the apparent ability of quantum particles to instantaneously 'know' about, and respond to, one another's state even when separated by vast distances. In simple terms, non-locality, or entanglement, refers to particles created in the same event that constitute a single phenomenon and respond simultaneously to measurement. Einstein famously derided this idea as 'spooky action at a distance' because he assumed it must violate his law of special relativity, a consequence of which is that nothing (not even information) can travel faster than the speed of light (1935). Entanglement seems to break this fundamental law since two particles separated by vast distances appear to instantaneously communicate. However, the law of special relativity is only broken if entanglement is misunderstood as involving two separate objects. Despite Einstein's objections, experiments in the 1960s and 1980s confirmed the theory of quantum non-locality, providing clear examples of entanglement, and revealing non-separability as constitutive of materiality at the quantum level.[2] The experiments confirm Bohr's hypotheses and suggested that the fundamental nature of reality is indeed relational.

Since the confirmation of Bohr's hypothesis, new interpretations of quantum physics have been developed that suggest entanglement is not only a feature of reality at a microscopic scale but that it has ontological status in the macroscopic world. Indeed, Barad herself insists that there is no division between differently scaled domains of reality, holding that the macroscopic world is continuous with the quantum (2007: 85). This follows from her insistence on following Bohr's logic as to the inseparability of subject and object. In the scientific context, this means that entanglement encompasses the entire experiment, that when an apparatus is introduced to resolve uncertainty, it becomes part of what is being described (2007: 118). Thus, the entire experiment becomes part of the original entanglement, rather than the entanglement remaining localized in some separate domain of the quantum. Schrödinger's famous thought experiment, in which a cat is placed in a box with a radioactive atom, provides a good example of this extension of entanglement. The cat's fate is entangled with the atom, the decay of which is probabilistic rather than determinate. In popular accounts of the experiment, opening the box collapses the indeterminacy, resolving the experiment to reveal the fate of the cat. However, Barad argues that opening the box (an act of measurement) is an intra-action in which the observer becomes entangled with the experiment (2007: 283). Barad's claim that entanglement extends outward is echoed by science writer Philip Ball in his account of QBism. In Ball's gloss on this theory, 'quantumness' is 'leaky' rather than prone to collapse. He argues that the entanglements that appear to decohere in the act of measurement in fact extend outward into the macroscopic world, and that this is how entanglement comes to produce the 'web' of spacetime itself (2018: 208, 188). Elsewhere, Jim Al-Khalili and Johnjoe McFadden (2014) argue that quantum phenomena, especially entanglement, are implicated in the genesis and evolution of biological life, likewise asserting a continuity between the microscopic and the macroscopic, the cold and stable world of quantum, and the hot, messy world of organic life.

The idea that reality is produced by entanglement is particularly resonant in the study of evolution. In a famous passage towards the end of *On The Origin of Species* (1859) Charles Darwin contemplates 'an entangled bank, clothed with many plants of many kinds, with birds singing in the bushes, with various insects flitting about, and with worms crawling through the damp earth', reflecting that each elaborately constructed form of life is dependent on the others, and that life is thus the product of a web of 'infinitely complex relations' (Darwin 2008: 360, 50). In more recent accounts of evolution, symbiosis is emphasized as the key process in producing novelty (Margulis 1998: 12). Lynn Margulis terms this 'symbiogenesis': the 'origin of new tissues, organs, organisms – even species – by establishment of long term of permanent symbiosis' (1998: 8). This account of symbiosis might first suggest interdependence between individual organisms rather than the ontic principle of entanglement as expounded by Barad, but the challenge to the conception of the *a priori* existence of individuals is sustained. Even the object we think of as a species only emerges from a complex tangle of relationships with symbionts, from other species, and is, as such, already a phenomenon, an entanglement in the sense expounded by Barad. Though they do not use the word 'entanglement', Scoff F Gilbert, Jan Sapp, and Alfred I. Tauber echo the claim that animal development and evolution are 'incomplete without symbionts' due to the role symbiosis plays in genetic inheritance and the expression of genes (2012: 325). Therefore, they claim, biological organisms 'cannot be considered individuals by anatomical or physiological criteria' due to the diversity of symbionts that comprise their being (2012: 325).

Similar challenges to the notion of the individual are emerging in discussion of the entangled nature of plant and fungal life. Mycorrhizal networks, which comprise fungal mycelia that connect two or more plants through the root systems of trees, are increasingly recognized as mediators in vegetal ecologies, crucial to tree survival and woodland biodiversity, for example (Simard and Durrall 2004; Whitfield 2007). As Merlin Sheldrake insists, summarizing decades of research on fungi-plant-animal relationships, 'human societies are no less entwined with fungi' than plants (2020: 4). This does not merely include the instrumental use of fungi by humans, nor the presence of fungi as symbionts and parasites in the human body, but also the complex ecological effects that are visited on plant and animal life as human agricultural and industrial practices affect fungi. Sheldrake explores these tangled relationships and uses fungi to rethink the idea of the individual. He says that '"we" are ecosystems that span boundaries and transgress categories' (2020: 19). Following Margulis, Sheldrake, describes the process of evolution from this fungal perspective as the 'intimacy of strangers' and that, as such, it punctures easy divides between species and other neat evolutionary categories (2020: 106). This description of organic life and evolution as a tangle of relationships echoes a paradigm long-established in sociocultural disciplines, such as anthropology, applying relational thinking across the continuum of life.

The ethics (and politics) of entanglement

As this discussion of relationality in the study of organic life shows, entanglement is not a synonym for the network or for the idea of interconnectedness between individuals. However, the image of a network of interconnected beings tends to underpin the very notion of the 'web of life'. This is because systems thinking has been very influential in the formation of ecology, which since the early twentieth century has been built on disciplines such as cybernetics, mathematics, game theory, and information theory. As Annette Voigt suggests, the influence of such theories in ecology has worked to cast organisms in the role of 'components of systems', such that the relationships between organisms could be represented by ecologists in the same way as electrical circuits (2010: 183, 187). However, nature is not a giant electrical circuit, nor a computer programme, any more than it is a clockwork mechanism, as imagined by early Enlightenment scientists. Moreover, the idea of the web of life implies a holism in which every component has its place in a stable system. Such holism is a legacy of colonial ideology, in which many systems theories are embedded, naturalizing hierarchies as intrinsic to organic life, as well as enshrining a myth of balance in popular ecological thought. As John Kricher argues, the notion of a balance of nature is 'not scientific in any way', but a teleological belief that 'what we call nature has a predetermined destiny associated with its component parts, and that these parts . . . all fit together into an integrated, well-ordered system that was created by design' (2009: 16). Entanglement punctures the myth of balance, the normative imperative of holism, and the very idea that the web of life is made up of (lesser) individuals, who come together to form a (stable) whole. Entanglement instead suggests a series of rolling 'cuts' that continually reconfigure relationships and the subsequent 'individuals' within a system, along with the form of the system itself. As philosopher Emmanuel Coccia argues, organisms are made by the world and, in turn, make the world, producing new conditions of life from which emerge other organisms. Nowhere is this more obvious than in the case of plants since to be – for them – means 'to make world' (Coccia 2019: 38).

Entanglement as world-making resists the idea of ecology as an ordered system, comprising discrete components, each in its proper place and suggests something more akin to what Morton names 'dark ecology'. They use the word 'dark because it compels us to recognize the melancholic wounds that make us – the shocks, traumas and cataclysms that have made oxygen for our lungs to breathe, lungs out of swim bladders' (Morton 2016: 180–1). Alenda Chang's summary of dark ecology is also helpful because it emphasizes that ecological thought is 'not solely about the bright optimism of interconnection and interdependence, a warm, furry, mammalian comfort in our cohabitation, but also a universe of waste, dirt, shit, and trash that does not disappear' (2019: 173). In terms of the climate crisis, to state that the biosphere is a wickedly complex tangle of interconnections is to name the problem rather than the solution. Mapping the systemic interconnectivity of climate change feedback loops, tipping points, and so on, helps scientists to trace complex relations of cause and effect, but systems thinking will not provide a utopian answer to the climate crisis in and of itself. Throughout this book, the concepts of ecology and entanglement entwine, and the readings of Fantastika seek to emphasize the ongoing conditions of violence and vulnerability, intimacy and estrangement, symbiosis and parasitism that are entailed in the making and unmaking of phenomena, and, concomitantly, of the world.

My approach to entanglement and ecology thus imputes an ethical responsibility at the heart of relationality. For Barad, the fact that matter is an entanglement, that each material intra-action reconfigures possibilities, suggests that an 'ethical call' is 'embodied in the very worlding of the world' (Barad 207: 160). Barad draws on Emmanuel Levinas's claim that ethical responsibility is the 'essential, primary and fundamental mode of subjectivity' (Levinas 1985: 95; Barad 2007: 391). Levinas locates the emergence of (human) subjectivity in an embodied, pre-logical responsibility to the other. This responsibility is not something taken up by a self from a position of freedom or will, but an *a priori* demand from which the self emerges and according to which it must account for its actions. The other of Levinas's ethics is not the 'other' of cultural discourse, which all-too-often functions as a marker of exotic difference, but, rather, an irreducible alterity at the heart of the self. Levinas's ethics begin with the relation itself and not with two terms (self/other), hence its influence on Barad's account of entanglement and intra-action, both of which relocate the idea of exteriority within phenomena. The difference between the I and the other is not, in other words, an opposition, and the ethical relation is not external, but emerges from within subjectivity. The entangled phenomena that comprise the (more-than-human) world, and the primary of relations and the intra-actions through which such phenomena materialize and evolve, imply just such a foundational ethical relation and its irreducible yet intimate alterity.

Although Levinas's work is taken up as part of the so-called 'linguistic turn' in cultural theory, already identified as a target of critique for the new materialisms, his insistence that ethics is embodied, an 'entwinement of thought and carnality', suggests an affinity with the materialist elaboration of entanglement offered here (Ziarek 2001: 50). Barad's development of Levinas's ideas to theorize the intra-actions that occur within phenomena elaborates on this notion of ethics as embodied, of 'having the other in one's skin', to include more-than-human beings (Barad 2007: 392). In her account of ethics, matter is 'entangled with the "Other"' (Barad 2007: 393). Subjects and objects are 'permeated through and through with their entangled kin; the other is not just in one's skin, but in one's bones, in one's belly, in one's heart, in one's nucleus' (Barad 2007: 393). The developments in evolutionary biology discussed earlier suggest that this is indeed the case, and that, therefore, ethical relations produce species, and cut across organic and inorganic life, entangling organisms and environments. The ethical responsibility entailed in entanglement is not, then, an act of conscious will, nor does it only occur through a human social or linguistic relation, but is instantiated through materiality itself.

I identify and develop entanglement as an ontoethical concept through my reading of Fantastika, characterizing this mode as one that is particularly engaged with ethical concerns around selfhood and alterity. As Sainsbury argues, 'ontological exchange' is a key metaphysical structure in children's fiction. Sainsbury describes this exchange as 'an ontic meeting of self and other during which being is tested and made aware of its status as being' (2021: 16). Although Sainsbury's idea is not analogous with entanglement because it preserves the notion of the individual prior to exchange, it does draw on Levinas's ethics and suggests children's literature as a particularly apt space for their exploration. Sainsbury notes Levinas's suggestions 'that there is a propensity for youth to open itself to the other through an essential recognition of what it means to be vulnerable' and that children's literature emphasizes 'this vulnerable openness to the other' (2021: 30). Certainly, children's literature is a space in which adult (re)writing of the matter of childhood tends to focus on vulnerability and on the indeterminacy of being, even if these are not (really) specific to childhood subjectivity. Indeed, the 'testing' of being Sainsbury traces in classic British children's fiction occurs in this corpus too, though the outcome is not always the shoring up of being. Moreover, I argue that entanglement should not be understood as a condition of childhood subjectivity, in particular, nor as a waypoint for negotiation in the process of maturation. The violence and precarity of entanglement as an ongoing condition of subjectivity, from childhood to adulthood, are emphasized in many of the texts I read here, with the openness of youth subjectivity not merely an opportunity for 'testing' the self but also, potentially, for its fracture. Like Sainsbury, I also show how children's fiction develops Levinas's ethics in relation to the more-than-human. Though she focuses primarily on the experiences of human protagonists, Sainsbury acknowledges the presence of the nonhuman in ontological exchange (2021: 12).

As well as imbricating human subjectivity in more-than-human worlds and ecologies, Fantastika also makes clear that entanglement has political and social implications. The texts discussed here respond to climate crisis, but also consider interrelated social justice issues and imagine the possibility of political and social transformation. Following the lead of the novels, then, I put the concept of entanglement in dialogue with Judith Butler's ethics of nonviolence. This idea entails a different critique of the individualism that prevails in Western politics. Butler opposes the dominant Hobbesian view, the idea that selves emerge into a social world from a state of nature in which dependence has been 'written out of the picture' (2020: 37, 30). The Hobbesian view of the individual shapes modern ideas about political and social contracts, naturalizing society as a site of contest and struggle for dominance. Though Butler does not mention either Levinas or Barad, the ethics of nonviolence they set out complements the idea of entanglement in its insistence that selves are 'implicated in each other's lives, bound by a set of relations that can be as destructive as they can be sustaining' (Butler 2020: 9). Butler understands the ethical relation to be potentially violent, and this serves as a correction to any utopian version of entanglement that would obfuscate parasitic or exploitative intra-actions. As Butler notes, 'relationality is not by itself a good thing' and interdependence is not an ethical norm, 'but a vexed and ambivalent field in which the question of ethical obligation has to be worked out in light of a persistent and constitutive destructive potential' (2020: 10). Moreover, this vexed field of relations encompasses far more than a 'dyadic human encounter' and pertains to 'all living and inter-constitutive relations' (2020: 9). Though Butler describes these as social relations, bringing their work into dialogue with Barad makes clear that the ethics of nonviolence are material and embodied, too. Indeed, Butler recognizes this in their critique of the Hobbesian view, in a description of the radical dependency that conditions material existence, a dependency that is defined as reliance on social and material structures as well as the environment (2020: 41). There is no overcoming such dependency, not even in the move from youth to adulthood so often imagined in texts for young audiences. As Butler notes, the adult is merely a being who 'imagine[s] a self-sufficiency', only to find that image repeatedly undermined during life (2020: 42). As I will show, Fantastika eschews normative maturation stories that value independence and models instead a move from the state of dependency to that of interdependency. For Butler such a developmental schema has political implications for understanding vulnerability, conflict, sociality, and violence, and promises a new idea of equality that has the potential to transform civic and political life (2020: 44). Paying attention to the entanglements entailed in the worldings of Fantastika is one way of considering this potential, and of imagining new modes of sociality and politics.

Fantastika: Planetary fiction

Entanglement is the philosophical concept through which this book responds to the ecological, political, and social crises of the present; Fantastika is the modality best suited to its elaboration. The umbrella of Fantastika includes children's and YA fiction, as well as a range of fantastic genres, all of which respond, I claim, to the condition of ecological belonging through imaginative speculation. John Clute, who coined the term Fantastika, claims that its genres, which include fantasy, science fiction, and horror among others, are modes of 'planetary fiction' that emerged in response to rational Enlightenment values by the mid-to-late eighteenth century in Europe (2016a: n.p.). Clute argues that the anxieties prompted by the scientific discoveries in this period, including the revelation of deep geological time, along with the terrors suggested by the future of industrialization, are given imaginative force in the genres of Fantastika, which, he says, 'vibrates to the planet' (2016a: n.p.). He explains that as 'science takes the ground from underneath our feet', Fantastika 'responds instantly to the vertigo' (2016a: n.p.). This is the fiction produced in what Clute – recalling the Fall myth – describes as an ever 'darkening garden', suggesting that an anxious and tragic disposition characterizes the genres of Fantastika from their inception, a concern with dark matters.

Although Clute does not discuss the contemporary climate crisis, his dating of Fantastika to the mid-eighteenth century, along with his evocation of the Fall myth, suggests an intimate connection between the two. Indeed, Sarah

Dillon notes that Clute's insistence that the genres of Fantastika were 'born at a point when it has begun to be possible to glimpse the planet itself as a drama' summarizes the idea of the 'Anthropocene', the term proposed by Paul J. Crutzen and Eugene F. Stoermer in 2000 to name a new geological epoch in which 'the effects of humans on the global environment have escalated' (Dillon 2018: 6; Clute 2016: loc 6237; Crutzen 2002: 23). Dillon also notes that Crutzen and Stoermer identify the latter part of the eighteenth century as the onset of the Anthropocene, connecting it to the Industrial Revolution and, so, roughly aligning the epoch with Clute's start date for the origin of the genres of the fantastic. Thus, says Dillon, 'fantastic literature would be, by definition, the Literature of the Anthropocene' (2018: 7). Dillon's comments are considered in more detail in Chapters 4 and 5, which examine the ecoweird and climate fiction respectively. These genres not only 'vibrate to the planet' but do so in a way that oscillates between dystopian and utopian imaginings of possible futures of climate change, refusing to capitulate to either what Clute calls elsewhere the bound and the free fantastic and, so, provide neither an escape nor the devastation of apocalypse (2016: loc 5799). Even in genres that are not so explicit in their engagement with environmental problems, Fantastika has, since the eighteenth century, anticipated the posthuman turn, intimated ecological anxiety, and negotiated the shifts in consciousness of the human–planet relationship prompted by developments in science and industry, each genre handling these anxieties and concerns in a different way.

This discussion of Fantastika as tragic in relation to its negotiation of planetary interrelations belies the complexity that emerges across its myriad genres. Certainly, Clute's account of the dark matters of Fantastika places it in contrast with the playful imaginings of children's literature, which emerges in the same historical period. Despite this seeming contrast between the way Clute describes Fantastika and the way children's fiction has popularly been perceived, as an imaginative escape, writing for young audiences, especially YA literature, is now routinely included under the umbrella of Fantastika. As the editors of *Fantastika*, a journal dedicated to the academic study of this literature, proclaim, '"Fantastika" embraces the genres of Fantasy, Science Fiction, and Gothic Horror, but can also include Alternate History, Steampunk, Young Adult Dystopic Fiction, or any other radically imaginative narrative space' (Palmer-Patel and Dodd 2016: n.p). The inclusion of 'young adult' in this list is significant, since children's fiction is a mode of speculation responding to the same historical conditions, albeit with often different ideological and societal drivers. Clute himself makes the connection, describing a 'fault line' that emerged in Western literary production after 1700 between mimetic work, which accorded with the rational Enlightenment values then beginning to dominate, and the great cauldron of irrational myth and story, which was now deemed primarily suitable for children (the concept of childhood having been invented around this time as a disposal unit into which abandoned versions of human nature could be dumped) (2016a: n.p.). Clute's language is cynical, but the connection between Fantastika and childhood is not spurious and explains the preference for fantasy in writing for young audience since the mid-to-late eighteenth century. I am more positive than Clute in the response afforded by writing for children to Enlightenment values, preferring to find in its imaginings a playful dialogue that has continued to have an impact on Western thought and culture since its inception. It is far from being a 'disposal unit'. From the classics to the present day, writing for young audiences is replete with imaginative counter-sites, figured as rabbit holes and wardrobes, spaces for ethical and metaphysical speculation, as Sainsbury's work shows, and for exploring alternative politics and possibilities for societal transformation.

Precisely because it emerged in response to the rational values of the Enlightenment, Fantastika is a modality of fiction suited to imaginings that challenge dualist conceptions of materiality. In this claim I interrogate the synergy between Clute's account of Fantastika as 'planetary' fiction and the ideas in the material turn, exploring how matter becomes vibrant and lively through the figurations found in Fantastika. As Clute says, the stories that surfaced in response to the Enlightenment re-imported all the 'old material' the scientific revolution had repressed, including the irrational, the impossible, the storyable, the prescience of things, magical objects, and so on (2016a: n.p.). Clute's account of Fantastika as a space for the storyable at a time when science sought to render the matter of the world mute accords echoes the language of contemporary material ecocriticism. Iovino and Opperman use the phrase 'storied matter' to describe materiality as a site of narrativity, further suggesting the entanglement of the semiotic with the material that has been elaborated through this introduction, emphasizing the vibrant, communicative character of matter (2012: 83). For thinkers contributing to the material turn, the genres of Fantastika are a resource. Coole and Frost note, for example, that science fiction 'may well be ahead of mainstream ethics' with regard to the instrumentalist appropriation of material resources, the question of synthetic life forms, and the supposed difference between humans and other species. Fantastika is particularly suited for the ethical concerns that drive this book, then, because it elucidates scientific and philosophical ideas without being bound by dominant modernist ontologies that deny agency to the more-than-human world. It also ventures beyond the strictly empirical, avoiding reductive forms of materialism and gesturing to more-than-human perspectives.

Finally, through this book I suggest that Fantastika, in its speculation as to the vibrancy of materiality and the agency of the more-than-human world, does important political and ethical work. I connect the literatures of Fantastika to worlding and describe them as engaging in the ontogenesis of our entangled reality. This claim builds on Haraway's concept of worlding, which is a particular blend of the material and the semiotic that refuses boundaries between subjects and their environment. As discussed, worlding is intrinsic to speculative fabulation and entails the imagining of the yet to come. The speculative work of Fantastika comprises a model of worlding not only attuned to anxiety, loss, and fear, which tend to dominate in Clute's account, but also of the not-yet foreclosed possibilities for transformation. Worlding outside of literary texts manifests itself in the same way, says Haraway, suggesting a continuity between text and world, rather than a representational divide. Matthew J. Wolf-Meyer makes a similar set of claims in his discussion of speculative fiction *as* social theory, describing both as modes that ask questions about 'the terror of the ongoing apocalypse' and seek to makes 'new futures possible' (2019: 3). Of course, as Wolf-Meyer acknowledges, the future is hard to imagine, and the multiple apocalypses threatened (and actualized) by the climate crisis are 'unimaginable' in many respects (2019: 4). Similarly, for Haraway, worlding via SF is always a 'risky game' because it must be attuned to 'staying with the trouble' as opposed to imagining impossible escapes or game over scenarios (Haraway 2016: 31). The texts in this corpus partake of some of the more tragic aspects of what Clute describes as the 'bound' fantastic in their refusal to provide escapes from planetary embeddedness, but, in staying with the troubled condition of planetary belonging, they also speculate as to the possible transformation of material conditions, and the upending of social rules and political structures, playing 'with theories of what might be' (Wolf-Meyer 2019: 15).

Methodology: Diffractive reading

The myriad modes that comprise Fantastika require an eclectic methodological approach, especially since Fantastika itself explores the intersection of science, philosophy, social theory, and politics. Following Barad (2007) and Haraway

(1992), I engage with my corpus through a diffractive reading process. Diffraction offers an alternative paradigm to reflection for critical thought and practice, rejecting a representationalist mode for a performative one. Where representationalism holds that words, concepts, and ideas are separate from, and reflect, the things to which they refer, a performative account 'insists on understanding thinking, observing, and theorising as practices of engagement with, and as part of the world, in which we have our being' (Barad 2007: 86, 133). A diffractive reading acknowledges this fundamental entangling of matter and meaning, refusing a division that consigns meaning to ideality and things to brute materiality. As Barad suggests, diffraction experiments in quantum physics disclose that mattering is 'a matter of what comes to matter and what doesn't' (2014: 172). Literary works, along with the various texts, ideas, and disciplinary practices read through and with them, are themselves material-discursive entanglements through which we produce and take account of this mattering. As Barad suggests, ideas make a difference in the world: they don't 'fly about free of the weightiness of their material instantiation' (2007: 55). Kai Merten builds on this claim, arguing that although Barad's work implies that diffractive reading might apply to either texts or matter, there is no need for such a separation since texts are always entangled with material 'referents' (2021: 13). For Merten, a diffractive reading discloses the ways in which texts are agentive with respect to mattering since they are 'capable of intervening into earlier texts and other language usages, and of thus creating more and more complex layers/entanglements of interventions' (Merten 2021: 15). Merten acknowledges that this idea of diffraction in relation to literary critique builds on existing interventions such as deconstruction and intertextuality (2021: 5). Indeed, in my earlier work I have discussed the reflexive intertextuality that characterizes contemporary children's fiction. Here, diffraction offers a more radical account of such intertextuality, since texts are always entangled with each other, and with the mattering that makes the world in which they are produced and (re) produced, without priorities or hierarchies.

If a diffractive reading respects the entanglement of matter and meaning that are literary texts, it also refuses to heed firm boundaries between disciplinary and discursive practices. For Barad, a diffraction pattern marks differences from within entanglements, which are material-discursive phenomenon. Diffraction is about taking account of the marks, cuts, and differences that matter within these phenomena, about reading insights through one another and illuminating differences as they emerge (2007: 89, 26). In terms of the practice of reading employed in this book diffraction is not about examining representations according to one framework or interpretation, then, but about taking responsibility for the practices through which the world materializes. This entails 'transdisciplinary engagement' rather than reading against some fixed target, which would privilege one discipline or material-discursive entanglement over another (Barad 2007: 90). Following Barad's account of diffractive reading, my work explores not only the ways in which literature thematically and imaginatively demonstrates the inseparability of culture and nature, I also consider the world itself as storied matter, engaging with scientific ideas about the nature of materiality through a discussion of philosophy and literature. That is, I read literary criticism, philosophy, and science through one another and through the novels, producing an 'interlacing diffraction of texts' (Merten 2021: 6). In terms of the mattering that is the world, these domains are non-separable. This point is especially important for thinking about scientific ideas and practices because it discloses that these are caught up in metaphysical and epistemological frameworks, as well as cultural and political conditions, and so cannot stand as objective truth claims against which other ideas and disciplines might be measured. Science is a cultural and imaginative endeavour, as Stephen Jay Gould asserts (1988: 6). As DeLanda suggests, too, the new materialisms demand 'transversality', a movement across the territories of science and the humanities in order to puncture the barriers of dualist logic, 'performing the agential or non-innocent nature of all matter that seems to have escaped both modernist (positivist) and postmodernist humanist epistemologies' (2006: 46). In other words, a diffractive reading becomes part of the performativity that is materialization, or worlding. Neither the act of reading nor the material-semiotic stuff this act explores is innocent; both are implicated in what is and what might be.

Scope and structure

In Chapter 1, 'Occult materialism: The landscapes of classic fantasy', I acknowledge the history of the speculative worlding carried out in children's fiction by examining two post-war British fantasies that prefigure the postmillennial fictions that comprise the remainder of the corpus. These post-war fantasies are paradigmatic in terms of a dark, inhuman mode of speculation that emerged in that period of writing for children. My reading acknowledges Jane Carroll's understanding of the landscapes of children's fantasy as more than setting. Carroll develops her concept of 'topoanalysis' through a close reading of Susan Cooper's *The Dark Is Rising* sequence (1965–77), attending to physical landscape features to understand their influence on character and story (2011: 14). I attend to Cooper's *The Dark Is Rising* (1973), the second novel in the sequence, as well as to Alan Garner's *The Weirdstone of Brisingamen* (1960) to further reveal the materiality of fantasy landscapes and the vibrant things that inhabit them. Where Carroll draws on psychogeography, I argue that Cooper and Garner's work suggests affinities with recent speculative and eco-materialist philosophies. Expounding a set of propositions that I call 'occult materialism', I identify in Cooper and Garner's fiction specific figurations of materiality that have persisted in contemporary Fantastika. Occult materialism is only one way to understand what emerges in this chapter as the 'hard problem' of matter, but it resonates with how Fantastika evokes and enlivens landscapes and their more-than-human inhabitants. I expound and evaluate the propositions of occult materialism in this reading of Cooper and Garner to show how it illuminates the various ethical and ontological problems that are developed in the rest of the book.

The second chapter, 'Animate worlds: Magical encounters in contemporary fantasy', moves into the twenty-first century but stays with the genre of fantasy. In contemporary fantasy I note elements of 'occult materialism', particularly in the still-popular trope of characters encountering a heretofore hidden world. However, the YA novels discussed in this chapter, *Akata Witch* by Nnedi Okorafor, *Children of Blood and Bone* by Tomi Adeyemi, and *The Lost Witch* by Melvin Burgess, develop the trope in new directions. These fantasy texts engage in ambitious world building, invent syncretic magic systems, and gesture to expansive animist cosmologies that reveal a spirit-infused materiality. In so doing, the novels eschew the malign feeling of the eerie present in the works of Garner and Cooper. Nonetheless, darkness remains present in the sense that encountering a world that is alive entails danger and vulnerability as well as magic and wonder. My reading suggests that these novels make apt companions for panpsychist, new animist and ecological thought since they engage in the (re) enchantment story prompted by the climate crisis. As Latour states, '[o]ne of the main puzzles of Western history is not that "there are people who still believe in animism," but the rather naive belief that many still have of a de-animated world of mere stuff; just at the moment when they themselves multiply the agencies with which they are more deeply entangled every day' (2014: 7). Each novel stages a conflict between that naïve belief in a world of mere stuff and those who are entangled with, and open to, animate matter. By selecting texts from writers who work with indigenous cosmologies from the majority world and a writer situated within British culture, I suggest that the de-animating thrust of so-called Western thought continues to be resisted in a variety of ways.

The ontologies of panpsychism and animism filtered through stories of witchcraft as discussed in Chapter 2 offer one rebuke to the divides inaugurated by Cartesian dualism. Aligning with what Thomas Nagel terms a general monism – 'according to which the constituents of the universe have properties that explain not only its physical but its mental character' (2012: 56) – panpsychism and animism posit 'mind' as a fundamental constituent of reality. In the ontologies explored in contemporary YA Fantastika a plurality of minds suffuses organic and inorganic matter. Without jettisoning the important ethical implications of this view, I introduce in Chapter 3 alternative ontologies to counteract dualism, thus exploring multiple perspectives on the dark matter of reality and, specifically, the problem of the mind and the emergence of consciousness in evolutionary history. I contend that the 'murky depths' of a persistent mind-body problem, as Deacon describes it (2011: 724), continue to find imaginative expression in contemporary Fantastika, particularly in science fiction novels about cybernetic, mechanical, and clockwork beings, whose autonomous minds provoke questions about consciousness and its origins in the evolution of organic life. Reading three such novels, Chapter 3 takes seriously the 'hard problem' of the mind, which, as many philosophers suggest, panpsychist approaches are not sufficient to solve. Terrence Deacon, for example, argues, that panpsychism evades the challenges posed by modern neuroscience and its physical account of the mind. When asked to explain how such objects as electrons 'think', panpsychism must resort to evasion tactics, offering notions such as 'combination' and 'emergence' to account for the appearance of unified, complex minds from lower-order components (2011: 137–8). Deacon's own solution to the problem of the mind, or the emergence of consciousness from materiality, echoes theories of entanglement in its view of the world as process rather than 'stuff', but he devotes much of his thesis to the consequences of dualism and its idea that mental properties must be something 'added to' physical processes (2011: 64). The children's books I consider in Chapter 3, *The Wild Robot* (2016) by Peter Brown, *Tin* (2018) by Pádraig Kenny, and *Wildspark* (2019) by Vashti Hardy, offer speculative depictions of artificial intelligence that likewise interrogate the consequences of mind-body dualism, and the problems it implies for understanding the emergence of consciousness.

In Chapter 4, 'Precarious Interdependence: The Oceans of the Ecoweird', I move from a discussion of consciousness and artificial intelligence to an analysis of the strange minds imagined in ecoweird fiction. The Weird is a different modality of Fantastika to that of either Fantasy or Science Fiction. Here I identify a specific articulation of the weird that has emerged in contemporary writing for young audiences, and that has a specifically ecological thrust. Contact with the 'alien' minds of the gods in Frances Hardinge's *Deeplight* (2019), or the strange being known as the 'Seamstress' in Sam Gayton's novel, *The Last Zoo* (2019), functions as a catalyst for characters to question their sense of earthly belonging in precarious worlds. Building on the ecological themes explored in my reading of *The Wild Robot* in Chapter 4, in Chapter 5 I explore the ways in which weird fiction imagines relationships of interdependence between humans and their environment, with a focus on oceanic spaces. The chapter considers the theme of entanglement in terms of the related ideas of 'interdependence' and 'planetarity'. Like entanglement, these require a conceptual shift from considering things in isolation to things as mutually constituted, emphasizing the contingency and precarity of ecological relationships, as well as the ethical responsibilities they engender.

Chapter 5 moves from the ocean to the woodland to consider contemporary climate fiction and its dialogue with the recent 'vegetal turn' in philosophy. As well as increasingly being recognized as vital actors in climate crisis and in possible solutions, plants have inspired a plethora of political writing that emphasizes collective subjectivity and agency in the Anthropocene. Immersive and open vegetal subjectivities, politics, and modes of collaboration suggest alternative futures to those imagined by mainstream environmentalism. Drawing on these debates, I read Sita Brahmachari's *Where the River Runs Gold* (2019) and Lauren James's *Green Rising* (2021), two dystopian climate novels in which plants, trees, and fungi play vital roles, to explore alliances between children and plants as material instantiations of Haraway's 'naturecultures' and Latour's 'collectives'. In so doing, I interrogate climate fiction's deployment of the catastrophe as a way of imagining the future otherwise to mainstream environmentalism. Since plant-thinking implies relational ontologies and ethics (Gibson and Brits 2018: 17), it provides an apt resource for concluding this investigation of the ontoethics of entanglement.

1

Occult materialism

The landscapes of classic fantasy

Fantastika in the second golden age of children's literature: The gothic turn

This chapter explores novels by Alan Garner and Susan Cooper, two influential writers who contributed to the development of Fantastika for children and young adult audiences. I examine their early work, Garner's *The Weirdstone of Brisingamen* (1960) and Cooper's *The Dark Is Rising* (1973), both of which were inspired by earlier fantasy works for young audiences, notably those by J. R. R. Tolkien and C. S. Lewis, but that introduce elements of the weird, the gothic, and the occult. Tim Jones identifies this moment in the so-called 'second golden age' of children's literature as a 'gothic turn' in the writing of fantasy for young audiences (2017: 179). What is also notable about these novels is their use of 'this-worldly' settings (Butler 2006: 19). Instead of imagining a discrete secondary world, such as in the case of Tolkien's Middle Earth or Lewis's Narnia, *Weirdstone* and *The Dark Is Rising* speculate as to the strange nature of real places and landscapes: Alderley Edge in Cheshire for Garner and the Thames Valley in Southeast England for Cooper. Rather than imagining magical worlds elsewhere, the novels conjure a nonhuman agency that inheres in, and animates, the topographical features of the landscape, its climate and weather conditions, and the flora and fauna. As familiar landscapes reveal their hidden fissures, they disclose their refusal to be controlled by humans. An unidentifiable intelligence is instead revealed, which is sometimes antagonistic to human life in ways that recall Algernon Blackwood's weird tale, 'The Willows' (1907). In my reading I suggest, then, that Cooper and Garner not only draw on a tradition of fantastic stories written for children featuring animate creatures and plants, but also on the modality of the weird as it emerged in the work of Blackwood, M. R. James,

H. P. Lovecraft and others. Indeed, the this-worldly setting of Cooper and Garner's fantasies accords with Maurice Lévy's assessment of early-twentieth-century weird fiction by Lovecraft, in which the objectively familiar locale of the stories is what allows for the irruption of the 'truly fantastic' (1988: 36–7). As suggested in the introduction, an interest in the weird has fuelled the speculative turn in continental philosophy and the mode is now routinely recognized as an ontological and metaphysical branch of Fantastika (Miéville 2008; Harman 2012; Newell 2020). Identifying the weird in Garner and Cooper's novels, I thus suggest children's Fantastika anticipates the metaphysical concerns of contemporary speculative philosophies.

I also follow Mark Fisher's delineation of the aesthetic modalities of the weird and the eerie in my reading of Cooper and Garner's novels because, like the texts Fisher explores in his essay on the topic, they exhibit a 'fascination for the outside, for that which lies beyond standard perception, cognition and experience' (Fisher 2016: 8). Fisher's definition of the eerie as a 'particular kind of aesthetic experience' constituted by a 'failure' of presence or absence is helpful for thinking through the paradoxical ways these children's fantasies disclose the inhuman presence of their landscapes. For Fisher, the eerie is apparent 'readily in landscapes' where it is tied up with questions of agency, in terms of both the nonhuman agents that inhabit those spaces and in terms of a more pervasive, impersonal agency that is the landscape itself (2016: 11). As Fisher notes, '[t]he sensation of the eerie occurs either when there is something present where there should be nothing, or there is nothing present where there should be something' (2016: 61). Fisher identifies Garner as an author of the 'malign Eerie' precisely because his characters are 'caught up in the rhythms, pulses and patternings of non-human forces' (2016: 81, 11). Unlike the fantasies of Tolkien and Lewis, then, whose secondary worlds might easily be interpreted as allegorical or political or, at the very least, structurally similar to the 'real' world, the this-worldly fantasies of Cooper and Garner gesture to the same 'natural-material cosmos' that their readers inhabit while simultaneously revealing a partially obscured beyond, or 'outside'. Unlike the sub-creations of high fantasy, which often entail detailed lore and history, eerie this-worldly fantasies remain shadowed, obscuring their structures, and so prompt feelings of what Fisher calls 'real externality' (2016: 16).

Garner's *Weirdstone* sets its child protagonists against supernatural powers of darkness that manifest from within and animate the natural landscape. The rocks, trees, hills, and cave networks of Garner's native Alderley Edge become combative and claustrophobic. *The Dark Is Rising* also animates a local geography, revealing an unhuman realm within the landscape of the Thames

Valley. In the novel, Will discovers he has the power of the 'Old Ones', a race of beings who occupy a different temporal dimension to humanity. On Christmas Eve, he is drawn into an age-old conflict between the powers of light and dark, tasked with finding and joining six talismanic symbols to prevent the dark from rising. In *Weirdstone*, two children (Colin and Susan) stumble upon the Wizard of Alderley Edge (a figure Garner takes from local folklore) deep in his underground cavern. The wizard, Cadellin, has been guarding a sacred stone of power, but this was 'misplaced' a century ago and accidentally passed down through the women in Colin and Susan's family. Garner borrows the name of the stone from the poetic Edda and Norse mythology: 'Brísing' was the name of a necklace possessed by the goddess Freya. The children join with the wizard and other fantastic creatures to reclaim the weirdstone and prevent the powers of darkness taking over the land. Both works, never out of print, have been hugely influential in British children's literature and much praised by critics since their publication. Their innovation of a symbiotic relationship between a fantasy realm and the real world finds its most famous expression in the Harry Potter novels by J. K. Rowling but can also be seen in the more explicitly weird novels of Antony Horowitz and Celia Rees from the early twenty-first century (Germaine Buckley 2020). In her infamous excoriation of the Harry Potter books, A. S. Byatt (2003) praises 'great writers' Cooper and Garner for the 'real sense of mystery' they evoke and encourages readers to (re)discover *Weirdstone* and *The Dark Is Rising* instead of reading Rowling. Certainly, many critics have claimed that the blend of landscape and history, fiction and folklore, developed by Garner and Cooper defined modern fantasy for children for many decades (Egoff 1981; Byatt 2003; Butler 2006; Carroll 2011).

I concur with these assessments of the authors' influence on children's literature, but my reading of these novels diverges from scholarship that positions Garner and Cooper as authors of humanist fantasy. Criticism of children's fantasy from the mid- to late-twentieth-century echoes the psychoanalytic account put forward by Joseph Campbell's *Hero with a Thousand Faces* (1949). Campbell identifies a heroic quest metanarrative across several myth cycles, reading it as a rite-of-passage metaphor for the universal subject's psychological maturation. Ursula Le Guin was also influential in connecting fantasy to psychoanalysis in her assertion that it represented 'a journey into the subconscious mind' (2004 [1973]: 153). Critics of children's fantasy have added a pedagogical gloss to this reading, suggesting an educational as well as psychological benefit. This is evident in Peter Hunt's formulation that describes the landscape of fantasy, including Cooper and Garner's, as 'a metaphor for exploration and education;

readers go, like Tolkien's hobbit, "there and back again" in a circle that enables them to gain knowledge [. . .] and to return to home and security and to a satisfying psychological "closure"' (1987: 11). Where later critics question the restorative nature of fantasy journeys, they continue to discuss it as metaphorical of human selfhood, even if this selfhood is, in Colin Manlove's reading of Garner, 'uncertain' (2003: 102). More recently, criticism of Garner and Cooper has moved away from humanist concerns and engages instead with elements such as the landscape and the writers' concern with sedimentary layers of history. This is an important shift in emphasis from a psycho-symbolic reading to one that examines materiality as in Jane Carroll's 'topoanalysis' of *The Dark Is Rising* sequence (2011) or Catherine Butler's interrogation of the role of archaeology and geology in Garner and Cooper's work (2006). As writers of the weird and the eerie, Cooper and Garner gesture in the opposite direction to the psychoanalytic inward turn. Considering the outside of human experience, their fiction views the 'inside from the perspective of the outside' (Fisher 2016: 10). Their plots are not propelled by, nor do they hinge upon, human psychology, but are precipitated by stranger agencies that inhere in the landscape and material objects, as well as in humans themselves. In this way, the novels intimate Jane Bennett's insistence that human power is really a kind of 'thing-power' (2010: 10). Thing-power is Bennett's way of describing the 'existence peculiar to a thing that is irreducible to the thing's imbrication with human subjectivity', the idea that 'things have the power to addle and rearrange thoughts and perception' (2004: 148). The idea that human agency is already a kind of thing-power is echoed in Fisher's account of the eerie, which he notes prompts the realization that 'there is no inside . . . I am an other, and I always was' (Fisher 2016: 12). It is this realization that Garner and Cooper's novels disclose through their characters' encounters with the thing-power that inheres in the landscape.

The 'hard problem' of matter

Developing fantasy with occult themes anchored in real landscapes, Garner and Cooper raise ontological and epistemological questions about materiality and humans-as-material. These questions have been debated in philosophy since antiquity, but I propose Bertrand Russell's work from the early twentieth century as a starting point for this reading. Russell defines and anticipates some of the problems speculative realism and new materialism also tackle, though he is not a key reference for either movement. This lack of dialogue comes from the fact that many current speculative thinkers are responding to the continental tradition rather than the analytic philosophy inaugurated by Russell. While I acknowledge this divide and its complex history, I seek to bridge it with an eclectic and somewhat impudent synthesis of approaches. Finding in Russell an expression of the 'hard problem' of matter, I suggest ways that his work intersects with the speculative realist project before reading Cooper and Garner to develop the concept of occult materialism as one possible imaginative response to problems expressed in both analytic and continental philosophy.

The Analysis of Matter (1927) applies Russell's analytic method to new insights emerging in the study of physics, including the theories of relativity and early work in quantum mechanics. Russell begins by probing these new theories to establish epistemological propositions. His key insight is to identify what science cannot know, asserting that physics 'allows us to infer a great deal as to the structure of the physical world, but not as to its intrinsic character' (1992: 400). Though the inductive inferences of scientific theory and method remain a good basis for knowledge of reality, there is a limit to their reach, a darkness that occludes the qualities and relations of things-in-themselves. David Chalmers glosses Russell's structuralism about physics, noting that scientific theories characterize basic entities relationally, producing a picture of the physical world as a 'giant causal flux' that 'tells us nothing about what all this causation relates' (1996: 153). I have already proposed relationality as a valuable basis for ontoethics and will develop this in later chapters, but it remains the case that a relational picture of reality, particularly as it finds expression in the physical sciences, renders the intrinsic nature of matter elusive. What is more urgent here, though, is that the practical success of modern physics' dispositional understanding of matter (what matter does rather than what it is) has produced a false confidence in the scope of scientific knowledge. As analytic philosopher Galen Strawson suggests, 'we're so very deeply committed to the belief that we know more about the physical than we do' (2016: n.p.). The dispositional account of matter offered by physics coincides with its willingness to 'annihilate' matter altogether, since it proceeds from inference to abstraction, rather than privileging the empirical data available in perception (Russell 1992: 402). In so doing, as Russell notes, physics moves further away from an account of the world as it is experienced (1992: 21). It is this experience that Fantastika explores, disclosing its occulted aspects and puncturing its edges.

Modern theories of cosmology and theoretical physics, such as those proposing the existence of dark matter and dark energy, mark this shift from perceptual experience to abstraction. Such theories arise from the form of scientific knowledge and practice identified by Russell – what might be termed a 'structural realism' (Ongley and Carey 2013: 104–5). The idea of dark matter and energy emerges, as I note in the introduction, to account for the fact that matter is not behaving according to accepted theories of gravity and energy conservation. Proponents of dark matter theories insist something must exist to account for the inconsistency, something occluded from perception and other forms of detection. The resulting picture of the world is very far removed from common-sense perceptions of it since it suggests that the sensible universe comprises only 5 percent of what exists. In popular scientific writing on these topics, confidence in the scientific method meets a hesitancy about this hiddenness and acknowledgement of the fact that such conclusions seem at odds with how we experience the world. Writing about the 'discovery' of dark matter, for example, Lisa Randall suggests that 'the big lesson of physics over the centuries is how much is hidden from our view' (2017: 5). Of course, since they have yet to be detected, it is very possible that dark matter and dark energy are erroneous theories introduced by assumptions based on existing understandings of the dispositional nature of matter (Clegg 2019: 129). That there is something dark out there awaiting discovery is an evocative narrative and one less likely to bruise the scientific ego than acknowledging that there is much we do not know about the matter we can see.

Despite these equivocations, dark matter is useful throughout this book as a metaphor marking the limit of scientific knowledge at the same time as revealing its hubris. In this sense, Fantastika is full of dark matter, proposing innumerable universes of weird and eerie materialities as yet undiscovered by science. However apt the metaphor is for Cooper and Garner's work, though, its invocation in this chapter should not be taken as a reformulation of the Kantian distinction between phenomena and noumena. That structure is, of course, what the so-called speculative realists have problematized, following Quentin Meillassoux's identification of Kant as the founder of correlationist thought in continental philosophy (Meillassoux 2009: 5). Meillassoux, and those who have taken up his provocations, seek to go beyond the limit inscribed by Kant. Meillassoux names the project 'speculative materialism' (Tuin and Dolphijn 2012: n.p.), but others have responded by delineating approaches such as speculative realism, object-oriented ontology and weird realism – to name a few. These approaches rail against correlationism as the 'philosophy of human access' (Harman 2009: 102–3). In its 'weak' form, correlationism denies human knowledge access to the world-in-itself, while 'strong' correlationism would hold anything outside the relation between thinking and being as entirely unthinkable, forever sealing off matter and objects in-themselves from philosophical investigation and, furthermore, engendering a suspicion of science and its methods. If philosophy holds that thought cannot get outside itself to the world-in-itself, then nonhuman relations, objects, and matter are abandoned to the natural sciences and never the twain shall meet (Meillassoux 2009: 3; Harman 2009: 156).

Here I put Meillassoux's account of correlationism in dialogue with Russell. The latter's structuralism about physics is not a correlationist argument or one that seeks to debunk science. Instead, it leads to a monist ontology in which the 'neutral stuff' of reality is present in sensation and perception, in the form of what Russell calls 'percepts'. Noting that physicists had dispensed with the need to speculate as to the concrete character of the processes with which they dealt in favour of mathematical abstractions, Russell seeks to validate the physical data through which 'we obtain knowledge which is not purely formal as to the matter of our own brains' (1992: 122, 382). This notion of the physical bridges mind and matter because percepts, present as physical data and perceptions, are a part of the physical world knowable 'otherwise than in the abstract' (1992: 402). Russell's insistence on 'bringing physics and perception together', giving scientific investigation of physical matter 'the greater concreteness which result for our more intimate acquaintance with the subject matter of our own experience', and his proposition that the traditional separation between physics and psychology is not 'metaphysically defensible' anticipate Meillassoux's project (Russell 1992: 10). Moreover, Russell's recoupling of perception to scientific investigations of physical matter seems germane to penetrating the darkness of noumena in all its guises.

Russell's ideas have also been influential in the philosophy of consciousness, his monism paving the way for panpsychist theories that argue that the intrinsic nature of matter is conscious or experiential. I examine these ideas in the next chapter, discussing Russellian monism and panpsychism alongside animism. Here, Russellian monism informs my analysis because it asserts that there are very real limits to what science can tell us about the physical world and that this physical world is actually more mysterious than consciousness, even though it is the latter that has been proposed as a 'hard problem' in modern science and philosophy (Chalmers 1996). As Strawson (2016) insists, it is in fact matter – and not mind – that is the real conundrum. Russell suggests ways to investigate this conundrum in his proposition that the physical world is available as percepts. Percepts are not merely mental events but exist at the head of a physical causal chain. Thus, experience and sensory perception provide access to the world-in-itself, bridging the gap instituted by Cartesian and Kantian metaphysics.

The access to the world that percepts provide go beyond the abstractions and structural descriptions of matter, which would deny us access to its intrinsic qualities and infer a picture of the universe very different to that which we experience.

Fantastika, as it was developed in the work of Garner and Cooper, echoes Lisa Randall's claim that much of reality is hidden from our view, revealing a world replete with dark matter, mysterious energies and objects that resist human understanding. Yet both writers also revel in the rich sensory experiences that connect us with this occulted materiality. Cooper and Garner are alert to the elusive nature of physical reality, while also speculating, often through perceptual means, via what Russell names 'percepts', as to its intrinsic qualities. They gesture towards occulted materiality through characters' perceptual experiences of the matter in which humans are embedded. Both writers have keen interest in the earth-bound sciences of archaeology and geology as forming part of these experiences. As I have suggested, the problem of understanding matter in its broadest sense is foundational for Fantastika as a mode. Clute asserts that Fantastika emerged as a subversive response to the Enlightenment, to that 'dangerous' point in the history of the West in which 'Enlightened Europeans were beginning to know it all, were beginning to think that glimpsing the world was tantamount to owning it' (2016: loc 6238). Cooper and Garner develop this subversion in a refusal of the easy knowledge of the physical world that sight seems to convey, leading their characters into various kinds of darkness that inhere in familiar places.

Cooper and Garner's Fantastika troubles anthropocentrism through recourse to folkloric, occult, and theological themes that gesture to more-than-human worlds. Their innovations in fantasy occur at a time when developments in quantum physics and relativity were filtering into popular culture. This period also saw the rise of 'New Age' ideas, which mingled with popular interpretations of quantum physics, as in the writings of so-called 'quantum mysticism' in the 1960s and 1970s. These writings do not directly influence the work of Cooper and Garner, but they indicate a zeitgeist in which ideas from popular science and new-age spiritualism abounded, challenging classical physics and common-sense local realism alike. Neither writer is explicitly scientific, nor are they an advocate of the 'new age', but their stories seek to destabilize local realist ontologies while maintaining an 'apprehension', in Clute's words, 'of the Earth beneath our feet' (Clute 2016: loc 5802). Where Garner and Cooper part ways with Russell is in their emphasis on enduring objects and earthly substance. Whereas Russell largely accepts physics' structural picture of reality, proposing a monism in which events rather than things form the ultimate constituents of reality, Garner and Cooper's interest in the land and what lies buried therein ensure their commitment to a materialism of objects and things, however strangely it might figure in their work.

'A world of darkness and silence': Locating occult materialism

In Garner and Cooper's writing materialism anchored in earth sciences and real landscapes synthesizes with the fantastic and the supernatural to produce what I term 'occult materialism'. Here I sketch the philosophical coordinates for occult materialism and summarize its key propositions in dialogue with Garner and Cooper's writing. The discussion encompasses tropes of occultism and the supernatural on which the writers draw, the gothic spaces that open in their landscapes, as well as recent philosophical writings including the materialisms proposed by Bruno Latour and Jane Bennett, and the horror (as) philosophy expounded by Eugene Thacker. The latter thinker, broadly a speculative realist, expands upon Meillassoux's concepts of the-world-for-us and the world-in-itself as designations of various encounters, and limits, between the world and the human subject, adding a shadowy third term, the 'world-without-us' that he delineates with reference to supernatural horror fiction, philosophy texts and medieval mysticism (Thacker 2011: 4–5). Thacker describes the world-in-itself as an occulted 'Earth', which can only make present its hiddenness without ever becoming fully accessible, hence his introduction of a third term that manifests this hiddenness (2011: 53). Occult materialism evokes both senses of the word 'occult', then, meaning both hiddenness and forbidden knowledge. Garner and Cooper's occultism reveals the world-in-itself in the hidden places of the earth, accessible only when characters access forgotten lore. Occult materialism is also interested in the nature of reality that Russell suggests physics' structuralism leaves out: the matter, and agency, of things-in-themselves. Garner and Cooper's fiction punctures the 'bounded surface' of the structure, wondering, as Russell does, 'what happens in the interior' (Russell 1992: 42).

The concept of occult materialism arises from my reading of the books' treatment of real landscapes, which follows Butler's account of Garner and Cooper's writing. Butler notes, for example, the influence of Jacquetta Hawkes's *A Land* (1951) on Cooper, describing the former's work as 'a history of Britain from the time of its geological formation to the present day, woven with digressions on consciousness, time and the relationship of human beings to geology' (Butler 2006: 47). She likewise emphasizes Garner's interest in geology, suggesting that for him it was as economics was for Marx, that is, 'the base of human life and culture' (2006: 48). Certainly, Garner's commentary on his work and the landscape that inspires it typically starts with what lies underneath the visible strata. Defining the human in relation to the geological, Garner describes Alderley Edge as

> a land of two worlds: above and below . . . a world of darkness and silence, so dark that you can see the lights of brain cells discharging; so silent that blood in the veins can be heard. Yet, shine a lamp and the eye is washed with colour; the colour of minerals with marvellous names: malachite, azurite, galena. They glisten in caves the size of a cathedral; and on the roof, in places, there are the marks of ripples in the sand, of a sea upside down and hung to dry. And, in that best sense, I came to know my place. (Powell and Garner 2010: n.p.)

In Garner's recollection, the experience underground connects body to earth; both are alive with energy, processes of transmutation and pulsing matter. The earth glistens with marvellous minerals and yet remains shadowy and occulted. In this description, Garner evokes the sacred and the numinous – a sense of the human confronting the world as wholly other – but he also suggests a recognition of one's embeddedness in this other. He comes to know his place through encounters with the land and the archaeological fragments of older peoples, but he understands theirs and his own insignificance in relation to the vastness of geological time. This is the 'human-lithic enmeshment' Jeffrey Jerome Cohen articulates in his ontology of stone, which reads inorganic matter alongside medieval and modern texts, recognizing 'earth' as encompassing living body, corpse, soil, minerals, planet, world, possessions, and grave (2015: 6). Garner's concern with the earth, then, anticipates the new materialist project. As Colin Manlove notes of Garner's fantasies, Garner is interested in 'the earth itself' and his child characters seem mere 'conduits' for the forces of the local area than figurations of human subjectivity (2003: 100, 101). Cooper's text, too, is less about the human self than it is about things, signs of power crafted from stone and wood, about the vitality that inheres in rivers and trees, about a familiar land made strange.

The estrangement from familiar landscapes staged in the fiction of Garner and Cooper undercuts any nostalgic or conservative tendencies that sometimes work through valorizations of folklore and local history. These are landscapes that invite ingress into their secrets for initiates or seekers, but they might also turn combative and violent towards the human interloper. Though neither writer is explicitly ecological, Garner and Cooper recognize the agency of the earth in eerie and uncanny encounters with the natural landscape. In *Weirdstone*, for example, features of the landscape act against the progress of the heroes with branches 'forming lancets of wood to goad and score the flesh' (Garner 2002: 210). Similarly antipathic animations of nature occur in the opening of *The Dark Is Rising*, including the 'shrieking flurry' of the rook attack and the subsequent terror Will feels as he sits in the darkness of his attic room, hearing the howling wind thumping against the skylight (Cooper 1994: 11, 21). The ecological resonances of this representation of a reactive land are noted by Butler, who suggests Cooper's work is in sympathy with ideas expressed by James Lovelock in *Gaia* (1979) (Butler 2006: 131). Lovelock's image of the earth as a 'mega-organism . . . a living planet' informed green cultural and political movements of the era and continues to inspire contemporary eco-materialist writers such as Bruno Latour, whose latest work, *Down to Earth*, describes an earth that stirs, strikes back, has become an agent (Lovelock 2000: xvi; Latour 2018: 17, 20, 41). As I have suggested, it is this terrestrial agency that manifests in Garner's trees and Cooper's rooks.

Of course, the landscapes described by Cooper and Garner are not always antipathic to humans, but they do contain objects, sources of power and more-than-human inhabitants that provoke the affective encounters described by Jane Bennett as 'enchanted materialism'. Bennett's theory of enchanted materialism locates sites of enchantment 'where matter is animate without necessarily being animated by divine will or intent' (2001: 14). This notion of 'animated' matter develops into a renewed vitalism in *Vibrant Matter* where the focus shifts from human encounters to the 'material agency of non-human or not-quite-human things' (Bennett 2010: ix). Bennett's 'thing-power' is anticipated in the work of Garner and Cooper, for whom not only is the landscape animate, but inorganic objects, tokens, and signs pulse with energy and significance. Bennett's materialism aims at dissipating binaries such as those between nature and culture, human and animal, organic and inorganic in order to counter fantasies of human uniqueness and concomitant images of dead or instrumentalized matter, which fuel the destruction of the planet (Bennett 2010: ix). *The Dark Is Rising* and *Weirdstone* are in sympathy with this eco-materialist project.

Anticipating this ecological impulse to decentre and dethrone the human, Garner and Cooper initiate their characters into unhuman worlds populated by hitherto unknown and powerful beings. Even though Will discovers he is an 'Old One', a being of supernatural power with the ability to learn things beyond human ken, he is caught up in events much larger than himself. As well as the existence of greater powers, the children also discover ecosystems of other-than-human beings, which includes, in *Weirdstone*, creatures such as Svarts and the ancient race of the Lios-alfar with whom the humans unknowingly share the Edge. This 'Copernican' shift is common in ecological materialism and other speculative philosophies, as it is increasingly in earth system sciences, where human hubris butts up against the complexity of vast interconnected systems to which we contribute but do not control, or, as in physics and cosmology, with the vastness of the universe and all that remains unknown within it. Such 'cosmicism' is a common theme elsewhere in Fantastika, of course, but here in Garner and Cooper's work it is evoked not by imagining the daemons of unplumbed space as in weird horror fiction (Lovecraft 2012 [1927]), but by a sense of embeddedness in the earth itself. It is this connection with the earth that grants ecological possibilities to the writing.

The books develop a connection with the earth through a downward movement that evokes a sense of the gothic and the grotesque. Justin Edwards and Rune Graulund associate the gothic and the grotesque as spatial terms, noting the etymology of the latter word as 'grotto', which is, 'like the labyrinth or the crypt, a disorienting and threatening place that inflames anxiety and fear' (2013: 5). It is also a potential place of spatial internment. In *Weirdstone*, the children discover the secret world of the Edge only by making ingresses into cave networks, becoming lost as they travel 'down, down, always down!' (2002: 129). The children's journey evokes gothic claustrophobia as they become 'jammed' into smaller and smaller faces, able to move 'neither up nor down' (2002: 177–8). This is the same 'lapsed topos' that Carroll identifies as central to Cooper's *The Dark Is Rising* sequence, which features an archaeologist as a central character and leads its child characters into newly opened spaces underneath the hills of the Thames Valley. Early in *The Dark Is Rising*, in one such underground space, Will feels 'the Dark, rising, rising to swallow' him as he pushes back against it, trying to force it 'down, endlessly down' (1994: 60, 61). Darkness, interior spaces, and downward movement are connected in both books, as the lapsed topos becomes the primary site of an encounter with the animated earth.

Garner and Cooper's interest in the darkness of this interior accords with its role in Thacker's writing on speculative philosophy where it takes on a metaphysical significance. In Thacker's work, darkness evokes the 'world-without-us', that is, the subtraction of the human from the world and the paradoxical gesture of trying to think the 'world-in itself' (2011: 5–6). Thacker reads darkness through horror and mysticism, tracing accounts of darkness that are ambivalent, contradictory, and radically nonhuman (2015: 19). This mystical darkness suffuses Cooper and Garner grotto-esque spaces, for their concept of the dark is also not a theological binary of good versus evil, even though the fantasy quest narrative frames it in these terms. Cooper evokes the language of mysticism in her descriptions of Will's initiation into the mythos of the Old Ones. Under the land he sees 'a dark light', an energy 'that could not be seen or heard' articulating a sense of the darkness as something that is and is not 'a nothing that is something' (Cooper 1994: 136; Thacker 2015: 18). The metaphysical connotations of darkness further evoke the eerie and its questions of existence and non-existence: 'Why is there something here when there should be nothing? Why is there nothing here when there should be something?' (Fisher 2016: 12). This is dark matter that provokes metaphysical hesitation and ambiguity rather than represents evil forces.

As its use of gothic spaces suggests, occult materialism also has to do with magic and the supernatural as much as with the rude matter of the earth. Garner and Cooper were writing during the period of the 'New Age' and Neo-Pagan boom, when *Man, Myth and Magic* magazine (1970) and *Fortean Times* (1973–present) circulated in British households and documentaries about real-life witch covens appeared on the BBC and ITV. The countercultural zeitgeist inspired the 'folk' horror film genre, typified by *Blood on Satan's Claw* (1971) and *The Wicker Man* (1973), and other occult-themed films such as *The Devil Rides Out* (1968). 'Folk Horror' is a relatively recent critical term to describe a 'loose collection' of films from the 1960s and 1970s that share a 'common obsession with the British landscape, its folklore and superstitions' (Jardine 2010). Folk Horror has since been the subject of academic criticism, notably in Adam Scovell's *Hours Dreadful and Things Strange* (2017). Scovell's formulation of the genre has much in common with Fisher's eerie, identifying its terrifying treatment of landscape combined with a sense of isolation (Scovell 2017: 17–19). Certainly, Cooper and Garner's landscapes resonate with the folk horror mode; their evocation of archaic rituals and ancient objects uncovered from within the earth anticipate its thematic concerns and plots. Scovell's short film *Weirdstone* (2015) explores 'the special relationship Garner has with the landscape of his native Cheshire, of Alderley Edge and the surrounding rural locations' as well as 'how this landscape allows the questioning of the role of time, its effect on space and the philosophy behind it' (Scovell 2015). The philosophy Scovell evokes here is that of nineteenth-century pessimist Arthur Schopenhauer, and he frames his exploration of Garner with a quotation from *The World as Will and Idea* (1891): 'It is for this reason that we find that coexistence, which could neither be in time alone, for time has no contiguity, nor be in space alone, for space has no before, after, or now, is established through matter'. Schopenhauer locates a material substrate of existence underlying human conceptions of space and time. Scovell's accompanying poem locates this substrate 'under my ground', not merely in rocks and earth, but also in 'the old world of magic and ritual', recognizing the irruption of archaic and occult practices and belief into the present, a key trope of both gothic and folk horror modes. Scovell's identification of Garner as a folk horror writer connects the latter to the countercultural currents of the mid-twentieth century. This dark occultism suggests fantasy's orientation away from humanist narratives of mastery, underscored by the reference to Schopenhauer's whose formulation of Will as an impersonal force underlying reality rejects human autonomy. Furthermore, Fortean mysteries and tales of the supernatural suggest there is much that humans do not know about the material world in which they are embedded.

As its connections with folk horror suggest, occult materialism concerns time as well as space. Carroll suggests that the lapsed topos and its chthonic spaces provide a space between the past and the present, noting that 'caves, graves and holes in the ground open up and expose the buried layers of both time and place, making the chronotropic correlation between time and space apparent without the need for excavation' (2011: 141). In the darkness of the caverns under the Edge scored with mineral veins, for example, Colin and Susan connect with 'the turn of wind and wave upon a shore twenty million years ago' (Garner 2002: 123). This is not human time, but, as in *The Dark Is Rising*, 'deep time . . . as old as this land and even older than that' (Cooper 1994: 47). The matter that lurks in these spaces is what Quentin Meillassoux (2009) calls the 'archefossil': objects that predate human being and so lie outside any possible correlation of thought and world. Archefossils show that it is not the world that is contingent on thought but thought that is contingent on the world in a reversal of idealist philosophies.

The spacetime of occult materialism is non-linear as well as unhuman, as Merriman tells Will in *The Dark Is Rising*, asserting that 'all times co-exist, and the future can sometimes affect the past, even though the past is a road that leads to the future', adding 'men cannot understand this' (Cooper 1994: 67). The simultaneity of events in time and the ability of the Old Ones to return to past moments and stretch or speed up time suggests an affinity with quantum theories and relativity, rejecting what Russell calls the 'old geometry' of 'static space' which assumes that space and time are separable (1992: 62). Fisher's account of the eerie, too, identifies 'twisted forms of time and causality . . . alien to ordinary perception' as germane to the mode (2016: 12). Garner and Cooper's lapsed topographies reveal this twisted time as classical views of space evaporate.

Walking in the darkness, Colin and Susan realize that 'time and distance mean little' (Garner 2002: 124).

Thus, through the trappings of the occult, folklore and Fortean mysteries, Cooper and Garner reveal a darkness that intimates an unhuman ontology and temporality. Though neither author quite embraces anti-humanist and pessimist attitudes sometimes found in dark Fantastika (the weird, the eerie, folk horror, and the gothic), they nonetheless draw on all these modes to evoke a potentially malign landscape, ambiguous darkness, and strange things from ancient times. Through these narrative elements, their occult materialism speculates beyond the 'world-for-us' in several ways. First, they consider a reality in which human subjectivity is decentred, experimenting with ways of accounting for materiality beyond human perceptions. At the same time, occult materialism recognizes that the human is embedded in nature, it being another instance of a material ontology that is profoundly unhuman. Occult materialism is not, though, a thoroughgoing materialism, since it points to the darkness at the edges of human perception, or, to use Russellian vocabulary, the revelation of the hiddenness of what is encountered as a percept. As such, it reveals the withdrawn nature of reality without collapsing into the dichotomy of noumena and phenomena. Hence its designation as 'occult' materialism, where occult stands for the hiddenness of the world. This is speculation without disclosure, a glimpse into the darkness without rendering all visible with the 'light of knowledge' (Thacker 2011: 53).

'We are for the dark': The limits of speculation

In what follows I develop the key propositions of occult materialism beginning with an exploration of Cooper and Garner's treatment of darkness. This is a concept at the centre of Fantastika in its various modes because it tends to operate, as Clute suggests, in antipathy to the Enlightenment. As my comments on 'occultism' suggest, darkness is often used as a dyadic representation ignorance and knowledge. Rather than embracing ignorance, though, Fantastika deploys darkness to illuminate what is not, or cannot be, known. This dialectical darkness often turns to the language of horror for its expression, as Thacker demonstrates in his 'prayers' to darkness, where he connects fears of the dark as they are often expressed in horror fiction to metaphysics (2015: 19). Similarly connecting horror to philosophy, Fred Botting locates noumenon 'outside categories of sense, knowledge, reason . . . a realm of horror, revulsion, nausea, dissolution' (2012: 283). Botting picks up on a trend in speculative realism towards characterizing the world-in-itself in negative terms. Botting echoes this discourse but injects ethics into his commentary on Kant's noumenon, describing 'an anonymous impersonal rumbling to be found in darkness and silence: preceding anxieties about death or nothingness and stripping objects of their separateness and things of their solidity' (2012: 284). This might be the realm of 'being-for-the-other' in Levinas's terms, a proposition I endorse in later chapters with readings of ethical entanglements of varying types, but if so, in Botting's terms, such entanglements take place in dark places that are haunted by monsters.

The danger here, aptly identified by Ebony Elizabeth Thomas, is that a certain discourse of darkness risks (re)inscribing a racially charged notion of a Dark Other as 'the spectacle, the monstrous Thing that is the root cause of hesitation, ambivalence, and the uncanny . . . the obstacle to be overcome' (2019: 3). Mindful of Thomas's critique of the Anglo-American fantastic tradition, I am wary of embracing Botting's image of the darkness as a realm where the self dissolves in screaming terror. In any case, it is quite a different conception from Garner's world of 'darkness and silence' in the caves beneath the Edge, a place where he comes to conceive of the human as emerging from relations with a vast, geological, material reality – without recourse to philosophical pessimism. Occult materialism negotiates the darkness of experience, finding in writers such as Botting and Thacker interesting provocations about the nature of darkness as a limit, but also seeking, through a reading of Cooper and Garner's work, figurations that guard against the aporia toward which such speculations tend. I follow Rosi Braidotti's caution about aporia, which, she argues, lead to critical stasis (2002: 3). Thus, occult materialism is interesting in tracing vibrant ontologies, albeit through a darkness that marks the limit of science, philosophy, and human thought.

Thacker admits that his (mis)reading of medieval mysticism settles on a notion of darkness that 'is not in any way an answer, much less a solution, to some of the issues we face today' and he wonders if 'thinking this type of darkness is doomed to failure' (2015: 42). Despite Thacker's pessimism, he develops productive ideas of darkness that aid in moving beyond the moralistic binary that children's fantasy seems to inscribe. The first is dialectical darkness defined against its opposite term, the light. Dialectical darkness figures in both texts, which explicitly conscript child characters into an age-old war between powers of darkness and light, the former threatening to take over the land. Dialectical darkness is not only moral, nor theological, and evokes numerous dyads such as gift/privation and knowledge/ignorance (Thacker 2015: 39). Dialectical darkness is also the ground for a concept of darkness that lies beyond: superlative darkness. Superlative darkness is explicitly metaphysical for Thacker, paradoxically making an anti-empirical claim (since it is beyond any experience) alongside an anti-idealist claim (it is beyond any conception of light and dark). It is the limit of thought itself (Thacker 2015: 40). In speculative realist terms, superlative darkness marks the limit of the human, offering a glimpse of the Great Outdoors in the form of the world-without-us, that impersonal zone that allows us to think, albeit briefly, the world-in-itself. Beyond superlative darkness, Thacker muses, lies a Divine Darkness marking the limit of the limit: 'it suggests that there is nothing outside and that this nothing-outside is absolutely inaccessible' (2015: 42). Divine Darkness is an expression of negative theology, a negative knowing that there is nothing and it cannot be known, a figuration of pessimist and aporetic philosophies.

Weirdstone and *The Dark Is Rising* open with descriptions of dialectical darkness, evoking a moral dyad as ravens, rooks, and stormy weather foreshadow dark powers that threaten the land. Here, a moral conception of darkness shadows the land as Colin and Susan look up at the Edge, 'high, sombre and black' (Garner 2002: 19), and Will wanders through the shadows of the trees worrying about the warning of a 'bad night' to come (Cooper 1994: 9). Though it seems that the landscape is itself a 'world of danger and shadows', darkness as evil does not inhere in the land. Rather, during the children's explorations, a moral dialectic gives way to darkness as privation, particularly when the characters venture underground. In *Weirdstone*, subterranean darkness provides an encounter that is more like Jane Bennett's enchantment than Fred Botting's terror, supporting Fisher's insistence that the weird and the eerie are not necessarily terrifying (2016: 8–9). Colin and Susan find themselves in a 'cathedral' like cavern that is utterly dark; above is a 'starless night' while below are 'unknowable depths' (Garner 2002: 123–4). To be sure, here be monsters as Botting suggests, but darkness as privation reveals something beyond evil, gesturing beyond the reaches of human sight. Cooper pushes this concept further, describing transformative experiences of the dark that also contain something more than an expression of evil. Watching the 'lowering sky over the spinney, dark with rooks', Will experiences 'a dreadful darkness in his mind, a sense of looking into a great black pit' (1994: 19). Here, superlative darkness marks a limit of knowledge and sight, but also connects the mind and the world in the sense suggested by Russell's notion of the percept. The darkness in Will's mind is the Outside, not merely a secondary sensation. This figuration of darkness as an experiential encounter with unhuman reality occurs multiple times in Cooper's novel. Darkness here is not defined in opposition to another term, nor merely as the absence of light, but as an external something 'hurtling against [Will] with such a force of dread that it flung him cowering away . . . he lay scarcely conscious, lost somewhere out of the world, out in blank space' (1994: 21). In speculative terms, this 'blank space' is the impersonal zone of the world-without-us.

In her intimations of a world-without-us and a world-in-itself, Cooper offers darkness as a metaphysical figuration. The superlative darkness Will experiences connects him to a force that is beyond the human and not simply antipathic in the dialectic sense of good and evil. Rather, it is an impersonal force. Servants of the dark are not so because they are evil, cruel, avaricious, or immoral. Rather, the dark is something like a puppeteer to whom its servants have ceded control. When Will meets an old friend, Maggie he quickly identifies her as one such servant; he doesn't know if she has 'always been one of them' but suspects that the words she speaks are 'nothing but the mind of the Dark' (1994: 82). In *Weirdstone*, Colin and Susan also meet human inhabitants of the Edge who are revealed to be agents of dark powers, known collectively as the 'Morthbrood'. Garner's terminology suggests that the darkness is a central intelligence that inhabits and animates its progeny, rather than a collection of individuals working in concert for evil ends. Garner evokes this idea again when Cadellin mysteriously warns the children 'we are for the dark', intimating that failure in their quest will take the form of absorption into the darkness (2002: 87). It is never clear exactly what the forces of darkness are, what they want, nor what they can do. In *The Dark Is Rising*, Merriman states that the Dark cannot actually destroy or damage but finds ways to work through individuals and extend its influence. Will feels this influence in the strange behaviour of the rooks and the menace of the trees, an impersonal and pervasive power.

The cry of the rooks that announce the coming of the Dark in Cooper's novel connects darkness to the eerie, prompting anxieties over agency. As Fisher notes, a bird's cry is particularly eerie if there is a feeling of something more in (or behind) the cry than biological mechanism (2016: 62). In its evocation of the eerie, the cry of the rooks figures not just the other-than-human agency we have relegated to 'nature', but, more than this, it questions the nature of agency itself as a property belonging to individual subjects. Behind the cry of the rooks and other animated servants of the Dark lies an impersonal force that desubjectivizes the human and more-than-human alike. In this reading, Will's name echoes the concept of reality formulated by Schopenhauer in *The World as Will and Representation* (1818), the pessimist work that Scovell evokes.

For Schopenhauer, reality comprises a hidden essence or striving working away under the representations human consciousness imposes on reality: a 'blind impulse, an obscure, dull urge, removed from all direct knowableness' (1969: 149). The blind striving of Will is unhuman; it has nothing to do with individual subjectivity. In a strange evocation of this unhuman agency, Robert MacFarlane's Twitter reading group that aimed to celebrate Cooper's novel during December 2017 used the hashtag #TheDarkisReading, offering an accidental, but apt, expression of the dark dissipation of human subjectivity intimated in these texts. Fisher identifies Garner as eerie precisely for his evocation of this transpersonal force, which Fisher names an 'eerie Thanatos' (2016: 82). Though this term denotes Freudian baggage, it names a process whereby the psychological is produced by forces from the outside. In both novels, a humanist notion of free will is undercut even as Cooper and Garner seem to evoke the hero quest and its metanarrative of maturation. Rather than exerting their will-as-mastery, the children are subsumed into mythic and cyclical patterns, following twisted paths of time and causality. This does not render their actions any less urgent, but it does place the idea of individual subjective agency in doubt.

Cooper's other-than-human darkness is a mode of negative transcendence akin to Thacker's Divine Darkness as both writers are influenced by Christian mysticism. Will only ascends to his role as an Old One after reading the occult tome, *The Gramareye* – a 'book of hidden things' (1994: 126). This learning isn't merely a matter of diligent study and understanding. He cannot give an account of reading it. Instead, the book gives Will 'a snatch of verse or a bright image, which somehow had him instantly in the midst of whatever experience was involved' (1994: 130). The experience of the book grants Will knowledge of earth, sky and stars, as well as affording him a glimpse into 'the infinite emptiness beyond' (1994: 131). Peering into this Divine Dark is a 'melancholy' experience and removes Will from theological binaries (1994: 135). Witnessing Will defend his parishioners from an incursion by the forces of the dark after this initiation, Will's pastor says, 'I am not sure whether you should be exorcized or ordained' (1994: 185). Despite the melancholic figurations of the dark as emptiness, privation, and negation present in both texts, Garner and Cooper pull back from the aporetic Divine Darkness with which Thacker ends his meditation, though they do use the figuration of darkness to explore that weird affect that Fisher calls 'unworlding, an abyssal falling away' of contact with reality (2016: 48). Though Garner's darkness as privation hints to an occulted world and Cooper's superlative darkness transports her characters to a world beyond the human, neither endorses the pessimism of darkness as a nothing that cannot be known. Rather, it is in the darkness that the characters in these texts encounter the vibrancy of materiality, be this the glistening minerals under the Edge, the luminous power of the Weirdstone, or the energy in the seven signs Will uses to fight the rising dark.

'The power of rocks and fire and water and living things': Vibrant matter

It is in the dark places of the earth, then, that the characters in these books encounter what Bennett calls 'vibrant matter' (2010). Bennett's theory recuperates matter from its status in anthropocentric thought as passive and inert. She calls attention to the 'agency of things that produce (helpful, harmful) effects in humans and other bodies', using the term 'thing-power' to identify traces of 'independence or aliveness' in other-than-human matter (2010: xii, xvi). Cooper and Garner express this in the shimmering minerals of aeons-old rock, flora and fauna animated by powerful forces, and, of course, specific objects of power: the Weirdstone that retains 'the strongest magic the world has known' and, in *The Dark Is Rising*, the 'six great Signs of Light' (Garner 2002: 49; Cooper 1994: 53). Talismans such as the Weirdstone and the Signs are not objects subordinated to human subjectivity. Rather, they accord with Bennett's account of things as 'vivid entities never entirely exhausted by their semiotics' (2010: 5). The Weirdstone, for example, goes by many names: 'tear', 'bridestone', 'firefrost' and eludes long-term possession by any one person. It even finds its way out of Cadellin's lair where it has been held for protection for many centuries, an event that precipitates the action of the book. It appears first as an adornment on Susan's wrist, a stone with strange capacities that responds to the conditions on Alderley Edge, sensing changes to the landscape beyond Susan's ken. In *The Dark Is Rising*, likewise, while Will successfully finds and holds the signs of power, he does not understand what power resides within them and, when facing the Dark, he simply lets 'the Signs work for themselves' (1994: 181).

There is what Cohen (2015: 6) calls a 'queer vivacity' to the Weirdstone and Cooper's Signs. Will finds the Sign of Stone because it emits a 'shaft of brilliance' in the local church (1994: 183). Will is awestruck by the 'glowing', 'smooth and beautiful thing': a stone circle quartered by a cross, though not made as such by any human hands (1994: 183). Will realizes that, despite its design, the Sign is 'natural flint, grown in the Chiltern chalk fifteen million years ago', challenging distinctions between man-made and natural materials (1994: 184). In Fisher's reading, the unearthing that is central to much of Garner's eerie fiction works in opposition to archaeology because it emphasizes rather than fills a gap in knowledge (2016: 77). The unearthing of objects that carry ancient threats is germane to the weird, the eerie and folk horror, which Garner's writing anticipates. Butler's reading of *The Dark Is Rising* echoes Fisher's account of unearthing, too, because she notes that Cooper's Old Ones value the objects they discover not as archaeologists would (though Merriman poses as one in later books in the sequence), since the artefacts do not grant knowledge but rather have a 'magical use' (Butler 2006: 499). The magical use of unearthed objects implies a mastery denied in the eerie texts Fisher examines, but my reading differs from both Fisher and Butler's account, since it identifies an equivocation, or hesitation, about human encounters with thing-power. These objects do not completely surrender themselves to human use or understanding, but nor do they entirely withdraw. Outside the church, when the Signs have done their work in repelling the forces of the Dark, another Old One remarks upon the fact that their 'minds' have not been required to engage in the encounter: it was the 'Things, this time. They did it alone' (1994: 181). In this case, the objects work in the humans' favour, but the Old Ones gathered around Will retain a degree of wariness about the thingness of the Signs that remain beyond their grasp.

Even occult practices are not enough to reduce these queer things to human use-value or to break them apart into their constituent pieces. In *Weirdstone*, the witch Selina Place casts a spell on the stone, enclosing it in a magic circle to break its power. However, the 'swirling mass' she conjures shudders, dies, and droops 'like the ruin of a mighty tree', leaving the stone untouched (2002: 114). The stone may be immutable, but it is not inert. Later, when Cadellin regains possession of firefrost, his occult knowledge unlocks some of the stone's power, repelling the dark forces that have gathered on the Edge. However, the hurried and chaotic scenes of this climax offer little exposition, with Garner opting for impressionistic descriptive fragments. The stone emits a 'cone of light' as Cadellin utters words in an unknown language and, all at once, 'the darkness passed and the blue light faded' (2002: 284). Within a few lines the novel draws to a close, leaving readers none the wiser as to operation of the stone's power. As Bennett notes of everyday objects, they issue a call even if we do not understand what they are saying (2010: 4). The things imagined by Garner and Cooper likewise allow for a momentary apprehension of thing-power, though this power resists full articulation. This is the nub of materiality as disclosed via Russell's percept: it is both the thing-in-itself and yet, also, something that remains partially withdrawn such that it is never fully integrated into a closed circle of human knowledge and use.

In the same way, the landscape in these novels does not function as an inert container for powerful objects but is itself a sliding 'bedrock of reality' that prompts 'shifts in perception, cognition, and environmental sensibilities' (Cohen 2015: 12). Following Cohen's ontology of stone, I read such talismans and objects as coextensive with the landscape, as are human beings. In sympathy with Garner's notion of geology as base, Cohen argues that stone is the 'foundation of story . . . history's bedrock as lithic agency impels human knowing' (2015: 4). Likewise, in Garner and Cooper's work, human stories and knowledge are enmeshed within an unhuman ontology of which they are a part, hence their evocation of romantic stories of stones and caves in which dragons, secret armies, and magical amulets slumber, or the emergence of a Viking Long Ship from its ancient burial in the swollen Thames, which comes to rest 'on the land that had once been an island' in order to give up the Sign of Water to Will in *The Dark Is Rising* (1994: 269). There is vibrancy in such objects of power but also in the earth from which they emerge.

The vibrancy of the earth expressed by Garner and Cooper also appears in Latour's recent writing. He returns to Lovelock's Gaia hypothesis as a basis for reorienting thought in relation to the climate crisis. Like Bennett, Latour does not advocate the old vitalisms that would add the property of life to inanimate matter. Rather, he endorses Lovelock because the Gaia hypothesis refuses to 'deanimate the planet' (2018: 76). As discussed, Cooper's writing contains something of the notion of Gaia, albeit expressed in supernatural rather than scientific terms. Will glimpses an animate earth in the story of the Old Ones, present 'from the beginning when magic was at large in the world; magic that was the power of rocks and fire and water and living things, so that the first men lived in it and with it, as a fish lives in the water' (1994: 133). This magical ecology echoes organicist conceptions of earth that, as ecofeminist Caroline Merchant (1980) argues, were eroded through early agricultural and industrial activities, giving way to mechanist conceptions of nature. Merchant notes, for example, that the demise of forests increased apace as trees became a resource for shipbuilding, soap, glass, iron, and copper refining (1980: 63). Rejecting such a mechanist view of 'nature', Old One Merriman scoffs at humanity's attempt to shape the landscape for their own ends, suggesting that 'forests are not biddable places' (1994: 68). Rather than the background for a story, or a container of resources, the landscapes in these tales become 'magic sites', a term Thacker devises in relation to occult fiction. The magic site allows an 'anonymous unhuman intrusion of the hidden world into the apparent world' (Thacker 2011: 82). In these novels, cave systems are threshold sites and doorways appear in stones and hillsides. Such portals are also, according to Fisher, key to the weird since they evoke the in-between, denaturalizing the world by exposing its 'openness to the outside' (2016: 29). This opening, or intrusion, occurs at the Earth's own convenience, as the dwarf Fenodyree notes in *Weirdstone* when he finds Colin and Susan desperately pounding on the stones outside the wizard's cavern begging them to 'open up!' (Garner 2002: 79). 'Rocks are old, stubborn souls', Fenodyree asserts, 'they were here before we came, and they will be here when we are gone. They have all the time there is and will not be hurried' (Garner 2002: 80). The magic site transports the characters from the 'world-for-us', revealing a partially withdrawn reality to which humans acquire only oblique access.

In these tales, as in Lovelock and Latour's writing, the earth strikes back. Stone circles suddenly fill with sinister mists, the earth itself 'shackling' the human characters 'in a net of blade and root' (Garner 2002: 77). Cadellin tells the children of the fate of those who thought they could drain and live upon Black Lake, a place suffused with dark power: 'the spirit of the place entered them, and their houses were built drab and desolate, and without cheer; and all around the bog still sprawls, from out of the drear lake come soulless thoughts and drift into the hearts of the people, and they are one with their surroundings' (Garner 2002: 89). These representations of the land echoes Bennett's assertion that vibrant matter might have either helpful or harmful effects with a latent ecological message about the negative effects of the destruction of the land. Indeed, Cooper and Garner's recourse to pseudo-medieval fantasy tropes along with local folklore and their assertion that magic suffuses the land itself harkens to an imagined organicist past. Though Merchant's thesis of organicism giving way to mechanism has been critiqued, both Garner and Cooper anticipate it, offering albeit oblique critiques of destructive modern land management, building, consumption, not to mention the tourists who come 'shouting and crashing through the undergrowth, and littering the ground with food wrappings and empty bottles' (Garner 2002: 97). Colin and Susan also learn that the elves, or Lios-alfar, were forced to leave the land because men 'turned from the sun and the earth and corrupted the air with the smoke of furnaces [and] the scab of brick tile' (Garner 2002: 226). Two eco-narratives mingle. On the one hand, there is a sense of grief for a lost arcadia, gone forever thanks to human activity. On the other hand, Garner suggests that the world-without-us endures despite destructive human hubris. *The Dark Is Rising* likewise mingles these two sentiments when Will brings the Signs of Power to Herne the hunter, a being associated with folklore of Southeast England. Herne's name signifies neo-pagan and New Age reconstructions of pre-Christian British mythology as well as a 'Merrie England' filtered through Shakespeare's staging of Falstaff's encounter with the deity in Windsor Forest (Shakespeare 1602). In Cooper's version, Herne is a terrifying and non-anthropomorphic creature belonging to neither the light nor the dark. It wears an 'abstracted' and 'cruel' visage that Will recognizes as 'the fierce inevitability of nature' to which humans must submit (1994: 279). The striking back of the Earth in these various guises offers a reminder that humans 'inhabit an ineluctably material world' (Coole and Frost 2010: 1), and it is this world that the objects of power in these stories belong, and to which they must return.

My reading of Cooper and Garner's landscapes as magic sites reiterates that children's Fantastika is an apt companion for the ecological materialist project since it intimates attitudes that Bennett argues are necessary to distribute value, agency, and subjectivity more generously between human and nonhuman actors, as well as between organic and inorganic matter (2010: 13). Bennett advocates naivety rather than pessimism since the limit marked by what she calls the 'outside of our own experience' need not be a terrifying black hole (2010: xvi). This reading of Cooper and Garner likewise does not seek to inscribe materiality-in-itself as an absolute outside, drawing on Russellian notions of the percept to resist the collapse into noumena to which talk of darkness and the Great Outdoors tend in speculative realism. As Cohen remarks, matter resists and rebukes epistemology but in this very reproach there 'inheres a trigger to human creativity and a provocation to cross-ontological fellowship' (Cohen 2015: 8). In *The Dark Is Rising*, the Signs of Power are ancient objects forged from the land, and from intimate relations between humans and other forms of matter. In each age Will sees 'the men who worked with stone and with bronze and with iron' forging the signs, evoking a pre-modern lineage of craftsmen working in symbiosis with their tools and materials (Cooper 1994: 133). The signs belong to this human history but not in the sense that they are produced by it, but because they reveal that this human history is already enfolded by an outside, a longer history that includes the long slow growth of forests and mountains.

The land as magic site also destabilizes boundaries, dismantling the quarantines between life and matter examined in both Latour and Bennett's work. This is a rejection of what Coole and Frost designate the Cartesian/Newtonian dual concepts of matter and subjectivity, in which the latter creates and dominates nature (2010: 7). As Thacker notes, the magic site 'creeps forth with entities that are neither animate nor inanimate, neither organic nor inorganic, neither material nor ideal' (2011: 82). Garner's descriptions of the landscape and its strange creatures contains this suggestion of mutability, of the breakdown of categorical distinctions. His underground spaces are apt for the disclosure of such taxonomical blurring since the aesthetic of the grotesque, of course, was first applied to paintings found on the walls of basements ruins in Rome underneath Nero's unfinished palace, called 'le Grotte' (the caves). The paintings and carvings called grotesque were a mixture of human, animal, and vegetable. Garner's *The Stone Book Quartet* (1983) returns to the caves of Alderley Edge, and the character Mary discovers an ancient cave painting of a bull along with the marks of many generations of human footprints etched into the clay. The bull seems to move, dying all over again as Mary traces the image with her hand, 'finger and thumb and palm and a bull' all merging in the darkness underground (Garner 2006: 30). In *Weirdstone*, when Colin becomes trapped in the cave network, he wonders if he is a 'living fossil' doomed to be stuck until unearthed by an archaeologist in the distant future (2002: 178). These encounters in the grotto complicate the neat line between living creature and fossil, between animal and human, image and being. In these spaces lie what Reza Negarestani calls 'inorganic demons' – relics of artefacts in the shape of objects made of inorganic material – bone, stone, metal. Inorganic demons are 'autonomous, sentient and independent of human will' as we have seen in the case of the Weirdstone and the Signs of Power, but they also take other forms (Negarestani 2008: 224).

Inorganic demons manifest as a myriad of strange creatures begin to 'creep forth' when Colin and Susan venture further into the Edge. The Mara are one such creature, attacking the children as they cross the snow-bound woodlands. Garner's description of the Mara cross-contaminates the human with animal and vegetable. The creature

> bore some resemblance to a woman . . . twenty feet high, and green. The long, thick-set trunks rested on massive legs with curving, bloated thighs. . . . There was no hair; the mouth was a shadowed line; the nose cut sharply down from the brow, between eyes that were no more than dark smears. It wore a single garment, a loose tunic that reached to the ground, and clung to the body in folds like wet linen. The flesh gleamed dully, and the tunic, of the same colour and texture, might have been of the same substance. A stone of polished malachite; but a statue that moved. (2002: 230–1)

This is a tree-woman-rock whose garment might also be her skin or may have emerged from the interior of her being in a process of mineralization.

Its mineral qualities suggest the Mara ought to be immobile, so the final revelation that it 'moved' provokes ontological shock. The malachite that gleams on the surface of the Mara recall the caverns through which Colin and Susan first travel, the veins of mineral that provide evidence of a world twenty million years away (Garner 2002: 123). As Manuel DeLanda (1997) insists, this geological history is not so distinct as we might imagine and there is a continuity between the minerals embedded in the rocks and those that comprise our own bodies. DeLanda theorizes 'mineralisation' as the process whereby fleshy matter evolved into bone, positing the 'mineral world' as the 'substratum for the emergence of biological creatures' (1997: 26). Glossing DeLanda's theory, Bennet notes that 'in the long and slow time of evolution . . . mineral material appears as the mover and the shaker, the active power, and the human beings, with their much-lauded capacity for self-directed action, appear as its product' (2010: 11). Mara, then, turn our sense of ourselves inside out, their mineral surfaces disclosing the ancient processes that forge organic bodies from inorganic matter and vice versa. Again, this undercuts a notion of exceptional human agency.

Conclusion

It is through eerie encounters with vibrant material agents, then, that Cooper and Garner probe the 'hard problem' of matter and speculate as to its intrinsic nature through perceptual imaginings. This extended analysis of their most famous novels aims to demonstrate how children's Fantastika echoes debates on matter from an older tradition of analytic philosophy and, in so doing, anticipates, and produces dialogue with, recent material and speculative turns, which have likewise taken up this problem. Furthermore, I have shown that children's Fantastika in its darker modes, where it hybridizes with the gothic, the grotesque, the eerie, and the weird, promotes the generous attitudes towards materiality Bennett proposes in her work. Despite the novels' evocation of darkness, they refuse the aporetic tendencies of metaphysical thought and exhort a willingness to be enchanted, to suspend one's disbelief and scepticism, and embrace a degree of naivety in wondering as to the agentic intrinsic nature of things. All told, they affirm Bennett's argument that an 'unrealistic imagination' is needed to open oneself to the outside of human experience (2010: 15). Bennett suggests that vital materialism already finds expression in 'childhood experiences of a world populated by animate things rather than passive objects', but in Garner and Cooper's work playful things also prompt metaphysical questions, doubt, and ambiguity (Bennett 2010: 15, vii).

My reading of these texts offers an alternative to anthropocentric, mythopoetic, or psychological interpretations of children's fantasy that would focus on human subjectivity. I propose that these novels gesture towards the revelatory impulse of speculation, to the 'ontological truth hidden behind the radical scepticism of modern philosophy: to be is not to be a correlate, but to be a fact' (Meillassoux 2008: 9). This is the revelation that the independent (in)existence of the 'in-itself' paradoxically includes the human. Despite the 'withdrawn' or occulted nature of the 'world-in-itself', this world contains the human, and is available, if only in part, through percepts that connect the inside of human experience to the Great Outdoors. Or, to express it differently, the human is embedded within an unhuman realm that philosophies of correlation would seal from access. Such is one reading available in Merriman's pronouncement to Will in *The Dark Is Rising*, that he is 'not bound by the laws of the Universe as we know them' (1994: 122). Yet, these books do not get lost in a noumenal darkness often found in speculative realist writings because they also propose ideas that accord with new materialist thought, especially with thinkers like Cohen, Latour, and Bennett who seek to decentre the human in an attempt to prompt new modes of engagement with nature.

My readings of Garner and Cooper serve here to initiate a much more expansive discussion of materiality. Their work is important because they innovated a form of Fantastika that has subsequently developed in myriad different directions. I have called Garner and Cooper's work occult materialism, but this is also the name of a set of ontological propositions that their work suggests when placed in dialogue with a particular philosophical synthesis drawn from analytic and speculative thinkers. These propositions might be found in some of the contemporary texts examined later in this book, but the different directions in which Fantastika has developed demands different kinds of engagements. In Chapter 2, then, we leave behind the dark places of the earth to focus on more expansive cosmologies developed in contemporary fantasy. The works discussed in the next chapter are more explicitly animist than Garner and Cooper's novels. If the hard problem of matter leads to speculation as to its intrinsic nature, one answer to the question, 'what is materiality?' has been to equate matter with consciousness as in new animist and panpsychist philosophies, to which I now turn.

2

Animate worlds

Magical encounters in contemporary fantasy

Cosmological fantasy: Panpsychism and animism

Moving on from fantasies from the Second Golden Age of children's literature in Britain, this chapter examines contemporary fantasy novels written for young adults in different cultural and geographical locations. *Akata Witch* (2011), written by the Nigerian American writer Nnedi Okorafor and set in contemporary Nigeria; *The Lost Witch* (2018), which is written by British writer Melvin Burgess and set in contemporary England; and *Children of Blood and Bone* (2018), written by Nigerian American writer Tomi Adeyemi and set in the secondary world of Orïsha, are pertinent to this developing discussion of the ontoethical affordances of Fantastika because of the ways in which they deploy the trope of magic to explore the intrinsic nature of materiality. Each novel uses magic to stage encounters between human characters and the more-than-human world. In so doing, they gesture to panpsychist philosophy and animist cosmologies, providing ethical reflections on being part of a world that is suffused with life and spirit. Despite hailing from distinct cultural and geographical locations, *Akata Witch*, *The Lost Witch*, and *Children of Blood and Bone* imagine similarly responsive entanglements of human witches and a more-than-human cosmos, and work to decentre modernist ontologies and epistemologies.

In what follows, I read the trope of initiation into a world infused with magic, which is common to the three novels, alongside concepts from the new animisms, a discourse that has emerged in anthropology in the last two decades. Often in sympathy with the new materialisms, new animism is an ontological turn in anthropology that is concerned with 'the relationship between modernist or cartesian approaches and the not-so-peculiar-after-all recognitions of the mutual constitution and generative interactivity of "persons" and "things"' (Astor-Aguilera and Harvey 2018: 1). As Miguel Astor-Aguilera and Graham Harvey suggest, new animism proposes a relational approach to subjectivity and social relations, echoing concepts central to the ontological principle of entanglement, including the mutual constitution of self and other. New animists reconsider colonial anthropology's application of animism to indigenous people as a 'belief in spirits' so defined by Edward Burnett Tylor in *Primitive Culture* (1871). New animists consider this definition a projection of mind/body dualism onto indigenous people, one that is grounded in the logic of inversion that pervades Western thought whereby beings are 'closed in upon themselves, sealed by an outer boundary or shell that protects their inner constitution from the traffic of interactions with their surroundings' (Ingold 2006: 11). This boundary is a conceptual apparatus that divides the world into subjects and objects and is precisely what new animists challenge as they write about the practices and beliefs of indigenous people in the majority world. As Alf Hornborg suggests, new animism is less about categorizing other beliefs as it is about challenging so-called 'modern' modes of knowledge production (2006: 21). Magic is of interest here precisely because of its similar status to animism in the popular imagination, a pre-modern belief that has been superseded by the rationalism of modernity. Like animism, magic punctures rationalism and its boundary-forming practices, revealing the entangled subjectivities of those who can sense and wield it.

Animism no longer means the imputation of spirit to non-living things. Rather, it describes a variety of subject–subject ontologies that contrast with the subject–object division that tends to characterize Western thought, science, and society. Suggesting the relationality of animism, Graham Harvey points to the influence of Irving Hallowell's article on Ojibwa Ontology (1960) and its phrase 'other-than-human persons', variations of which now abound in new animist, new materialist, and ecological writings. Harvey credits Hallowell with developing the idea that relationality is not merely theoretical, but strongly pervades the praxis of many cultures, arguing that 'to engage with animism necessarily involves being provoked to think more carefully about what it means to be a person' (2014: 15). Such thinking characterizes Eduardo Kohn's writing on indigenous people in Amazonian Ecuador, for example, leading him to theorize reality as a mutually constitutive 'ecology of selves' comprising human persons, more-than-human persons, and the spirits of the dead (2013: 16). The cosmologies developed by Adeyemi, Burgess and Okorafor exemplify this extension of human sociality to a more-than-human world; their witches sense the spirit that infuses other creatures and ecosystems, which lurks beyond the world of the living, and binds powerful beings of the sky with those who dwell on earth. There are varied theorizations of animism developed by anthropologists working across different continents, but most identify a divide between largely Western ontologies, which posit autonomous and bounded individuals, and largely non-Western ontologies, which posit relational and interdependent 'dividual' persons (Astor-Aguilera and Harvey 2018: 4).

Although the novels discussed here cleave to this broad divide between Western thought and animism, with Okorafor and Burgess levelling accusations about the destructiveness of Western capitalism, they also complicate the divide. They suggest that animism is not a quality particular to pre-modern societies and indigenous cultures, but rather that it suffuses modernity. Writing from South Africa, Harry Garuba makes a similar claim, suggesting that animism is a materialist mode of thought 'embedded within the processes of material, economic activities and then reproduces itself within the sphere of cultural and social life' (2003: 269). Garuba's 'animist materialism' refuses a divide between pre-modern and modern worlds; he identifies an animist unconscious that pervades life in modern Africa. Such an animist unconscious manifests dramatically in all three texts, but especially in *Akata Witch* and *Children of Blood and Bone*, which draw on West African mythologies. Animism is not only identified as an African mode of thought, of course. Burgess' writing develops the cosmology of *The Lost Witch* with reference to Norse myth and neo-pagan practices particular to Britain. In all cases, the writers' use of magic as a signifier for an animate world rebukes the simplistic idea that there is a 'Western worldview that is singularly scientific, rational and mechanistic' (Braddock 2017: 72).

Animism is also evoked in new materialist discussions of the implications of quantum physics, further blurring neat distinctions between cosmological 'belief' and 'rational' science, so-called 'primitive' ontologies and so-called 'modern' ones. Christopher Braddock, for example, recognizes a 'striking collusion of anthropology and quantum mechanics' especially in the ways in which theorists such as David Bohm translate the implications of quantum entanglement into concerns about agency and ethics (2017: 74). Braddock further contends that Bohm's interpretation of quantum physics echoes a Māori cosmology in its 'emphasis on holism in entanglement' and 'collective phenomena' (2017: 76). He glosses Bohm's 'Wholeness and the Implicate Order' (1980), stating that 'ultimately the nature of the world is that all is mutual participation – everything is everything . . . everything "enfolds" everything' (Braddock 2017: 76). As Braddock suggests, mutual participation is the ontoethical implication of the science of entanglement *and* many animist cosmologies. A refusal of a neat distinction between the two ontologies is apparent in this reading of Fantastika, which finds corollaries of both in Okorafor, Burgess, and Adeyemi's work.

To emphasize Braddock's point about drawing comparisons between indigenous cosmologies and Western science, in order to refuse a caricature of the latter, I also bring the philosophy of panpsychism into dialogue with these texts. Arising from discussions about the nature of the mind in nineteenth-century European and American philosophy, panpsychism argues that consciousness is ubiquitous in the world. The theory has enjoyed a resurgence in the twenty-first century thanks to developments in the philosophy of mind and neuroscience. Proponents of panpsychism often derive their arguments from Bertrand Russell's propositions about the structuralism of physics and his resulting monism, discussed in the previous chapter (Seager 2006; Coleman 2009; Strawson 2016), and advocates have also pointed out panpsychism's sympathy with quantum physics. Though the claims of panpsychists differ from one another, and from new animism, the unifying theme is that the 'world is alive' and 'that to be means to participate in this aliveness', or, alternatively, that the 'world is awake' (Vetlesen 2019: 16; Seager 2020: 1). There are competing theorizations of panpsychism but a relevant distinction for this chapter is between micropsychism, which accords consciousness to small units of reality (down to quantum particles in some cases), and cosmopsychism that holds that the universe as a whole has an inherent consciousness or subjectivity. In this chapter, I focus on cosmopsychism, exploring its sympathy with animism and tracing imaginative renderings of its ontoethical propositions in the novels by Okorafor, Burgess, and Adeyemi.

Despite panpsychism emerging as a response to the 'hard problem' of consciousness, in which human thought is privileged, I find it more useful as a philosophy that engages with the liveliness of the more-than-human world. To that end, cosmopsychism is compelling because it describes a universe that is itself a subject, from which individual selves emerge and to which they are connected. This living universe is a communicative order that reaches out to itself in the form of the differentiated beings it has produced. Freya Mathews finds inspiration for her articulation of cosmopsychism in the enchanted ambience of the fairy tale (2003: 18). Although she is dismissive of connecting panpsychism to magic, 'where magic is understood in the sense of sorcery' that would manipulate the world to do its bidding, her elucidation is replete with references to characters in fairy tale and myth being 'initiated' into 'magic', which stands for the communicative impulses of the living universe (2003: 68, 115). The texts discussed here also position magic as a communicative order that connects its users with a living world. The descriptions of characters in the novels who embrace this enchanted way of being contrast with those characters who refuse to see magic or, worse, use it for the purposes of exploitation. 'Good' magic, then, produces an enchantment with the world that emphasizes relations of obligation and responsibility, and witches must learn to control their powers to reduce the harm they might commit. This ethics of responsibility relates the trope of magic to animist concepts of personhood, which extend human sociality (and its obligations) to the more-than-human world. Mathews' cosmopsychism is furthermore instructive for my reading of Fantastika because it acknowledges its debt to animist ontologies, myth, and fairy tale. This is unusual in the literature of panpsychism, which generally credits white European philosophers for its revelations.

As the chapter progresses, then, I draw on various concepts from the writings across panpsychism and new animism. My approach is not to privilege either, but to develop a dialogue that reveals the multiple possibilities available in the texts' use of the trope of magic. Though Adeyemi and Okorafor are influenced by their West African cultural heritage, and draw on Yoruba, Igbo and Efik cosmologies, I do not restrict my discussion of animism to this geographical context. Following Harvey and Astor-Aguilera, I take animism not as a description the social reality of indigenous peoples, nor as a specific African cosmology, but as a 'heuristic tool' for finding alternatives to anthropocentric modes of thought (2018: 3).

Animism in the Anthropocene

With respect to the ecological concerns of this book, animism is a compelling means to think through the crisis of the Anthropocene towards modes of being that offer better futures for all life on the planet. The inclusion of indigenous perspectives and ideas from the majority world is particularly important in developing such ecological thought. As Jason Moore's concept of 'cheap nature' shows, colonial and capitalist societies are founded on metaphysical assumptions that sanction the exploitation of both human and 'natural' resources (2016: 2). Moreover, as multiple ecological thinkers and activists point out, Western nations have presided over growing global inequality and climate chaos, the effects of which are not evenly distributed. Moore draws on Bruno Latour's concept of the Great Divide, discussed in the introduction, one of the operations of which was to de-animate the earth. Latour's claims about the subsequent re-animation of the earth in the coming to notice of the climate crisis, discussed in Chapter 1, accord with animists' diagnoses of the Anthropocene as a period of anthropogenic climate chaos that also brings into focus our obligations to a more-than-human world. Vetlesen, for example, identifies the crises of the present as emanating in the way Western thought has denied to 'concrete units of nature any inner duration, inner motion, and internal becoming' such that we have come to regard nature as 'something we are set deeply apart from rather than being a part of' (2019: 72). He suggests that 'if the Anthropocene is the historical product of anthropocentrism, it is also what forces us to abandon it and search for alternatives – alternatives whose first assignment is to be less destructive to the natural world that humanity depends upon' (2019: 9). For Vetlesen, animism and panpsychism offer alternatives to much of Western philosophy, which finds itself 'ill-equipped' for the crisis (2019: 6). Mathews gestures to a similar conclusion in her suggestion that the 'refusal of Western thought' to countenance panpsychism and its implications for subjectivity explains 'many of the current crises and regressions occurring in our techno-industrial civilisation' (2003: 150). Both writers suggest the urgent need for re-engagement with modes of thought that have been marginalized and repudiated, modes that emphasize intersubjectivity, relationality, and entanglement rather than identity, individuality, and division.

To an extent, new animists and panpsychists repeat warnings about the destructive nature of Western thought already uttered by indigenous scholars and activists. Anthropologist Philip Arnold, for example, credits 'A Basic Call to Consciousness', an address given to the United Nations in 1977 by representatives of the Six Nations Council, an indigenous group in the United States, for bringing important tenets of animism into the political sphere, including the ecological claim that human beings are not the only, nor the most important, beings in the world (Arnold 2018: xii). The Six Nations Council admonish the way of life known as 'Western Civilisation', arguing that 'Western technology and the people who have employed it' have 'been the most amazingly destructive forces in all of human history' (Hau de no sau nee 1978: 77, 90). For the Six Nations Council speaking in 1977, Western culture has 'no viable answers' to the crises it has manufactured; indigenous peoples hold 'the key to the reversal of the processes in Western civilisation that [. . .] promise unimaginable future suffering and destruction'; their spiritualism is the 'highest form of political consciousness' (Hau de no sau nee 1978: 90–1).

Though these words went unheeded in their day, recent turns to animism in philosophy, anthropology, and science seek to reconcile Western ways of knowing the world with other perspectives. For example, the botanist Robin Wall Kimmerer emphasizes the importance of combining indigenous and scientific knowledge to find better relationships between humans and their environment (2013: 41–2, 45). In philosophy, Vetlesen relates new animist thought to sympathetic currents in Western philosophy. He reframes Alfred North Whitehead's observation that 'any physical object which by its influence deteriorates its environment, commits suicide' within the context of the Anthropocene, finding in Whitehead latent ecological philosophy in sympathy with the cosmologies related by anthropologists such as Ingold, Kohn, and others (Whitehead 1967: 109; Vetlesen 2019: 59). Such connections suggest that the ontological turn in anthropology, along with the writing of indigenous scholars and activists in different disciplines is contributing to the development and dissemination of ecological thinking. The cosmologies of those who found themselves on the other side of the Great Divide, then, those called 'animists' by colonial anthropologists, identify, and suggest solutions to, the crisis of the Anthropocene.

Breaching the divides: Decolonizing fantasy

Akata Witch, *The Lost Witch*, and *Children of Blood and Bone* complement the decolonizing impulses central to new animism and ecological thought. All three complicate the literary legacy of high fantasy as it has been developed by white Anglo-American writers through the twentieth century. Nonetheless, it is important to recognize that the genre of fantasy is rooted in European imperialism and colonialism. Specifically, it has ties to the Imperial Romance of the nineteenth century, a connection that William Green explores in his analysis of the resonances between J. R. R. Tolkien's *The Hobbit* (1937) and the colonial adventure narratives of Henry Rider Haggard and Robert Louis Stevenson, calling Tolkien their 'most influential and innovative heir' (Green 2001: 53). Examining the development of children's fantasy in the post-war period, Michael Levy and Farah Mendelson suggest these imperial roots lingered even as the British Empire dissolved, through stories in which children took 'colonial values through portals' to other worlds (2016: 115). Ebony Elizabeth Thomas recognizes the impact of this legacy for readers of the fantastic, arguing that 'when people of colour seek passageways into the fantastic, we have often discovered that the doors were barred' (2019: 12). Drawing similar conclusions for the related genre of science fiction, Jessica Langer identifies its central myths of 'the stranger' and a 'strange land' as the very same myths of colonialism and critiques the racialized othering mechanisms of science fiction narratives (2011: 3). Thus, 'imagination gaps' persist in the genres of Fantastika, especially in the representation of Black female characters (Thomas 2019: 19). Thomas suggests that the 'marginalisation of [. . .] dark fictional girls is analogous to the marginalisation of people of colour in schooling and society' (2019: 24). Although Okorafor, Burgess, and Adeyemi all write from Western societies in the Global North (America and the UK), they occupy complex positions within this location and recognize the operations and effects of the Great Divide in the way their fantasies, all of which centre on marginalized young women, offer commentary on contemporary issues surrounding race, class, and the environment.

Witches, of course, are one of those 'principal Others to man' that Haraway describes as being 'whelped' in the Great Divide; they go among the throng of 'gods, machines, animals, monsters, creepy crawlies, women, servants and slaves' that reside outside the 'security checkpoint of bright reason' (2008: 9–10). Adeyemi, Burgess, and Okorafor likewise emphasize the witch as a figure of the margins. The dîviners of Orïsha are brutally repressed and forced to labour for the elites in *Children of Blood and Bone*, who fear the return of their power. The magical 'Leopard people' of *Akata Witch* have suffered global persecution and so now reside mainly in the spirit realm. Similarly, the Hebden Bridge coven in *The Lost Witch* hide; they are among only a handful of witches who have not been routed by 'the Hunt', an establishment conspiracy. In different ways, these characters are endangered and oppressed but nonetheless inspire 'panic in the centers of power' (Haraway 2008: 10). In this sense, the writers all draw on a negative witch stereotype, which, as Ronald Hutton's history of the European witch trials attests, 'provided a kind of human being whom it was not only proper but necessary to hate actively and openly' (2017: 23). In the wake of this hatred and fear, of course, revisionist myths have worked to recuperate the witch as a cipher for differently imagined relations of humans in nature to those of modern patriarchal capitalism. Caroline Merchant's polemic history of the loss of the 'organicist' world view in the wake of the European Enlightenment, for example, romantically describes the world of the witch as 'anti-hierarchical and everywhere infused with spirits. Every natural object, every animal, every tree contained a spirit whom the witch could summon, utilize, or commune with at will' (1983: 140). This world did not exist for the women and men scapegoated across Europe in the historical witch trials of the middle ages, but the retroactive imagining of a pre-Modern animist world provides ecology, feminism, and fiction with a material-semiotic figure in the witch that exposes the repressive operations of power. As Merchant states, linking sexual politics, the subjugation of nature, and the witch trials, 'disorderly woman, like chaotic nature, needed to be controlled' (1983: 127). The hybrid nature of the witch figure, her ability to confound categories, that is, to act as a scapegoat but also as a subversive provocation to power, make the witch an effective challenge to dominant structures of thought and feeling, as well as to the false divides erected between humans and nature, and between so-called pre-modern and modern people.

As the witch shifts from being an antagonist to protagonist, the ontologies of Fantastika shift around her. The magic-infused worlds of these texts refuse a sense of the eerie present in the twentieth-century fantasies discussed in Chapter 1. Such a sensibility, which attributes a malign or unsettling presence to the landscape, is an effect of the puncturing of an anthropogenic perspective that is surprised to find something other than itself inhabiting the world. Indeed, in those texts, witches were agents of the Dark. In contrast, an animate world is not a container, so there cannot be 'something where there should be nothing' nor 'nothing present where there should be something' (Fisher 2016: 61). Life, in the form of agency and presence, does not arise within nor enter into an already existing world, but is 'immanent in the very process of that world's continual generation' (Ingold 2006: 10). As I will show, Adeyemi, Burgess, and Okorafor imagine magic as a force moving through the world and the bodies of the characters, vividly rendering Ingold's idea of animism. Such magic is not the province of impersonal and malign forces working against human characters, but a part of them.

In this chapter, then, I move away from the aesthetics of gothic and horror, though I continue to recognize the darkness negotiated by Fantastika. Animism locates the ground of human subjectivity in a larger ecology of selves and while this is indeed enchanting, the intimacies and obligations it affords are not without their violence and difficulties, as the texts reveal. Likewise, though the novels do not overtly refer the climate crisis, they are concerned with the persistent inequalities and destruction inaugurated by metaphysical and societal divides. Violence emerges in the conflict between ways of knowing and being, as those who reject magic, or else wish to amass power for their own ends, persecute those who embrace its enchanting effects. What plays out in each novel is a fantastic version of the warnings uttered by indigenous thinkers and activists as the impoverishment of the land and the destruction of other ways of life increasingly limit the ways of knowing and being that the land affords. Vetlesen suggests just such an interconnection between biological and cultural destruction in his exhortation for philosophy to embrace panpsychism and animism as antidotes to Anthropocene thinking (2019: vi). I offer the analysis of these novels as a further contribution to these debates, suggesting that the tropes of Fantastika are well suited to the task of recovering the openness of the world that has been lost to Western thought.

Re-traditionalization: *Akata Witch*

The title of *Akata Witch* evokes a racist slur suffered by the protagonist, Sunny, an albino Igbo girl who has recently returned to Nigeria after spending her childhood in the United States. An outsider by virtue of her appearance and American upbringing, Sunny is further isolated when she discovers that she possesses magical powers. She is a 'Leopard Person' able to wield magic. Her family and most of her peers at school have no access to the magic-infused world that Sunny begins to inhabit, which has much in common with the spirit world, or the 'Wilderness of the Bush', of West African cosmologies. Sunny gains access to places that lambs cannot go, including the town of Leopard Knocks, which exists in both the spirit world and the physical world and is home to the most powerful Leopard scholars. Along with three other young people, Sunny is initiated into this community so that she can learn to use her magic to stop a ritual serial killer, Black Hat Otokoto. Black Hat is a witch gone bad who is using the spirits of the children he murders to raise a powerful masquerade that will bring about the end of the world. Although the threatened apocalypse is magical not ecological, Sunny learns that Black Hat was 'a Nigerian oil dealer who did big business with the Americans' and that his 'hunger for power and wealth has made him vulnerable to terrible forces to whom he has lost himself' (Okorafor 2011: 308). In the novel, the characters who wield 'black juju' are associated with oil-fuelled capitalism while the Leopard people, who help Sunny and her friends, are those who reject the 'toxic' extravagance of contemporary Nigerian culture, choosing instead to 'live by the philosophy of modesty' (Okorafor 2011: 210, 224). However, this turns out not to be a wholesale rejection of so-called modernity in favour of traditional practices and ways of life, a stance that would echo a colonial framework imputing 'primitivism' to magic. Instead, the child witches of the novel straddle multiple worlds that overlap one another and, in so doing, refuse the hierarchies and binaries imposed by the 'great divide'.

The child protagonists of *Akata Witch* are initially marginalized characters whose 'in-between' status suggests a meeting of cultures, cosmologies, and modes of thought. Alice Curry argues for a reading of Okorafor's protagonists as 'quintessentially hybrid figures' who can negotiate invisible and visible spaces and give a 'view from both sides', including that of the nonhuman (2014:

38–9). My reading of the novel suggests that such a notion of hybridity is not a reconciliatory meeting of colonized and colonizer, nor human and nonhuman, but a rejection of any such divide. This rejection recognizes the difficult histories inaugurated by the divide, but points to the ways in which forms of matter and being were never really divided, but continually entangled. In this reading I am informed by Okorafor's commentary on her work, which she has terms alternatively 'organic fantasy' and 'African Jujuism' (2009, 2019). Both terms relate a concern with what this book identifies as 'dark matter': the problem of human interrelations with the other forms of matter and being, in which they are embedded and with which they are entangled. Okorafor's account of 'organic fantasy' argues that a combination of the cultural shifts she negotiates in her movements between Nigerian and American cultures, along with her own animist world view, which blends spirituality with an interest in science, means that her writing 'blooms directly from the soil of the real' (2009: 278). Here Okorafor echoes Garuba's notion of animist materialism developed in relation to the African context, as well as ideas of new animist thinkers informed by studies from other cultural locations. Like those thinkers, Okorafor does not wish to refute Western science, only to 'recover the sense of astonishment' banished from its official doctrines (Ingold 2006: 9). In Mathews's terms, Okorafor's blend of realism and fantasy 'suggest[s] new modalities of enquiry' in which humans encounter rather than interrogate the world (2003: 6). Sunny's magic does not give her power over her world but renders vividly the maxim repeated by her mentor Anatov: 'the world is bigger and more important than you' (Okorafor 2011: 54). The term African Jujuism, as theorized by Okorafor, centralizes African epistemologies and ontologies over European modes of thought in these new modalities. 'This is not Harry Potter,' she cautions, emphasizing the fact that there are people who believe elements of what she incorporates into her fantasy (Kelleher and Okorafor 2019). Elsewhere, Okorafor defines African Jujuism as a 'subcategory of fantasy that respectfully acknowledges the seamless blend of true existing African spiritualities and cosmologies with the imaginative' (2019: n.p.). She recognizes that this blend incorporates plural cosmologies, something represented by her diverse cast of young Leopard initiates in *Akata Witch* all of whom hail from different cultures, and, also, that it evokes Africa as a construct, an 'ethereal idea' (Okorafor 2019: n.p.). Thus, Okorafor's work is also in sympathy with the new animist project in that it mobilizes animism as an imaginative (and political) strategy that brings together literary modes and mythologies.

Okorafor's animism rejects the evolution narrative proposed by colonial anthropology and suggests instead the possibilities emerging from non-linear temporal interactions of different modes of thought. Colonial anthropologists writing about animism in the nineteenth century characterized it as a 'primitive' belief system that would evolve, in time, to proper religion, which itself was in the process of being superseded by scientific rationalism (Arnold 2018: xii). This narrative is rejected by the new animists in their recuperation of the term from Tylor. In *Akata Witch* this process of recuperation plays out when Sunny finds a book from Nigeria's colonial period, 'In the Shadow of the Bush by P. Amaury Talbot', which her friend Chichi says carries 'many secrets', even though it was 'written by a white man': 'Shadows, bushes, jungles, the Dark Continent. Sounds so stereotypical, but [. . .] the man who wrote it managed to preserve some important information – unbeknownst to him' (Okorafor 2011: 27–8). The girls' reading of the book emphasizes the decentring of Western modes of thought, rendering Talbot's rationalist account outdated. The discovery of the book also suggests the possibilities that emerge in a rejection of a division between the so-called 'modern' and 'pre-modern' worlds. Adding to this texture of temporalities, the title of the invented book and the name of its author recall the real-world text, Amos Tutuola's *My Life in the Bush of Ghosts*, an Anglophone Nigerian novel published in 1954. Here Okorafor acknowledges the influence of literary forebears in her weaving of the real and the fantastic. Tutuola's novel comprises a series of fragmented narratives about a young boy becoming lost in the wilderness. In part historical, recounting the period in which slavery operated in West Africa, in part metaphorical, the book contains nightmarish and fairy tale elements as the boy negotiates strange beings in the liminal space of the Bush, something Sunny herself experiences when she is initiated into the world of the Leopard people. The blurring of Tutuola's legacy with colonial narratives of the 'Dark Continent' refutes simple binary and linear accounts of Nigeria's history and development.

What happens to Sunny on her return to Nigeria in her discovery of the Leopard world is a form of what Garuba calls 're-traditionalisation', a process of the re-emergence of traditional cultural beliefs and practices occurring across post-Independence Africa (2003: 265). This includes the 'manifestation of an animist unconscious' in an ongoing and 'continual re-enchantment of the world' (Garuba 2003: 265). Countering Western narratives about the disenchantment of the world such as that offered by Max Weber, Garuba identifies in African literatures and cultures a process whereby developments in science and technology are assimilated with 'magical elements of thought' (2003: 266). Here Garuba echoes arguments made by Jane Bennett, who also refutes Weber's 'disenchantment story' by identifying the 'enchanting events and affects residing within or alongside scientific calculation, instrumental reason, secularism, or disciplinary power' that 'induce a more visionary and expansive mood' (2001: 14). Garuba and Bennett's use of the concept of 'enchantment' accords with the sensibilities developed in Okorafor's writing and given political vibrancy in the trope of magic. The fictional Talbot assumed magic was not real, but he was wrong. Okorafor's African Jujuism and New Animism, then, both suggest the possibility of simultaneous and continual processes of (re)enchantment and reject linear accounts of history that claim a 'pre-modern' world has been superseded by a 'modern' one.

The entangling of worlds in *Akata Witch* also reveals that the so-called modern world is neither rationalist nor disenchanted after all; rather, it employs its own form of magic. This revelation is bound up in Okorafor's ecological concerns, which play out in the rift between the traditional Leopard scholars and those, like Black Hat, who have embraced Western capitalism. The children's mentor in *Akata Witch*, for example, is called 'Anatov, Defender of Frogs and All things Natural' (2011: 42). Whereas, as Deborah Williams argues, Black Hat is a mixture of 'dark' Nigerian magic and Western capitalist exploitations, with the West significantly more to blame (2020: 10). That is, Black Hat's power has been amplified by his dealings with the so-called modern world. Building on Williams reading to interrogate the dialectic of enchantment and disenchantment this conflict between the West and Africa evokes, I suggest that Otokoto is an example of the way in which both processes are integral to Western thought and capitalist production, especially in the extraction of fossil fuels such as oil. Yes, there are impulses towards disenchantment through the de-animation of the earth and the application of a mechanist ontology, as Latour and Weber both suggest, but a different kind of magic arises in place of the outlawed animist sensibility: a magic that suggests that the extraction of resources incurs no cost and that there is no reciprocal obligation binding humans to the earth. Capitalism thus appropriates the 'manipulative magic of the sorcerer', which makes demands and imposes its will (Mathews 2003: 68, 151). Otokoto's magic is a manifestation of this logic: he uses it to accrue power and wealth and seeks to give nothing in return. However, the spirit that takes over his will, and which appears at the climax of the book in his place, punctures such a fantasy of something for nothing. The spirit is composed of oil and toxic filth, a stark reminder of the costs of Western capitalist exploitation. Re-traditionalization and re-enchantment in *Akata Witch*, then, comprise a strange remixing of worlds and world views that suggests no hard divide exists as such, but that worlds are entangled. This is an animist realism that recognizes the different kinds of magic at work in the world.

A cosmology of land and sky: *Children of Blood and Bone*

Tomi Adeyemi's novel *Children of Blood and Bone* develops the notion of enchantment through the invention of a secondary world, Orïsha. The cosmology of Orïsha features a pantheon of deities whose power infuses different clans of 'maji' with specific magical powers according to the deity's sphere of influence: water, fire, air, earth, mind, and life and death. As in *Akata Witch*, the protagonist is a teenage girl in whom magic is awakened. Zélie is a dîviner of Orïsha, marked by her white hair as someone with the potential to wield magic. Unfortunately, magic abandoned Orïsha a decade before the events of the main narrative, on the night of a brutal raid carried out by the King on the maji population. Zélie's mother was killed in the raid along with many others. The King's soldiers left many dîviners alive, their latent magic seemingly destroyed, but they continue to be persecuted. The novel opens when magical artefacts, which the King had sought to destroy, resurface, and awaken magic in the dîviners, including Zélie and the King's own son, Inan. While Inan is tasked with hunting down the artefacts and the dîviners who wield them, Zélie must wield her new powers to ensure the survival of her people and bring magic back to Orïsha permanently. The novel relates these two intersecting journeys and the fraught intimacy that develops between the warring protagonists.

Adeyemi's world-building relies on a blend of West African cosmologies with other elements of high fantasy. Yoruba, for example, appears in the novel as the outlawed tongue of the maji and the language of spells. Orïsha, the name of Adeyemi's secondary world, is itself a collective noun for the deities of Yoruba mythology, which inspire Adeyemi's pantheon, though are not analogous with it. The pantheon is an original creation, blending elements of Greco-Roman mythologies, in its emphasis on the elements, Zoroastrianism, from which Adeyemi takes the word 'maji', and aspects of Yoruba and Igbo deities. The supreme deity, the 'Sky Mother' has commonalities with indigenous North American spiritualities. Adeyemi's mixing of these mythologies with the genre of high fantasy, building a secondary world in the tradition inaugurated by J. R. R. Tolkien, contributes to the 'renovation' of Fantastika being undertaken by contemporary authors. Afro-Caribbean Canadian writer Nalo Hopkinson recognizes that 'to be a person of colour writing science fiction', for example, 'is to be under suspicion of having internalised one's own colonisation' (2004: 10). However, Hopkinson disputes Audre Lorde's missive that the master's tools won't dismantle the master's house, saying, 'I don't want to destroy it so much as I want to undertake massive renovations' and 'build me a house of my own'

(Hopkinson 2004: 10). The bricolage approach to the cosmology of *Children of Blood and Bone* testifies to a similar impulse.

Building a house of her own within YA, Adeyemi has done much to popularize West African–inspired fantasies for this audience with her politically aware fiction in which the fantastic evokes contemporary crises and inequalities. New directions in Fantastika along such lines are diverse and include other forms of Anglophone African and African-diaspora SF, Afro-Futurism and Indigenous Futurisms. The focus on Okorafor and Adeyemi in this chapter limits its concern to the Nigerian diaspora, but this choice reflects the fact that West African mythologies and storytelling traditions are prominent in YA publishing. Other successful examples include Tochi Onyebuchi's *Beasts Made of Night* (2017), Rena Barron's *Kingdom of Souls* (2019), and Roseanne A. Brown's *A Song of Wraiths and Ruin* (2020). Of these, Adeyemi's work is most explicit in its engagement with the politics of resistance in the wake of the Black Lives Matter movement. In a postscript she dedicates the book to all the African American children shot by the police in the United States (2018: 526). Adeyemi's characterization of Zélie is particularly important in this context since, as Thomas points out, 'black adolescence as both category and lived experience is clouded in the United States by [. . .] troubled signification' (2020: 4). Zélie's suffering at the hands of the King's soldiers, her social marginalization, and the bodily markers (such as her white hair) that reveal her as a dîviner bring to the trope of magic an acute social commentary about whose lives matter. As Adeyemi suggests, although riding giant lionaires (powerful, sentient creatures in the novel) and performing sacred rituals might be in the realm of fantasy, all the pain, fear, and loss in the book are real (2018: 526). The fantastic elements function to raise consciousness about exploitation, inequality, and suffering in the context of the Black Lives Matter movement, but they also work within the story-world to infuse those who feel powerless with the confidence that they 'have the power to change' things (Adeyemi 2018: 527). Thus, processes of (re)enchantment through the blending of animist cosmologies are more than a rebuke to Western narratives and modes of thought. Nor is animism a flight from the problems of Western modernity, a retreat into an idealism about the world, but a way of engaging with lived experiences and real inequalities.

The politics of *Children of Blood and Bone* crystallizes in the visual metaphor of 'rising' that repeats through the book. The metaphor appears in the blurb of the hardback edition: 'They killed my mother. They took our Magic. They tried to bury us. Now we rise.' It expresses the revolutionary spirit embodied by Zélie and her conflict with King Saran that drives the plot of the novel. This language of 'rising' also appears in critical commentary on Black-authored Fantastika, with Thomas's recent survey of YA fiction in light of the Black Lives Matter movement concluding with the subheading, 'and still we rise', suggesting the work ahead for Black authors (and critics) from African diasporas (2020: 13). The metaphor of rising is given dramatic force in Adeyemi's elaboration of magic in Orïsha. To return magic to the dîviners, Zélie must reforge the severed connection between the land, its people, and the Sky Mother, a supreme being from whom the universe (and its gods) spring. The figure of the Sky Mother recalls the Skywoman, a mythological figure common to various North American indigenous groups, whose coming to earth formed 'Turtle Island', the domain of humans, animals and plants. This aspect of Orïshan mythology is related to Zélie by a priest she discovers hiding in the ruins of a temple destroyed by the King's soldiers; he is the last in a line of a group of maji whose task it was to maintain the link between 'the Sky Mother's spirit' and 'the maji below' (2018: 161). The story he relates to Zélie makes explicit a connection between earth, body, and sky and the tethering ritual revolves around the magical artefacts the protagonists have discovered. The sun stone retains a fragment of the Sky Mother's soul; the scroll awakens the dîviners' latent magic; and the bone dagger creates the 'blood anchors' that will restore the connection to the goddess (2018: 164). The political uprising and social emancipation of Zélie's people depends on the successful enactment of this ritualistic tethering, making explicit an intimate connection between cosmology and politics, body and environment.

I foreground the word 'rising' and its dramatic enactment in *Children of Blood and Bone* as a rebuke to currents in new materialism that are too anchored in Western thought. Both Latour and Haraway, for example, relate their thoroughgoing materialisms to the ground and soil, expressing disdain for 'out of this world' thinking unconnected to 'the realities of [the] earth' (Latour 2018: 34). Haraway associates arrogant 'sky gods' with the human exceptionalism of the Anthropocene; they must be given up for chthonic beings residing in the 'compost pile' of the Earth (2016: 53, 57). Such a rhetorical strategy that rejects sky gods for an association with earth and soil suggests the privileged position of those for whom an association has not been bound up with oppression, as it has with people whose histories include being subject to European colonization and slavery. This binary separation of land and sky also contrasts with indigenous thought. Wall Kimmerer's retelling of the Skywoman story, for example, emphasizes the interconnectedness of the 'Skyworld' with life on 'Turtle Island': the seeds of the Tree of Life growing in the world above turned the earth from brown to green as 'sunlight streamed through the hole from the Skyworld' (2013: 4–5). Wall Kimmerer suggests that the story of the Skywoman makes clear the 'responsibility that flows between humans and the earth' (2013: 5). This responsibility is dramatized in Zélie's task to remake the connection between the people of Orïsha and the Sky Mother: it will emancipate the dîviners and restore the land, which is degrading as a result of King Saran's rule. This is the 'fundamental indissolubility of the connection between persons and landscape' that characterizes new animist thought (Vetlesen 2019: 173). Curry's reading of Okorafor's West African children's novels suggests their attention to invisible forces, spirits and unearthly being likewise demands what Cameroonian writer Jacques Fame Ndongo has called '"cosmocriticism" in place of the more western "ecocriticism"' (2014: 37). Curry's reading of *Akata Witch*, discussed in the previous section, might suggest that the 'organic' elements of Okorafor's work include the earthly and the spiritual (2014: 38). This conjoining is marked in Adeyemi's novel, too, since looking skyward is a necessary part of the characters' emancipation, while also connecting them to the blood that has been spilled as part of this struggle, in Orïsha as well as in the real world.

The cosmology of *Children of Blood and Bone* also echoes the new animism elucidated by Tim Ingold, which likewise refuses a binary separation between land and sky. He argues that 'the equation of materiality with the solid substance of the earth creates the impression that life goes on upon the outer surface of a world that has already congealed into its final form, rather than in the midst of a world in perpetual flux' (2006: 10). In *Children of Blood and Bone*, magic functions to propel beings through a world composed of earth and sky, rather than across a grounded surface. That Orïsha is a world-in-flux is indicated by the fact that the ritual Zélie must complete lasts only for a hundred years; the connection between earth, blood, and sky must be reforged each century in an ongoing commitment to the Sky Mother. Adeyemi takes Fantastika, then, from the grotto-esque caves of Garner and Cooper's folklore-inspired magical worlds to a cosmos that incorporates expansive lands and sky. Her synthesis of African animisms with other cosmologies dramatizes new animism as a way of understanding the common ground between a range of non-Western beliefs and practices, even as it locates that common ground in a secondary world built in the tradition of high fantasy.

Finding common ground: *The Lost Witch*

Using the new animisms to understand commonalities between diverse cosmologies allows me to trace connections between works by Nigerian diaspora writers with *The Lost Witch* by Melvin Burgess. Published in 2018, Burgess' novel develops the trope of magic as a form of communication with an animate world in similar ways to *Akata Witch* and *Children of Blood and Bone*. The novel focuses on a teenage girl living in the North of England who discovers that she has magical powers and belongs to a society of witches that live in 'a second world hidden behind this one' (2018: 62). The protagonist, Bea Wilder, discovers her magic when she rescues a trio of hares (witches in animal form) from a troop of huntsmen on the Yorkshire moors. Bea summons spirits from deep in the earth, animating a herd of deer with powers that she didn't know she possessed, which rout the hunting party. Bea's summoning powers illustrate the ways in which the witches are aligned with the natural world, with the spirits of individual animals and plants as well as with ecosystems such as rivers, while their enemies, the Hunt, are associated with capitalist interests and the exploitation of humans and animals in their acquisition of money and power. This conflict echoes the struggle in *Akata Witch*, between the Leopard people and those who use magic to extract wealth. Okorafor and Burgess also integrate the real-world witchcraft trials in Early Modern Europe into their invented histories. Both novels refer to the trials as a massacre of genuine witches that forced the survivors into hiding, rehearsing the now-debunked 'Witch Cult' hypothesis put forward by Margaret Murray (1921) and later popularized through the occult revival and neo-paganisms of the 1960s and 1970s. Murray's witch-cult thesis, especially as retold in various neo-pagan traditions, posits the existence of witchcraft as a continuous tradition from ancient pre-Christian Europe to the present. Neither writer endorses the witch-cult thesis, of course: this is fiction. Rather, in connecting an individual witch's struggle to a wider history of persecution, *Akata Witch* and *The Lost Witch* seek to make vivid a clash of world views. Like Okorafor, Burgess deploys a latent animist mode of thinking and being in Western culture that contests the environmentally destructive anthropocentrism that appears to dominate society today.

The political sensibilities of *The Lost Witch* echo that of *Children of Blood and Bone*, too, with its focus on persecution and marginalization. Bea learns that the persecution that began in the Middle Ages never stopped, with witchfinders simply moving into 'the government, the army, the police and the justice system' (2018: 85). Witches die in police custody, or in car crashes that are not investigated; they are sentenced to crimes they haven't committed, or are taken by the Hunt when they are admitted to hospital. In his suggestion that none of the country's institutions are safe, Burgess evokes the systemic oppression suffered by marginalized groups in Britain. Adeyemi's depiction of the persecution and suffering of the dîviner population in Orïsha likewise examines their social and economic marginalization and the punitive state-sanctioned violence they suffer, drawing on histories of colonialism and slavery as well as the present-day inequalities and violence endured by African Americans. Both novelists are interested in the ways that such oppression gives rise to further violence, and a violent conflict over the control of magic drives the plot of each novel. Violence emanates from characters who reject the relationships of obligation and responsibility that persist in an animate world, but also in the response of those who are the target of persecution. Zélie and Bea both suffer trauma and respond by using their magic in aggressive and self-destructive ways. Zélie is a Reaper, her magic linked to Oya, the goddess of death, who grants her the power of the spirits. Similarly, Bea is a Summoner: her power lies in her ability to call the spirits of the dead and the living from their resting place and their bodies. Having made herself a target for the Hunt, who would use these powers to accelerate their destruction of the remaining witches, Bea must leave her family (who believe she is suffering from mental illness) and go into hiding. Her escape is hijacked when she is seduced by the ancient witch, Lok – a character named for the Norse trickster God, Loki – who works with the Hunt. Manipulated by Lok, Bea uses her summoning powers against her own kind. The final third of the novel follows Bea's return to the witch community, her reparations to them, and her final confrontation with Lok. Burgess's interest in the interplay of intimacy and aggression echoes the difficult interpersonal relationships of *Children of Blood and Bone*. These include the abusive relationship between King Saran and his children, and the fraught romance between Zélie and Inan, the King's son. Inan's childhood history of abuse results in his inability to commit to his feelings for Zélie, and to her cause, as he is taken over by a fervent belief that magic should be destroyed. In both novels, then, magic functions to dramatize conflicts that have their roots in real-world oppressions and divisions, but these are given emotional force in the depiction of intense interpersonal relationships that include moments of intimacy, betrayal, and abuse.

In all three texts, the enchanted world the characters discover is precarious and threatened by forces that would destroy it. In *The Lost Witch*, the world of the witches is endangered, its liveliness being drained by the Hunt, who enslave the spirits of surviving witches inside machines and golems, repurposing magic to manipulate people's voting and buying habits, 'remak[ing] the world as they want it' (2018: 53). As in *Akata Witch*, capitalism is associated with its own kind of toxic magic, which functions precisely because its proponents have convinced most people that such magic would not possibly exist. That the Hunt are so effective in their attempts to remake the world is testament to the disenchantment story, and Bea finds that her own father is so indoctrinated in mechanistic thought that he denies his own latent witch abilities. Although Burgess' work is not explicitly allegorical, in this link between dark magic and political institutions he suggests something of anthropologist David Graeber's assertion that 'politics is very similar to magic', though its efficacy depends on never acknowledging this fact (2012: 342). Burgess's use of mythology lends imaginative force to this conflict between different uses of magic. Echoing Garner's syncretic approach in *The Weirdstone of Brisingamen*, Burgess reimagines the characters of Odin and Loki in the witch brothers, Odi and Lok. Their rivalry dramatizes a conflict between different ways of using magic and of being in the world. Other elements of the witches' powers and their non-hierarchical social organization recall aspects of neo-pagan spiritualisms, including Wicca. Burgess's engagement with neo-pagan spiritualties takes further the occultism present in Garner's work; here the idea of an old religion functions to critique social inequalities and forms of oppression apparent in British society, not least the dominance of the landowning classes, corporate interests, as well as interpersonal forms of coercion and violence that those interests perpetuate. As do Garner's child protagonists, Bea learns that seemingly normal people around her may be in league with the Hunt, including the doctors in the hospital where she attends a psychological assessment. Unlike Garner's 'morthbrood', however, these individuals are not possessed by some inhuman and impersonal darkness whose motivations are opaque, but by a political conspiracy that seeks all-too-human ends.

Burgess's use of a revivalist witchcraft story and Norse mythologies also complements his recourse to deep green philosophies, suggesting the ethics of biocentrism and ecocentrism in his animist depictions of animals, plants, rivers, and even stones. These elements of the text's cosmology are not conservative, as sometimes such mythologies can be, nor is his version of old religion fetishized as regressive as in many examples of folk horror. In terms of the rebuke of the new animists to colonial anthropologists, for example, the Hebden Bridge witches critique the idea of animism as a 'primitive' imputation of spirit to matter. Though Bea learns her powers reside in her spirit, and that this can be separated from her body by the Hunt's machines, to undergo such a binary separation of spirit and body, is something violently imposed by the Hunt. For the witches, spirit and body are one. To divide them is to remove 'all the love' from the world (Burgess 2018: 124). Burgess's depiction of the witches' spirituality thus has much in common with the *Basic Call to Consciousness* and its claim that Western modes of thought and being are anything but 'civilized'. Burgess's evocation of the witch-cult thesis also resonates with a claim made by the Six Nations Council. This is the claim that the world view on which Western Civilisation rests, and which underscores the ecological devastation and human exploitation it has perpetrated, is a relative newcomer in the history of human thought (1978: 68). The Six Nations Council accuse early forms of Christianity as beginning the process of the de-spiritualization of the world. Odi relates a version of this story to Bea, recounting how the invasion of Christianity and its 'jealous god' recast the spirits as 'devils, sprites, fallen angels, evil things', turning people away from the 'Second World' (2018: 34). What the Hunt began as religious persecution, intended to drive out 'evil' beliefs, continued as an establishment conspiracy premised on a love of mechanization and money. Both the *Basic Call* and Burgess's novel use this story of disenchantment and persecution to invert the violent hierarchy imposed by the Great Divide, positioning mechanistic anthropocentrism as the aberrant mode of thought. Burgess's reworking of the witch-cult myth goes further, though, reanimating landscapes and communities at the heart of the Western world, revealing a lingering enchantment in the heart of the former colonial centre.

Having drawn out these connections between the texts, I want to further interrogate the way magic functions in each, elaborating the theoretical connections between YA Fantastika, new animism, and panpsychism. The remaining discussion examines the moments of awakening to magic experienced by each character. I identify these moments as 'encounters', as discussed in the introduction, developing the idea here with reference to the panpsychism of Freya Mathews as well as various accounts of the responsiveness inculcated by animism in anthropology. I also analyse magic in each text as the language of animacy, a mode of accessing the communicative order of a living universe. Once awakened, magic is also movement, a force that propels beings through an animate world in a continual process of becoming, as in Ingold's elaboration of animism. Such movement entails relationships of intimacy and obligation, apparent in each text in the fraught interpersonal connections between characters. I conclude by gesturing to the further sense of animism as a mode of being that extends human sociality to a more-than-human world. This notion of animism hails from the mid-century anthropology of Alfred Hallowell and 'refers to ways of living that assume that the world is a community of living persons, all deserving respect, and therefore to ways of inculcating good relations between persons of different species' (Harvey 2014: 20). The widening kinship relations embraced by witches in these novels anticipate the more-than-human relationships discussed in Chapters 4 and 5.

A call to consciousness

Each of the characters in these novels awakens to magic through strange encounters that inaugurate new ontologies and dispositions towards the world. Magic inculcates human characters into the 'heightened sensitivity and responsiveness, in perception and action, to an environment that is always in flux' that Ingold suggests characterizes animism (2006: 10). The protagonists' use of magic in these novels is not as sorcery that would impose human will upon the world, but is cultivated as a response to what Vetlesen describes as the 'liveliness and manifestations of agency' that comprise the 'very fabric of the world' (2019: 17). Prominent examples of this agency include the 'faces hiding in the rocks, green arms and twiggy fingers' spied by Bea in *The Lost Witch* (2018: 27). As her perception deepens, she senses the liveliness woven into the fabric of her world, such as the cells on the leaves opening and closing 'like tiny mouths' (2018: 58). For Zélie in *Children of Blood and Bone*, heightened sensitivity emerges through the awakening of a connection between her body, the land, and the gods, forged through magic that flows through the words she speaks and the blood in her veins. In an instant, she feels magic as a 'surge', inking itself 'into each cell, staining my blood, filling my mind' (2018: 171). As is the case with Bea, magic connects Zélie to other lives that she can now sense, and the 'unbreakable connections' between them (2018: 171). For Sunny in *Akata Witch*, too, the world 'shifts' when she first encounters magic, as though 'reality was blossoming, opening and then opening some more' (2011: 39, 33). Each of these moments function to call the girls into what David Abram calls the 'vital presence' of the world (2011: 33).

These encounters with magic disclose the subjectivity of the world, a presence that enfolds different forms of matter and being, from highly conscious organisms to plant life, from ecosystems like rivers that disclose a unitary presence to individual agency at the cellular level, and from the spirits of the long dead to the spirit that inheres in inorganic forms such as stone. The coven in *The Lost Witch* blend such different forms of matter in their machine, the Spook, which hides them from the Hunt. The Spook is an assemblage of domestic machinery, folk talismans, living tissue, and spirit. Each part exhibits agency, but the machine as a whole is also a subject with a face that is 'gasping and panting to the rhythm of [a] great beating, bloody heart' as it maintains the spell that hides the coven (2018: 94). The Spook serves as an apt image of the ways in which magic in all three novels entangles all kinds of beings and matter and the ways in which magic functions to disclose the world as a subject in flux, a source of continual movement and becoming.

Reading *The Lost Witch* through Mathews's concept of panpsychism emphasizes the ethical dimension of these magical entanglements. Bea's first experience of magic is an 'encounter' as described by Mathews as an epistemological and psychological disposition that recognizes the 'subjectival dimension of matter' (2003: 10). To encounter involves recognition of, and contact with, an independent subjectivity, and so gives rise to 'a certain respect for their integrity and sympathetic concern for their fate' (Mathews 2003: 10). The encounter contrasts interrogative modes of approaching the world that lack such respect, such as in modern science. The dramatic opening of *The Lost Witch* exemplifies Mathews's notion of the encounter. The witches in the form of hares are chased by the Hunt across the rain-soaked moorlands. Bea is alerted to their plight and opens the car door just in time for a hare to fall bloody and sodden into her lap. She feels its heart beating 'furiously' and understands that she must 'give sanctuary to this wild creature' (2018: 6). There is a moment of recognition and sympathy with a more-than-human being, of course, but, as Bea looks into the eyes of the hare, who is really the witch Odi, the encounter deepens. She sees a cosmic vision of 'worlds upon worlds within worlds' nested impossibly inside one another (2018: 5). The reader later learns that Odi is an ancient witch who lives between all possible worlds, the keeper of a portal to multiple realities, but this initial image of many worlds enfolded in one another echoes Mathews's description of the universe as a 'conative unity' that realizes itself through infinite self-differentiation (2003: 9). That is, Odi manifests as what Mathews calls 'the one and the many'; he is the locus from which many finite centres of subjectivity emerge through the continual self-differentiation of one primordial subject (Mathew 2003: 55). Thus, Bea's encounter discloses a heretofore unknown cosmic order of which she is a part.

Locking eyes with Odi effects a shift in Bea's perspective from the interiority that Ingold suggests characterizes Western thought to an openness to other beings. As discussed, this interiority maintains a barrier around the self, outside of which everything is reduced to appearances: a world of objects. Kohn's elaboration of the term 'soul blindness' diagnoses a similar disposition: an 'isolating state of monadic solipsism – and inability to see beyond oneself or one's kind', a failure to recognize the 'soul stuff' of other beings that inhabit the cosmos (2013: 117). It is particularly prevalent in Western thought because of the Cartesian cut that privileges symbolic thought and isolates the human mind, rather than conceiving of it as connected to a larger mind, to the thoughts of the world (Kohn 2013: 49). A world of external appearances perceived by a disconnected mind cannot be experienced as real unless it is granted a subjectival dimension. For Mathews, only panpsychism recuperates realism because it grants a 'palpable sense of the world from within' (2003: 31). Bea's encounter with the hares discloses just such a sense of the world, revealing the meaning and intention behind appearance, allowing her to experience material reality in a new way. She is acutely aware of 'every drop of water, every hair on her arm and on the hare's back [. . .] the pelting rain' and the wind (2018: 6). She is in the presence of another subject, the hare, and recognizes its soul stuff, an act that, in turn, discloses a broader subjectival dimension that Bea feels in the rain and the wind. Bea is in the presence of the world as a communicative subject and active co-respondent, whose responses are conveyed by appearances but not reducible to such. Burgess expresses the idea very simply when he states that 'a witch is just someone who can see the life inside things' (2018: 112). Bea's encounter with magic, then, is not merely an ecological fable about one's ethical responsibilities to more-than-human creatures. Nor is it only a vehicle for revealing her own magical powers, though she does find, after locking eyes with Odi, that she is able, somehow, to summon the spirits of a herd of deer that rout the hunting party. Rather, the encounter discloses a new ontology, revealing to Bea that the material ground of her own being is itself alive, and that this subjectival dimension of reality enfolds her world within multiple others and connects her subjectivity to others.

The language of animism

Zélie's awakening to magic in *Children of Blood and Bone* is another encounter in the sense that it discloses the subjectivity of the world, but here that disclosure is initiated by magic in the form of language. Magical language in all three novels manifests as an animist mode of speech that connects its speakers with a more-than-human cosmos. In this reading of *Children of Blood and Bone*, I elaborate on the way in which the trope of magic illuminates new animist concepts of the world as a communicative subject. I draw on work by Abram and Kohn who suggest that neither language nor thought is exclusive to humans, nor even to individual animals, but is, in Abram's words, 'a property of the animate earth' (2011: 33). For Kohn, following work on biosemiotics, 'all life is semiotic, and all semiosis is alive', a formulation that suggests that the world communicates, and that communication is itself a form of life (2013: 16). These ideas are dramatized in the syncretic magic system developed in *Children of Blood and Bone*. Magic is a physical property that moves through the bodies of maji as 'ashê', but this can only be harnessed through speaking Yoruba, the language of the gods. Zélie is overwhelmed when she hears Yoruba spoken for the first time in a decade, describing the silver light that the maji Mama Agba conjures between her fingers as an exploding 'cosmos' (2018: 91). The words have a powerful effect, and Zélie describes the sensation of hearing and seeing magic conjured as 'a floodgate opening in my heart, an endless wave of emotion rushing through my entire being. The gods are back. Alive' (2018: 91). Yoruba is a language that reanimates Orïsha and its suffering people. Seeing the effect of her incantation, Mama Agba breaks into sobs and says, 'I feel like I can breathe again' (2018: 91). The importance of the language of Yoruba in this moment exemplifies Kohn's thesis about the liveliness of signification.

The suppression of Yoruba in the novel recalls the real-world suppression of indigenous languages by the US government and by colonial administrations elsewhere in the world. In making this real-world connection, *Children of Blood and Bone* points to the functional differences between the official language, Orïshan, and the suppressed Yoruba. To elaborate these functional differences, I turn to Robin Wall Kimmerer's elucidation of the grammatical differences between English, especially scientific language, and of indigenous languages. She recalls her experience of learning the American language, Potawami as an adult, one of the languages that suffered suppression during the nineteenth and twentieth centuries and is in danger of dying out. She says that the experience of learning Potawami revealed to her the ways in which English and Western scientific languages reduce beings to their working parts and erect boundaries between humans and others (2013: 49). Abram likewise suggests that Western languages, like English, function by constructing hierarchies of objects and beings (2011: 92). Though Zélie does not discuss the grammar of magic in this way, she nonetheless emphasizes the contrast between the flowing sound of Yoruba and the 'harsh stops and guttural sounds of Orïshan, the tongue we are forced to speak' (2018: 90). The 'pang of longing' that stirs in Zélie when she hears Mama Agba speak suggests that being denied access to Yoruba for so long has barred Zélie from the ground of her being: the experience reveals a 'gaping hole' in her body that aches to be filled (2018: 90, 77). When maji speak Yoruba, the earth responds, as Zélie discovers when she utters incantations to summon spirits from the water and watches it 'writhing with life' (2018: 250). Magic in *Children of Blood and Bone*, then, is expressed as a language that awakens the body and connects its speakers with a more-than-human world from which they have been severed.

Magical encounters reveal the communicative order of the more-than-human world and disclose the speaker's ethical obligation to it. When Bea first uses her summoning powers in *The Lost Witch* it is in a voice that appears to come 'from deep, deep down – so deep it felt to her as if the earth beneath her had spoken' (Burgess 2018: 9). Other objects and beings speak, including the fetish Odi gives Bea for her protection, which whispers in 'a voice like dry leaves' as it works its magic (2018: 45). In *Akata Witch*, Sunny encounters magic in the form of a written language that pulses with life and energy. Reading the signs of 'nsibidi', an early indigenous form of writing from south-eastern Nigeria re-imagined in the novel as the language of spirits, Sunny watches as the writing pulses and migrates about the page (2011: 154). She also learns to communicate with more-than-human creatures who express their desire to be treated as human beings despite not speaking in a tongue Sunny understands. These communicative encounters disclose an animist notion of sociality in which not only language but also relations of reciprocity and obligation extend beyond the human. In these texts, magic in the form of language suggests what Levinas supposes about language: that it is not a description of the world but instead signifies generosity and openness to the other, presupposing the presence of interlocutors to whom the speaker is obligated (Levinas 1991: 73). In all cases, learning the language of magic requires that the protagonists confront their responsibility to the world, whether this be their responsibility to fellow witches and maji who suffer persecution, or, in the case of Sunny, to all those who would be affected by the toxic spirit conjured by Black Hat.

Levinas discusses the speech act as an encounter with the other without reference to a specific language, but his idea is given specificity in the notion of a grammar of animacy elaborated by Wall Kimmerer. This grammar is exemplified by Potawami, which allows the speaker to address other beings through verbs rather than objectifying them as nouns (2013: 55). Such a language 'reminds us, in every sentence, of our kinship with all of the animate world' (Wall Kimmerer 2013: 56). Magic in the form of animate words, as well as in the form of words with the power to animate, makes language into the site of a reciprocal encounter. This is language as a form of expression that is 'addressive rather than representational' (Mathews 2003: 210). For Mathews, because it is addressive, panpsychism is expressed best through music and song. This idea is given vibrancy in *The Lost Witch* through the magical voice of Bea's friend, Silvis, which has the power to unlock clasps, cages, and other forms enclosure. When Silvis sings it sounds more 'like a musical instrument than a human voice', and this sound resonates through the trees, the grass, and the air, searching for something to unlock (2018: 80). Though Silvis thinks her voice is nothing more than a parlour trick, it is the key to defeating the Hunt at the close of the novel. Bea commands Silvis to sing, their combined power filling the valley with music, freeing all the spirits who have been separated from their bodies and trapped inside golems and machines. Indeed, all the locks in the area 'burst' open (2018: 325). Here, magic as the song of animacy penetrates barriers and boundaries that would maintain human-imposed hierarchies, divide life and matter, and separate body and spirit.

Magic as movement

Magic as the language of animism can work to loosen divides great and small, but it is not only through words and voice that magic manifests in these novels. Sunny's awakening in *Akata Witch* emphasizes movement over language, though the different modes are connected through her initiation rite. Movement is implicit in Abram's elaboration on the concept of an 'animistic style of speaking' because such a language opens the possibility of interaction and exchange,

> Allowing reciprocity to begin to circulate between our bodies and the breathing earth [. . .] such a language makes evident the consanguinity between ourselves and the enfolding terrain, invoking an explicit continuity between our lives and the vitality of the land. (Abram 2011: 116–18)

I have given examples of the consanguinity Abram describes in *Children of Blood and Bone*, with its emphasis on magic flowing through Zélie's blood, but it is differently expressed in *Akata Witch*, where the emphasis is on Sunny's fluid position between worlds and states of being. Okorafor suggests a movement of enfolding that Abram says is mobilized by animistic speech through the placement of the nsibidi symbol for 'journey' at the beginning of the novel, and then the symbol for 'welcome' at the head of Chapter 3, which is the scene of Sunny's initiation. The initiation begins with Anatov drawing a symbol in the air that descends on Sunny. She is warned to hold her breath, but before she can do so, she is 'pulled down. Yanked like a rag doll. First through the hut's dirt floor and then into sweet-smelling earth' (Okorafor 2011: 49). The initiation is a physical trial: the earth pushes 'its way down her throat, pulling up her eyelids, scratching her eyeballs, grating her clothes away, and pressing at her skin' (Okorafor 2011: 49). Sunny moves down through the living and dead parts of the earth and then upwards again, through the river that separates the Wilderness of the Bush – the spirit realm – from mundane reality, before appearing once more in Anatov's hut. This initiation emphasizes magic as movement in and through bodies and the world, rather than a power that can be used by a person upon the world. The magic is set in motion by the magical language commanded by Anatov and reveals what Abram calls a 'carnal knowledge' through an encounter between flesh and the landscape (Abram 2011: 136). The scene also exemplifies Ingold's idea of animism as an ontology of the world as a weave of living beings. Sunny discovers just what Ingold describes: that the world is not a surface upon which her life plays out, but a texture in which she is embedded (Ingold 2006: 13). Sunny's initiation, then, is another magical awakening that refutes the logic of interiority explicit in Cartesian dualism; it reveals the interiority of matter, literally taking Sunny into the interior of the earth, as well as the infusion of spirit and life through matter.

Sunny's descent into the soil invites an ecomaterialist reading of magic. The descent through soil anticipates the call of philosophers to pay attention to the earth, from Haraway's insistence on collaborations 'in hot compost piles' to Claire Colebrook and Jami Weinstein's articulation of the 'posthumous' as a response to the climate crisis, a word that derives its meaning from the Latin for 'ground, soil and earth' (Haraway 2016: 4; Colebrook and Weinstein 2017b: 6). *Akata Witch* exemplifies a trend in YA literature in its evocation of 'an ecopoetics of earthy belonging' (2013: 32). However, the focus on the earth in this text is not an endorsement of a reductive materialism, nor a rejection of the immaterial, since spirit remains vital to the book's ecological message. I have already made a similar argument about *Children of Blood and Bone*'s cosmology. Here the appeal is not to the sky, but to spirit, since Sunny's initiation takes place in the spirit plane, in the Wilderness of the Bush. The children enter Anatov's hut through the 'out' door, leaving the mundane world behind, and leave through the 'in' door, returning to their world having been transformed by their encounter with both soil and spirit. Things in the earth are not wholly to be embraced, either, including the 'oily, greasy' being, Ekwensu, conjured by Black Hat in the novel's closing scenes (Okorafor 2011: 314). To defeat Ekwensu, who embodies the corruption of Black Hat and the greed of American capitalists who have polluted the Niger Delta, Sunny must enter the 'green' spirit world, speaking the language of spirits to conjure the power that will send Ekwensu back into the 'wet, red mud' (Okorafor 2011: 327). Animism complicates ecomaterialism, then, by suturing the parts of reality that have been denied by reductive materialism or divided by dualism, with everyday matter.

Suturing earth with spirit is not without its difficulties, and the transformation Sunny undergoes involves a painful unmaking of herself. Again, I draw on Curry's analysis of the novel which links the 'organic underpinnings of Okorafor's fantasy' to the ways in which her hybridized protagonists give voice to 'a specifically ecological other' (2014: 3809). I think this notion of hybridity is useful but want to add that the lens of new animism allows for a reading that reveals the unmaking of the binaries instantiated in Western dualism and takes us beyond hybridization to a different ontology altogether, one that rejects divides and quarantines. Sunny's unmaking begins as soon as she enters the earth, which threatens to 'rip her apart' (Okorafor 2011: 49). When she returns, the process that began in the spirit world and under the soil takes hold: 'All through the night, she battled herself. Or battled to know herself. She fell apart and then put herself back together and then she fell apart again [. . .] over and over' (2011: 92–3). For Curry, this scene suggests a 'dismantling [of]the barriers between the human and the nonhuman, earthly and spiritual' as Sunny battles to 'embody – in the truest sense of the word – both her humanity and her spirit' (Curry 2014: 42). Sunny's spirit face manifests, a carved wooden mask that is hard to the touch: 'It was her, but it felt as if it had its own separate identity' (Okorafor 2011: 92). Curry notes the 'linguistic slippage from "its" to "her"' as Sunny negotiates identification and reads the scene as a moment in which Sunny becomes more than human, gaining a 'view from both sides', and access to the 'ecological other' (2014: 43, 39). I would add that new animist thought allows for the scene to be read as a remaking of the self that refuses an ontology in which there are such 'sides'. Drawing on field work with Siberian communities, Rane Willerslev argues that animists reject Cartesian dualism identifying with the world without distinction between subject and object. Animists are 'betwixt and between: their souls are both substance and non-substance; they are both their bodies and their souls, their selves and reincarnated others' (Willerslev 2007: 12). Moreover, this condition of inbetweeness 'seems to have no ending' (Willerslev 2007: 12). In animist cosmologies there is no stable hybrid position that the self might reach, then, and the notion that there are distinct sides or states being traversed dissolves. Sunny's encounter with magic, especially with her spirit face, similarly rejects the assumptions of dualism and its 'distorted' perception of an 'impermeable barrier' between the human mind and objects in the world (Willerslev 2007: 12). Sunny's initiation into magic also defies the law of non-contradiction, allowing her to both be and not be at the same time. This allows her continual movement between modes of being and seeing, into the green place through her connection with the earth and with spirit, which are not, in the end, disconnected states or substances.

Conclusion: Vulnerability and violence in magical entanglements

Through this chapter I have elaborated the entanglements inaugurated by magic, reading the trope of magic with new animism and panpsychism to argue that these texts argue for a conception of materiality that acknowledges its interiority, subjectivity, and responsiveness. Though there is much that is positive in this reading, not least its disclosure of a green, lively, blossoming world-as-subject that reaches out to humans and more-than-human others alike, magic is also a dark matter. The call to consciousness prompted by magical encounters entails vulnerability, danger, and suffering for those that answer. As Mathews suggests, panpsychism welcomes a disposition and mode of being that might be called 'erotic' in the sense that it includes a desire to immerse oneself, an appetite for connection (2003: 58). Each of the witches in these books experiences this appetite, but also recognizes that it leaves them vulnerable (Mathew 2003: 78). In *Children of Blood and Bone*, for example, Zélie finds that magic reveals her connectedness to others, and allows her to forge a particularly intimate connection to Inan. Yet, when she wields blood magic, she feels the danger of magic's intimate interconnection with her body: it 'tears' through her, 'ripping my organs apart', shredding her muscles. Magic is visceral and powerful, can eviscerate as well as empower. As Mathews states, the intersubjective encounter of panpsychism involves exactly this kind of vulnerability, since the body opens itself to the possibility of pain and suffering in its experience of the world (2003: 96, 199). There is no shortage of suffering in *Children of Blood and Bone*, of course, particularly for the persecuted dîviners. Thus, even as magic empowers Zélie to act on behalf of those who suffer, it renders her uniquely open to experiences of such suffering. Sunny's encounter with magic also endangers her, and not only because it brings her face to face with Black Hat Otokoto. The danger is also metaphysical. As Willerslev argues, the danger of the animist self is that though people can transform themselves into others, both human and nonhuman, they risk total participation and confusion (2007: 12). Kohn also notes that selves in an animist cosmology are ephemeral and ambiguous, and that they might be subject to dissolution through the processes of transformation and interrelation in which they are embedded (2013: 103–4). Such is the danger Sunny encounters as she struggles through her initiation. She successfully navigates the danger and finds her true 'Self', though this contrasts with the fate of Otokoto, whose self has been completely consumed, or, as Anatov describes it, 'lost' (20122: 308).

Whereas the encounters with a hidden world discussed in the last chapter brought protagonists into spaces of inhuman darkness, here the danger is from human violence. In *Children of Blood and Bone* violence arises from an antagonistic response to the revelation of a world that is alive. That is, the witch who responds to the call to consciousness with an erotic disposition, and all that entails, is persecuted by those whose responses to the entreaties of the world are denial and aggression. Magic is, in this sense, the 'metaphysical encounter' described by Mathews as requiring sacrifice: 'We must surrender something if we are to answer the call, and this something is, as it turns out, nothing less than the many means at our disposal to control the world, to keep at bay the threat it harbours for us' (2003: 21). King Saran's antipathy to magic comes from his refusal to make just such a sacrifice. He sees magic as a direct threat to his own power and his response is nothing less than genocide. He tells Inan that 'every maji had to die' and describes how he was able to 'break' their connection with spirit, effectively de-animating Orïsha in order to preserve his control. Though Inan feels the call to consciousness as magic blossoms inside himself, he views it antagonistically. Magic is a 'virus', a 'curse' that must be pushed 'down' (Adeyemi 2018: 173, 134). Inan briefly shifts into an erotic disposition towards the world when he meets Zélie, but their union does not last. Returning to his father, Inan acknowledges that he wants to be 'a solider. A great King' (Adeyemi 2018: 476). Inan's rejection of Zélie and his aggressive response to magic recall not only Mathews's account of a 'repressive' response to panpsychism, and its 'compulsive' defensive strategies but also Levinas's account of violence as the 'allergic reaction to the face of the other' (Mathews 2003: 94–7; Large 2015: 83). Both Saran and Inan reject the pleasures and risks of sustained intersubjectivity, which magic entails, and engage in war. Inan's repeated refrain throughout the book is 'Kill her. Kill magic' (Adeyemi 2018: 222). His compulsion to destroy magic is an attempt to bring about a totality that completely denies the subjectivity of the world and, so, leaves him able to reject its demands. The many deaths that he causes in his pursuit of Zélie are justified by an appeal to the safety of the 'kingdom', or else by his 'duty' – both are signifiers of a totality that denies the ethical relations implicit in magic. In *Akata Witch*, too, Black Hat's desire to wipe out the world might be read as another form of the totality sought by Inan and Saran, a complete erasure of the self and the ecology of selves to which it belongs, a repudiation of the difficulty of being in the world.

In *The Lost Witch*, Bea's response to the call to consciousness meets with resistance from her parents, who refuse to give up their mechanistic view of the world. Bea experiences first infantilization and then pathologization when she refuses to recant her story about acquiring magical powers. Vetlesen notes that the idea that the world is alive is, of course, socialized out of adults such that they become alienated from its truth; it is 'culturally banished' (2019: 16, 17). Bea's insistence that the world really is alive leads to her rejection by her immediate family who take her to the hospital to be assessed by psychiatrists. This puts Bea into danger, exposing her to the Hunt and then to abuse by Lok, who poses as her saviour. Lok is a witch, like his brother Odi, but has turned against his kind, using his power to thoroughly de-animate the world, stealing the spirits of witches and putting them to work in machines and golems. The revelation of Lok's spirit face at the close of the novel suggests his violence against his own kind comes in part from a repressive self-hatred. In the climactic scene, Bea summons Lok's second face, the visage that he always hides in shame. The face appears and tells Bea, 'He hates me. He will show you no mercy now' (2018: 322). Like Inan, Lok justifies his aggressive actions to Bea in the language of 'war' and, for a time, turns her into a 'child soldier' (Burgess 2018: 208, 205). However, through the character of Lok, *The Lost Witch* complicates any sense that magic is wholly good while those who would destroy it are wholly bad. Indeed, in the sections of the book where Bea uses her power against other witches on Lok's orders, the emphasis is on consumption and death. Lok gorges himself on piles of meat and swallows the spirits Bea collects for him. Though Bea's vulnerability is what allows for her manipulation by Lok, she cannot deny that 'she had felt exhilarated by her power' and that she 'enjoyed the cruelty' (2018: 268). Similar moments occur in *Children of Blood and Bone*, too, when Zélie encounters newly awakened maji 'hungry' to use their power to destroy their enemies (2018: 336).

Throughout this chapter, I have considered the political potentials of magic as a metaphor in YA Fantastika and, in dialogue with panpsychism and the new animisms, have also sought to elaborate its metaphysical and ethical implications. In addition to empowering those who are marginalized and oppressed, magic entails opening oneself up to interrelations with a more-than-human world. This call to consciousness brings with it vulnerability and exposure to aggression, particularly from those who want to deny such connections and the ethical demands they imply. Magic is not a solution to the world's ills, then, nor its ecological crises, so much as a disposition to be cultivated, an ongoing relation with the world that acknowledges the difficulties of reality and one's embeddedness therein. This chapter has also considered an ontology that posits the world-in-itself as a subject, or mind, from which individual minds congeal and emerge. The next chapter continues to trace philosophical and scientific elaborations on the problem of mind, moving from fantasy to the genre of science fiction to consider the problem of other minds and artificial intelligence.

3

Minds, machines, and ghosts

Consciousness in science fiction stories

Introduction: The haunted 'hard' problem

The previous chapters examine how children's and young adult fantasy imagine the liveliness of materiality, scaling up the focus of its analysis from objects and artefacts, to the landscape, and, finally, to the cosmos as a whole. The philosophies discussed so far, which include speculative realism, vital materialism, animism, and panpsychism, eschew a dualism that imagines a separation between mind and matter, preferring instead to focus on the 'hard problem' of matter in itself. Freya Mathews's cosmopsychism, for example, suggests that 'mind is not a mysterious entity in its own right but the reflexive, purposive aspect of a self-directive, self-realising system' (2003: 65). In this account of the world, intersubjectivity is inextricable from consciousness. Elsewhere, Karen Barad suggests a similar conception, describing minds as material phenomena that emerge through specific intra-actions (2007: 361). While these ontologies deny that there is any mind-body 'problem' for philosophy and science to solve, just such a problem remains very much in focus in contemporary philosophy, in the sciences, and in the speculations of children's Fantastika. The latter is replete with cybernetic, clockwork, robotic, and otherwise artificial beings whose development of an independent mind drives the plot of many stories. I examine three such recent science fiction novels here: *Tin* (2018) by Pádraig Kenny, *Wildspark* (2019) by Vashti Hardy, and *The Wild Robot* (2016) by Peter Brown. Exploring additional philosophical and scientific ideas to those already discussed, I continue to develop my conception of entanglement through an interrogation of these novels' depictions of what has come to be known as the problem of the 'ghost in the machine'.

At the climax of *Tin*, the villainous engineer, Richard Blake, is punished for his scheme to make an army of vicious mechanical 'Beserkers' animated by the souls of the human dead. In the climactic struggle to foil the engineer's plan, Blake's own soul is wrenched from his body and trapped in a rudimentary brass mould. He ends up, as one of the protagonists maliciously exclaims, 'a stupid ugly metal head rusting in the dark' (Kenny 2018: 310). The scene concludes as Blake's silent scream merges with the darkness, and 'finally for Richard Blake there was nothing but darkness. And the darkness became forever' (Kenny 2018: 310). This scene recalls similar in contemporary science fiction where a disembodied consciousness suffers in an endless void.[1] The mind is rendered dark matter indeed in this Cartesian tale of a 'ghost in the machine' where artificial intelligence and human consciousness are imagined as the mind stuff (res cogitans) that animates the brute matter of the body (res extensa), be it meat or metal (Descartes 1968 [1637]). Unlike much contemporary science fiction, however, the locus of anxiety in Kenny's story is not technology, but the mind itself. The dénouement occurs not in a factory where Blake's war machines have been constructed, but in a graveyard that is rapidly filling with the 'black and smoky' shadows of the souls of the dead (Kenny 2018: 287, 291). Trapped in a brass mould, Blake becomes one of the 'pre-cybernetic machines' rejected in Haraway's seminal manifesto, 'haunted' by the 'spectre of the ghost in the machine' and by the materialism-idealism dichotomy that has determined much of Western philosophy and science since the seventeenth century (Haraway 1991: 152). However, despite decades of poststructuralist thought, on the one hand, and research in neurobiology and artificial intelligence, on the other, the image that Kenny evokes in *Tin* remains potent in the cultural imagination.[2] This is because there is yet to be any consensus among scientists and philosophers about what constitutes consciousness: it remains dark matter.

Descartes's dualism, dubbed the 'doctrine of the ghost in the machine' by Gilbert Ryle (2000 [1949]: 17), persists in the modern imagination and has shaped scientific theories. Susan Blackmore contends that most people are dualists, dividing the world into mental and physical things from a very young age because dualism fits well with the way consciousness feels (2005: 5, 43). In the sciences, Don Favareau suggests that Descartes's 'bifurcation' of mind and body 'amputated from the natural world of material and logical relations from which it came, "the mind" and all of its internal relations' (2010: 26). The 'polar opposition' between res cogitans and res extensa theorized by Descartes suggests that bodies are subject to mechanical laws and available to inspection by external observers while qualities of mind are private 'occult episodes' (Ryle 2000: 15, 14, 26). A lasting consequence of the opposition has been the partition of the humanities from the sciences. The objects of study of the humanities are 'ruled unfit' for scientific enquiry, and the truth claims of science are deemed not to be accountable to those made by the humanities (Favareau 2010: 26). As discussed in previous chapters, this disciplinary divide is a consequence of dualism. Here, the effect has been the proliferation of the idea that the meaningful world can be reduced to physical processes without the need for reference to any other phenomena (Deacon 2011: 22). The resulting eliminative theories of consciousness, which appeal to the physical substrate of the brain, postulate counterintuitive conclusions such as the idea of the self as a fictional abstraction (Dennett 1993), that 'nobody ever was or had a self' (Metzinger 2004: 1). Moreover, as Blackmore asserts, 'we still have no idea' what it means to say that consciousness is generated in the brain or why some cells give rise to consciousness and others not (2005: 24). Those seeking a unified explanation of the emergence of life, consciousness, and subjectivity, then, maintain that physical theories have not solved the so-called 'hard problem'.[3] As Terrence Deacon argues, eliminative physical theories of consciousness superficially appear as explanatory victories but end up creating more difficult problems (2011: 147). In bracketing out the mental half of the explanation, denying what he calls 'absential' phenomena, physical theories remain haunted by *homunculi* (little men in the brain) and *golem* (the being that acts without understanding) (Deacon 2011: 88, 140). Science has not yet dealt with Descartes's ghost story. How to do so without falling back into either materialism or idealism, or reconstructing the divide in another form, continues to be the subject of enquiry and debate.

Humans, machines, ghosts: From the posthuman to the posthumous

The novels considered in this chapter negotiate the philosophical problem of Descartes's ghost story in varied ways, exploring the mind-body problem through the depiction of clockwork mechanicals, human and animal ghosts, and by comparing animal minds with artificial intelligence (AI). The first two novels discussed, Pádraig Kenny's *Tin* (2018) and Vashti Hardy's *Wildspark* (2019), make most evident the figure of the ghost in the machine. *Tin* evokes a neo-Edwardian setting in which pioneering engineers have mastered the art of conferring intelligence and sentience on mechanical objects. Mechanicals powered with 'basic propulsion' – the use of glyphs that imbue the object with commands much like in the medieval story of the *golem* – fulfil manual and service roles.[4] Whispers of 'refined propulsion', a process by which the machine is animated by a human soul, are repressed by the 'Agency' that controls the production of mechanicals in England. The story opens with the discovery that the protagonist, Christopher, is not a 'proper' boy as he believes, but a highly life-like mechanical, powered by refined propulsion. When he is kidnapped, his friends – including a human girl and a rag-tag group of 'basic' mechanicals – must rescue him and prevent 'refined propulsion' from being used to animate an army of deadly war machines. Blake's berserkers recall the vicious 'Sir Ironsoul' from Philip Pullman's *Clockwork or All Wound Up* (1996). Ironsoul is a relentless clockwork knight powered by 'some kind of goblin [. . .] a spirit or a devil' who seemingly acts without understanding or sentience (Pullman 2010: 328). The idea of the golem works in Pullman's story to evoke a sense of the uncanny, with the creepy Dr Kalmenius – a character inspired by the nineteenth-century stories of E. T. A Hoffmann – able to command Sir Ironsoul with 'one word and one word alone' (Pullman 2010: 329). The golem figure in *Tin* is no mere monster, however, and its use by humans elicits ethical questions. Blake blithely demonstrates the principles of basic propulsion by scrawling a simple command onto a rudimentary marionette, which he then discards. Though the marionette does not have eyes and cannot speak, it becomes Christopher's friend, and he is devastated by its cruel destruction in a later scene. The incident reveals that the mechanistic notion of the golem, a being that acts without understanding or internal experience, is far from a satisfactory explanation for the experiences of the mechanicals in the book, be they 'refined' or 'basic'.

Whereas 'ensoulment' is a source of terror in *Tin*, it is the basis for a supposedly utopian technology in Vashti Hardy's *Wildspark* (2019). In this neo-Victorian story set in the fictional town of Medlock, inspired by Manchester at the height of the Industrial Revolution, cybernetic animals – called 'personifates' – are animated by the souls of the dead. The 'wildspark' of the soul is plucked from the spirit world and harnessed into the preformed bodies of the personifates on the night of a full moon. However, the personifates that awaken after this process remember nothing of their first life. Mourning her recently dead brother, Prue passes herself off as an apprentice at the Personifate Guild of Medlock, hoping to learn the secrets of harnessing so that she might bring back the soul of Francis and restore his consciousness and memory into the body of a personifate. Prue and her friends – another mixed group of children and cyborgs – uncover a plot to hijack the Guild's grand harnessing event. Unhappy with the way humans exploit personifates, the antagonist, Craftsman Primrose – actually a personifate posing as a human – attempts to ensoul an army of artificial 'Stag Men' to bring down the Guild and the human society of Medlock. Unfortunately, foiling Primrose's plan makes Prue realize that she cannot bring back her brother from the dead. Hardy's personifates have their predecessors in the *Oz* books written by Frank L Baum (1900–20). According to Margaret P. Esmonde, Baum 'introduced the first cyborgs to children's literature' (1982: 86). As Zoe Jacques suggests, Baum's cyborgs are amalgamations of the human and the mechanistic, fusions of organic and inorganic substances (2015: 178). However, while the cyborgian creatures of Oz suggest a 'fruitful coupling' of 'tin' and 'meat', the nature of thought that inhabits them is not explained (Jacques 2015: 191–2). In *Wildspark*, however, Prue leaves the design of the cybernetic bodies of personifates to her fellow students, focusing her research instead the informational signals that constitute the 'wildspark' itself.

Information as consciousness is explored in Peter Brown's *The Wild Robot* (2016), which differs from the other novels considered here in that its main character is a representation of artificial life (A-Life) inspired by modern robotics. Set in a future world affected by climate disasters, *The Wild Robot* tells the story of Roz, the sole survivor of a shipment of service robots that washes onto the shore of a remote island. Roz is an example of symbolic AI, in that she operates from a pre-programmed dataset and internal representations, but also of 'connectionism' and evolutionary programming, because she can adapt to her new environment. Roz becomes embedded in the ecology of the island, learning to communicate with its animal inhabitants. Just as she embraces her 'wildness', reclamation robots, called 'recons', arrive on the island seeking to deactivate the stray and return her to the factory for a reset. In its ecological theme, *The Wild Robot* draws on elements of Ted Hughes's *The Iron Man* (1968) and *The Iron Woman* (1993), both of which offer negative depictions of a human world in which technological progress is destructive. In the more explicitly ecological *Iron Woman*, 'humanity is a villain and nature innocent' (Jacques 2015: 195). Though humans are antagonists, this binary is complicated in *The Wild Robot*. The arrival of the recons reframes the remote island as part of a global ecology shaped by human action; its status as an Edenic garden, cultivated by the animals and Roz, cannot hold. *The Wild Robot* suggests a necessary ongoing exchange, then, between the human world and the island. At the close of the book, Roz recognizes that she must return to her 'makers' to seek repairs and to stop them from sending more robots to the island (Brown 2016: 262). Unlike Hughes's iron beings, who function as fabled figures, Roz's provenance is no mystery. Hughes's iron giants appear as if from nowhere and disappear once the fable is complete. In Roz's case, though she must leave the island at the close of the story, she promises to return, and her story continues in further novels in the series. Brown carefully traces her transformation from artificial machine to wild organism, physically as well as through the emergence of her autonomous consciousness. Indeed, evolution and adaptation are key themes of *The Wild Robot* as Roz responds to the environment and vice versa. Though Jacques suggests that *The Iron Man* closes with the robot's 'quasi-evolutionary return' to the sea (2015: 190), Hughes's story leaves untouched the mystery of how life and consciousness might have come from this same source, as well as how these relate to the possibility of machine consciousness embodied by the Iron Man himself.

I connect these contemporary children's science fiction stories through the way they complicate a dualist ontology despite their rehearsal of the 'ghost in the machine' metaphor. Where *Tin* and *Wildspark* imagine the possibility of life after death, of the continuation of consciousness in more-than-human materials, *The Wild Robot* explores the possibility of life from non-life, of intentionality from meaningless computation, or what the theoretical physicist Sara Walker calls 'bio from bit' (2018). Each book begins with a dualist ontology, instantiating the classical divide between body and spirit in *Tin* and *Wildspark*, with a more a subtle divide between inorganic information processing and self-organizing organic bodies in *The Wild Robot*. In each, this dualism is compromised by problems and conflicts that require solutions not available to an ontology that would separate the mind from the body, and both from the wider world from which they emerge. Rather than falling back into one half of the Cartesian divide, such as the reductive materialism of neuroscience and eliminative interpretations of the mind-body problem, my reading of these books traces a productive interpenetration of the material with the incorporeal, developing the concept of extramaterialism discussed in the introduction. Ecological concerns also persist throughout this chapter. Though the books are about machines, the notion of 'wildness' is emphasized in their concern with animals, ecosystems, and evolution. Thus, my reading moves through artificial intelligence and cybernetics to consider an evolutionary perspective, exploring how mind emerges from (and is embedded within) what Timothy Morton calls the 'mesh' of nature, a sprawling network of interconnection between life forms of all types (2010: 28–30, 2016: 143).

My reading of these novels about cybernetic creatures and robots acknowledges the insights of posthumanism as a critical approach but synthesizes a different framework that focuses on the specificity of the 'hard problem' of consciousness. There are existing critical readings of robots and cyborgs in children's and young adult fiction that draw on posthumanism, of course, notably those by Victoria Flanagan (2014) and Zoe Jacques (2015). Both are instructive in charting developments in the representation of the posthuman and of technology in children's books and in their assertion of the efficacy of the mode in challenging the tenets of humanism. Flanagan builds on work by Clare Bradford et al. (2008), arguing that representations of posthuman entities in twenty-first-century young adult fiction disturb the binary classifications that shore up humanism and that they produce an optimistic vision of a technologically mediated subjectivity (2014: 40). Her observations hold for the books considered herein since the stories are positive about the effects of technology. Likewise, her assertion that recent writing for young adults uses the theme of technology to redistribute subjectivity to nonhuman subjects is applicable (2014: 53). These books focalize their narratives through humans, machines, and animals, conferring upon each an internal and autonomous subjectivity. Jacques also reads children's texts that explore the fluidity of the borders between the human and the nonhuman, though she is more cautious about a lingering 'anthropocentric conservatism' in the mode (2015: 3, 5). Here, Jacques builds on Robyn McCallum's argument that children's and young adult fiction is dominated by humanist conceptions of the individual but contends that the 'subversive elements of these fictions nonetheless possess a transformative power' (McCallum 1999: 257; Jacques 2015: 5). I differ in my framing here since the humanist inheritance in *Tin* and *Wildspark*, which includes their recourse to notions of individual subjectivity and the possibility of transcendence beyond human finitude, is not overshadowed by a subversive counter-current in the stories. Rather, the characters' evocation of the limits of humanism is what makes them such apt conceptual personae for this study.

While acknowledging the valuable insights offered by Flanagan and Jacques on a range of classic and contemporary children's fiction, my approach offers distinct analytical tools from those of posthumanism. I concur with their identification of disrupted boundaries in children's texts, but do not pursue an ideological critique of the humanist subject. Rather, I want to focus on the specific problem that inheres in any cartography of posthuman subjectivity: what constitutes a self-directed, autonomous organism and how has such a thing emerged from seemingly mindless matter? I am not as interested in a discussion of fluid borders between humans and others as I am in the specificities of what Braidotti calls the 'mind-body continuum' or 'the embrainment of the body and embodiment of the mind' (2018: 31). Flanagan, for example, argues that cyborgs in young adult fiction advocate a non-Cartesian subjectivity, emphasizing the role of the material (albeit metal) bodies of its characters (2014: 53). What is not traced in her reading, though, is the genealogy of the Cartesian divide nor its continuing influence in scientific and philosophical investigations that seek to understand consciousness, whether this is identified as an exceptional human trait or not. Since the trend in the physical sciences has been to reduce subjectivity to the 'pushes and pulls of physical interactions' (Deacon 2011: 54, 52), it is not enough to challenge humanism with discussions of embodiment. There must also be consideration of the incorporeal phenomena that have been excised from reductive materialist discussions of consciousness. The challenge is to achieve this without recourse to idealism. As it finds expression in these recent studies of children's fiction, then, posthumanism offers a radical, sometimes utopian, reformulation of concepts of subjectivity within a humanities framework, but it does not interrogate the specificity of the mind-body entanglement across the disciplinary divide. Its grounding in a humanist/posthumanist dialectic also limits its efficacy as a conceptual framework.

This latter critique is advanced by Jami Weinstein and Claire Colebrook, who argue that posthumanism has become a stable discourse and no longer articulates the problems of mass extinction, ecosystem destruction, and global heating. This, they state, might be better expressed as the problem of the post*humous* (2017b: 1). Among Weinstein and Colebrook's critiques of posthumanism is its expression as an 'ultrahumanism', expounding the distinctiveness and expansion of the human (2017a: xiv). Bound up with this claim is the related idea that 'whatever might have passed as posthumanism has always been a form of humanism' and that the 'human, or man, has never been one being or animal among others but is precisely the being who believes himself to be in command of his own open, self-creative, and purely potential being' (Weinstein and Colebrook 2017a: xvi). They suggest that posthumanism does not subvert humanism, then, but is an intensification of its logic (2017a: xvii). In this sense, the mechanicals of *Tin* and *Wildspark* are posthuman figurations that reveal their 'residual humanism' (Weinstein and Colebrook 2017a: xvi). The persistence of a human soul in a void beyond the material world that might be recalled into existence by the ingenious scientist is a humanist narrative *par excellence*. Yet, the mechanicals in these stories function as more than a hyperbolic posthumanism; they embody the problematic of the post*humous* in their paradoxical iteration of Cartesianism. On the one hand, the persistence of a human soul or consciousness is a hyper-Cartesianism which the hero protagonist of *Wildspark* (Pru) and the villainous antagonist of *Tin* (Blake) seek to manipulate for their own ends. On the other hand, the mechanical constructions in which the human spirits become embedded suggest decay and degradation. From Absalom's rusting workshop in the opening of *Tin* and the mouldy, scuffed, and dented components of his mechanicals, to the precarious qwortzite crystals of *Wildspark*'s personifates, which only sustain consciousness for a few short years, the life of the mechanicals counter the radically futural and expansionist claims of posthumanism. Their anachronistic aesthetic, which emphasizes mechanical rather than digital technology, points to the thermodynamic entropy wearing away at the gears, joints, and internal wiring of the precarious reincarnations. The spirits themselves also manifest in a fleeting and disruptive way that punctures ultrahumanist conceptions of pure potentiality. Blake's 'diviner' machine, which he hopes to use to harness the souls of the dead to his war machines, seems to elicit this potentiality, exploding in a column of blue light and 'luminous fractures', exerting a huge physical force on the heroes as they struggle to break it apart (Kenny 2018: 286). However, the power of the diviner is fleeting. Once the device is smashed, the light suddenly contracts and – 'as if all the air was being squeezed from the world' – the tattered wisps of the souls are sucked back into the void (Kenny 2018: 303–4). The scene suggests a sense of the posthumous described by Weinstein and Colebrook as 'a disturbance and a vibration orienting around the chaotic intensities that swirl in the absence of a concept of life as a controllable, containable, nameable force attributed to humans [. . .] life as excess and privation but decidedly not posthuman' (2017a: xxiii). For all their efforts, neither Blake nor Prue can control or harness life, which manifests as a chaotic excess before swiftly vanishing into the dark.

While *Tin* and *Wildspark* suggest the posthumous in their evocations of death, *The Wild Robot* does so in its engagement with the Anthropocene. Weinstein and Colebrook argue that it is the height of hubris and narcissism to talk about the senses in which the human has been surpassed, or the end of human exceptionalism, or the breaching of the borders of human life, in the midst of the sixth great extinction event (2017a: ix). The problem of the posthumous requires instead a 'critical study of life' that considers, among other things, the possibility of a world without humans (Weinstein and Colebrook 2017a: x). The failure of the human techno-society and the scattering of its detritus opens *The Wild Robot* with the scene of a 'robot gravesite' and the 'broken' bodies of the rest of Roz's shipment smashed against the rocks (Brown 2016: 4). Later, Roz's friends, the migrating geese, report seeing 'dirty and crumbling' buildings 'leaning' out of the ocean, which suggests the ravages of climate change on human society (Brown 2016: 208). The 'recos' that come to the island at the end of the book are evidence that humans continue to live, produce technology, and affect the planet, but their demise – along with the potential demise of the animals on the island threatened by rising sea levels – is vividly rendered.

The problem of the posthumous also necessitates confronting life in its contracted sense of mere survival and the 'no exit' warnings of climate scientists (Weinstein and Colebrook 2017a: xi). Brown emphasizes this in the precarious lives of Roz and her friends due to the uncertain conditions in the local ecosystem. Though the island is remote from human interference, its winters are 'colder', the summers 'hotter', the storms 'fiercer' and the ocean higher than in the animals' living memory (Brown 2016: 191). The story engages with the paradox of the Anthropocene as stated by Weinstein and Colebrook: never has it been more necessary to forge affinity with nonhumans and non-life, but never has it been more apparent that humans are 'well and truly distinct in our earth-destructive capacity' (2017a: x). My reading of *The Wild Robot* as speculation on the hard problem of consciousness contributes to critical life studies in the face of the crisis of the Anthropocene because the problem of the mind, in the sense of the environmental causes of mind and its concomitant effects in shaping that environment, is inextricably linked to the emergence of life on the planet and the possibility of its continued existence. This is the post*humous* as post*humus*, relating to the earth (*humus*), and the exploration of what Weinstein and Colebrook name a 'wild life': the very condition of the possibility of life in all its forms (2017b: 6, 7).

The critical study of life and mind in this chapter builds on the concept of entanglement developed throughout the book. There are three distinct senses in which entanglement operates here: first, the interpenetration of the material with the ideal, which provides a way of resolving dualism without reductionism. Extramaterialism is given specificity here in the biosemiotic and cybernetic studies of the mind that inform this chapter. They locate the mind in the dynamical emergence of form through evolution, the feedback and feed-forward signals of neural networks, the semantics of information, and in the 'strange loops' produced by perception and affect. The second entanglement is, as Peter Godfrey-Smith suggests, the emergence of mind from the interactions of an organism with the complexity of its environment (1996: 3). Here the chapter is informed by evolutionary biology, which takes the human mind as one case among many. The mind is the product of dynamical interactions that shape the *phylogenic* and *ontogenic* becoming of organisms. These include the development of membranes internally and externally and the expansion of bodily boundaries to incorporate previously independent beings, as well as the signalling and sensory processes developed in response to the demands of social interaction (Godfrey-Smith 2016: 153). This last point suggests the third entanglement at work, which is encapsulated in the notion that 'the mind evolved in response to other minds' (Godfrey-Smith 2016: 36). Although the image of Blake's mind alone in a dark void is evocative, it suggests the 'soul blindness' discussed in Chapter 2 (Kohn 2013: 117–18). Though human symbolic thought produces the feeling of 'radically separate' minds, all individual minds are nested within a 'larger mind', which just is the semiotic processes of the world beyond the human (Kohn 2013: 49). Making a similar point from the perspective of neuropsychology, Max Velmans argues that

> it is a mistake to think of the brain as an isolated system. Its existence as a material system depends totally on its supporting surround, and the contents of consciousness that it in turn supports, arise from a reflexive interaction of perceptual processing with entities, events and processes in the surrounding world. (2012: 155)

These entanglements point to a dynamic unity of mind, brain, and world, the understanding of which has been frustrated by the persistence of Cartesian dualism in Western thought. The remainder of the chapter, then, examines the pointed resurrection of this dualism in *Wildspark* and *Tin*, where ghosts literally inhabit machines, showing how the tensions of the premise point to alternative extramaterial concepts of consciousness. In the final section of the chapter, I move on from the metaphor of the ghost in the machine to examine *The Wild Robot*, developing an ecological concept of mind in response to theories from biosemiotics and evolutionary biology.

Spectres or signals: What haunts the concept of mind?

Tin and *Wildspark* literalize Ryle's critique of Cartesian mind-body dualism by imagining highly 'life-like machines that contain *people*', 'ensouled' machines animated by spirits 'harnessed' from the world of the dead, which in both books is described as a sort of 'void' (Hardy 2019: 268; Kenny 2018: 304). In this way, the books exactly repeat Ryle's description of the Cartesian doctrine: that every human being is both a body and *anima*, ordinarily harnessed together, though, after the death of the body, the mind may continue to exist (2000 [1949]: 13). As Ryle notes, this idea derives not solely from Descartes but is testament to the fact that Descartes was reformulating prevalent theological doctrines of the immortality of the soul using the 'new syntax of Galileo' (Ryle 2000: 24).

This synthesis of mechanism and theology is made clear in *Wildspark* when the characters visit the 'Hall of Lost Personifates'. The phrase *Capax Infiniti* is engraved on the cases which house the 'empty' personifates. Edwin tells Prue that the phrase is

> a reminder that the thing that makes us who we are is not the outer body, but something deep insider, and that our bodies, whether flesh or ghost machine, are just a shell. It's a stage in our history and future, which is, you know, infinite? Or something? (Hardy 2019: 140)

This accord between *Wildspark*, *Tin* and Descartes seems to exemplify Weinstein and Colebrook's point about the way in which a centuries-old transcendent ultrahumanism is re-packaged in the figure of the 'posthuman' – in this case Hardy's animal-machine 'personifates' and Kenny's child-like mechanicals. The note of doubt raised by Edwin here, though, points to the eventual failure of Prue's project to return her brother to the world of the living, suggesting the necessity of accepting human finitude.

The books' uneasiness with posthumanism also manifests in intra-story-world taboos against the construction of adult-sized life-like machines endowed with human souls. In *Tin*, mechanicals must not appear as fully grown humans, whether basic or refined, so most are built in child-like dimensions. In *Wildspark*, the personifates are constructed to resemble animals: human forms are strictly forbidden. The taboos, which are broken only by the novels' villains (Primrose and Blake), suggest an unease in the story-world with the doctrine of the ghost in the machine. The injunction against human adult sentient machines complicates the binaries in which the notion of mind as 'intellect' has been conceived since Descartes, which would place animals (and children) on the side of the body (Ryle 2000 [1949]: 27). In *Wildspark*, the housing of *anima* in animal bodies further probes such tensions, apparent in Descartes's language. After all, as Gregory Bateson points out, 'the very word "animal" means "endowed with mind or spirit"', which is precisely what is denied in Descartes's schema (1979: 5). This tension about the status of *anima* plays out in the form of political strife in Medlock, pitting 'anti second lifer' groups against those campaigning for 'rights for personifates'. In *Tin*, the uneasiness manifests through Blake's dastardly plans to misuse 'refined propulsion' in his 'war machines', and in the strange reverence of the basic mechanicals for those who are 'proper', or alive. This section interrogates such tensions in Cartesian metaphysics and so unpicks the books' seeming endorsement of mind-body dualism. I follow the threads of the stories that produce alternative cybernetic conceptions of the mind, which include recognizing its loopy, entangled structure, as well as considering the role of information in the production of subjectivity. I also contend that there is value in the metaphor of the ghost as it finds expression in *Tin* and *Wildspark* because it refuses to capitulate to eliminative physical theories of consciousness and makes explicit the homunculi that haunt those theories, revealing science's theological inheritances.

Wildspark proposes a kind of Cartesian vitalism, endorsing consciousness as res cogitans, a 'spark' added to organic and mechanical bodies. However, that this something added is the dead, producing what Prue's mum scathingly calls 'mechanical ghosts' (2019: 15), points to a metaphysical problem as to what constitutes life. This has ethical and political consequences. Prue is made aware of the tensions brewing in Medlock almost as soon as she arrives: 'it's best not to use the term "life-like"', Primrose warns, 'with the whole philosophy on what defines the term "life"' (2019: 42). This comment registers unease despite the pointed efforts of the Guild to promote 'respectful' language about the personifates (2019: 43). Prue's personifate friend, Edwin, expresses his anxiety not merely with the politics of his status as a 'second lifer', but concerning the precariousness of that life: 'it could be snatched away again so easily' and he might 'go back to being a frequency lost in some world beyond' (2019: 128). Edwin does not have the confidence expressed in the formulation, 'I think therefore I am'. Instead, the personifates' 'sense of self is quite fragile', and, as Edwin notes, this makes them vulnerable, like 'putty in the hands' of the human technicians who have made them (Hardy 2019: 154, 215). The mechanical 'Round Rob' in *Tin* increasingly feels this unease, questioning the power that engineers have over their creations. His accusatory question to Cormier, after the engineer destroys what seems to be an ensouled mechanical in the basement of the Agency, pointedly exposes the fragility of the 'life' conferred upon Rob and the others: 'You wanted it dead, and you made it dead, and it's gone now, and you did that. Why?' (Kenny 2018: 212). The recourse to a *telos ex machina*, whether in the form of a spark animating the machine, or life conferred by an engineer, breeds ontological anxiety about the self not being at one with, and 'proper' to, itself, but instead determined from outside.

Deacon suggests that the consequence of Descartes's machine metaphor having influenced physical accounts of the mind is that such accounts implicitly 'beg for a watchmaker even as (they) deny his or her existence' (2011: 56). *Wildspark* and *Tin* render visible this paradox in their depictions of scientists having unlocked the secret of conferring life and intelligence on machines only by consorting with 'occult' forces. The dividing lines between science and superstition are redrawn by *Wildspark*'s Hannah Woolstenbury, head of the Medlock Guild and the 'greatest technician and inventor that the world had ever known' and, in *Tin*, by a lineage of engineers from the 'great' Joshua Runcible, who makes the first mechanicals, to Philip Cormier, who devises the principles of 'refined propulsion' (Hardy 2019: 64; Kenny 2018: 59). In both texts, full moons, ley lines, 'fractures in the world' or locations where the walls between 'our world and the spirit world are weaker' suggest a recapitulation of the occult materialism seen in the children's fantasy discussed in Chapter 1 (Kenny 2018: 277; Hardy 2019: 117). Here, though, instead of occult materialism working through an archaeological uncovering, a 'mechanical revolution' has proceeded alongside the development of 'ghost theories', producing hybrid technologies (Hardy 2019: 149). In *Tin* the secret to consciousness is in the glyphs devised by Runcible and in the now illegal, and highly secretive, method developed by Cormier for the 'melding of a soul with a mechanical system' (Kenny 2018: 66). This framing of ostensibly occult explanations as scientific method and achieved by means of scientific apparatus such as Woolstenbury's 'spectral oscilloscope', exposes and reconfigures what Ryle terms the 'para-mechanical hypothesis' inaugurated by Cartesian dualism (2000: 21). This hypothesis proposes that the 'substance' of the mind, having been divorced from the material world, is nonetheless of a similar type such that it must conform to the 'grammar of mechanics in reverse' (Ryle 2000: 21). The para-mechanical hypothesis casts spirit in the same mould as mechanics, suggesting minds are 'spectral machines' (Ryle 2000: 22). Ryle's excoriation of Descartes is written in the early days of cybernetics, but it predicts the ways in which theories of artificial intelligence come to describe the mind as a 'virtual machine' (Boden 2018: 3–5). Deacon suggests that this proliferation of mechanism and its metaphor of the world 'as an immense machine full of smaller machines' has eroded notions of material causality such that they are insufficient to explain the emergence of life and mind (2011: 74–5).

Such dissatisfaction with scientific mechanism is not explicit in these novels, but they do exhibit suspicion for the figure of the scientist who would claim to control life through mechanical means: clockwork gears, springs, and coils. Hannah Woolstenbury is revered by Medlock society, but Prue rejects her authority and ignores her injunction against investigating the wildspark for a way to recover the personifates' memories. Carrying out research in secret, Prue proves that, contrary to Woolstenbury's claims, memory loss is not 'a natural part of the process' (Hardy 2019: 202). The other Guild members whisper that perhaps Woolstenbury is not 'completely right' and that 'perhaps there are new things to come . . . that need to be discovered by others (Hardy 2019:

204). The suspicion of engineers' authority is more marked in *Tin*. The first engineer that readers encounter is Absalom, the cruel master of the scrapyard where Christopher and his friends live and work. His claims to greatness are derided by the mechanicals, though they have little choice but to do what he commands. Throughout the book engineers are viewed from the point of view of the mechanicals themselves in narration focalized through either Jack – a basic machine – or Christopher – who is ensouled. Being held captive by Blake, Christopher cannot bear to hear the engineer 'expounding on his own greatness', nor witness the callousness with which he treats his machines (Kenny 2018: 137). Even Cormier, who helps the mechanicals find Christopher, is hated by Jack for his 'self-congratulatory' arrogance (Kenny 2018: 196). The toppling of the engineers at the end of both books, with Blake trapped forever in a machine body and Woolstenbury and Cormier having learned humility, suggests that they have not fully grasped the complexity and value inherent in the sentient machines, and that their injunctions about what is a proper object of study ought to be ignored.

In their rejection of an engineer's insistence on minds as virtual machines, the books' use of spirits of the dead residing in a 'void' beyond the physical world intimates the importance of what Deacon calls 'absential phenomena' in the emergence of consciousness. Deacon notes 'that there is more than what is actual. There is what could be, what should be, what can't be, what is possible, and what is impossible' (Deacon 2011: 848). Absential phenomena, or absence-based causality, include the predictions arising from perceptions of the environment (events yet to occur), future possibilities for action (things the self might do in response to its perceptions), memories (of past events and actions), and goals and desires. Such absence-based causality gives rise to consciousness through the creation of loops that run within the body, outside the body, and between body and environment. Godfrey-Smith calls these 'looping causal paths' and suggests they include immaterial elements such as communications between present and future selves (2018: 82, 154–5). Philosopher of mind, Douglas Hofstadter (2006) goes further, characterizing the conscious self as a 'strange loop' built around a paradoxical absence: the very self to which it gives rise. A reductively materialist view of consciousness as a brain would suggest that the combination of its components gives rise, somehow, to sentience, which in turn produces memories, goals, and desires. Hofstadter and Godfrey-Smith suggest, instead, a downward causality, via the strange referential loops produced by communication and perception, loops that twist back on themselves, such that 'the microstuff' inside brains 'is pushed around by ideas and desires, rather than the reverse' (Hofstadter 2006: 294). The reference to a void from which consciousness emerges, and to ghosts enlivening bodies, in *Wildspark* and *Tin* suggests this 'absence-based causality' that is central to human experience (Deacon 2011: 38). The selves they imagine are in some senses 'as non-material as Descartes might have imagined, and yet as physical, extended, and relevant to the causal scheme of things as the hole at the hub of a wheel' (Deacon 2011: 755). Prue learns, for example, that Woolstenbury made her breakthrough in the harnessing of the wildspark after searching for a way to bring her daughter back from the dead. In the same way, the emotions of grief, described as a 'void inside' Prue, drive her to the Personifate Guild in Medlock in a quest to bring back her brother (Hardy 2019: 16). Absential phenomena are not, however, *telos ex nihilo*: these are not ghosts in the machine in the sense characterized by Ryle. In the case of Christopher, in *Tin*, at the end of the novel, when the conflicts have been resolved and he has been reunited with his grandfather, he continues to feel 'a curious sense of absence, as if he was lacking something' (Kenny 2018: 317). The conferring of a soul upon his mechanical body has not settled feelings of unease that have persisted throughout the book. In this case, the something missing is, as Hofstadter and Deacon describe it, the paradoxical form that is the self, a form that comprises absential phenomena and absent causes, including memories.

One important absential phenomenon in the production of a conscious self is information. The idea of information as cause, and that life and consciousness arise from a mutually constitutive entanglement of matter and information, is increasingly considered likely in evolutionary chemistry and biology (Küppers 2016; Walker et al. 2017; Rovelli 2018; Davies 2019), though it has its basis in quantum physics and John Wheeler's famous formulation 'it from bit' (1989). Wheeler argues that every 'it', including the spacetime continuum itself, derives its existence:

> from the apparatus-elicited answers to yes or no question, binary choices, bits. It from Bit symbolizes the idea that every item of the physical world has at bottom . . . an immaterial source and explanation . . . that all things physical are information-theoretic in origin. (Wheeler 1989: 355–6)

Wildspark suggests such an information-theoretic basis to consciousness in its representation of the soul as a 'signal', a complex information pattern that can be measured by the GODAR (ghost observation detection and ranging device) and channelled through the 'parabolic reflector' into the personifate bodies (Hardy 2019: 194–5). In studies from evolutionary biology, artificial intelligence and quantum biology, information is accorded a causal role in the emergence of life, complexity, and mind, not as a vitalist 'life force', but 'instantiated in matter' as chemical exchange, energy transfer and the molecular shuffling that keeps living organisms in a far-from-equilibrium state in defiance of the second law of thermodynamics (Davies 2019: 7, 47, 64). Paul Davies argues that it is 'tempting to suppose that some aspect of information will form a bridge between mind and matter as it does between life and non-life' (2019: 186). Though Davies states we should not think of information as a 'ghost' or a 'life force', *Wildspark*'s imaginative rendering of the ghostly self as 'data' frequencies that flow through the personifate's body to produce speech, 'movement' and 'thought' does accord with the idea of life as information processing instantiated in matter (Hardy 2019: 220). In one scene, the Guild apprentices work with a signal simulator, wiring feed-forward and feedback 'loops' to form the 'inner connections and workings' of the personifate bodies. The 'movement data' comes from the wildspark, the technician tells them, but its causal power emerges from the 'constant stream' of information flow through the cybernetic body (Hardy 2019: 185–6). This description of the personifates resonates with the notion of feedback loops discussed earlier, and with modern theories of life defined in terms of information processing.

Prue's secret investigations on the wildspark with her specially modified GODAR also attests to contemporary theories of information that locates causality – and consciousness – not in individual processing units like cells and neurons but in the integration of the whole (Tononi et al. 2016; Davies 2019: 187). Integrated Information Theory, which proposes a mathematical measure of connectedness and integration in a system [Φ] as an indicator of consciousness, is endorsed by Prue's findings which disclose 'complex patterns within the wave: waves within waves, within more waves' (Hardy 2019: 240). This is compatible with Deacon's 'absential' thesis, which locates consciousness in the dynamical emergence of patterns and relations, here informational in nature. Although Prue modifies her device to 'separate' specific frequencies in the signal, it is clear that the wildspark is a complex, integrated phenomenon. When Prue attempts to isolate what 'she hoped was the history data', the introduction of her specially modifies apparatus and her intentions obtains unexpected results: she can recall the personifate's old name but no other details from their first life (Hardy 2019: 281). In a sense, Prue encounters the quantum measurement problem as she tries to break the entangled wildspark into its constituent parts. As is the case in all cases of measurement, Prue's experiment asks questions that determine what is knowable in that particular instance, producing a new phenomenon as it makes a 'cut': in this case, the restoration of the name, but no other information. Recasting the measurement problem in the field of cybernetics and bioinformatics, Deacon suggests that the information about a system is not exhaustible since 'signal receivers' limit what information can be captured (2011: 400). Prue wants to discover who the personifates once were and so modifies her physical apparatus (we are not told how). The modification produces one piece of meaningful information, but this does not mean that the wildspark is reducible to individual computational tokens. The self as a highly complex integrated informational system resists mereological analysis, explainable by relating 'parts' to a 'whole'. Thus, Prue is never successful in her aim to be able to 'read' the signal and 'select who comes back' and must accept her brother's death at the end of the book.

Information-theoretic and downward causality theories of the emergence of mind resist dualism by emphasizing what Braidotti calls 'the mind-body continuum – i.e. the embrainment of the body and embodiment of the mind' (2018: 31). Of course, as strange perceptual loops suggest, this continuum extends to the environment in which the body is embedded, and to the other minds that inhabit that environment. Hardy's engineers intimate they understand this continuum of mind, body, and nature, when they tell Prue that they've 'melded' their personifate technology 'with the wild' since 'nature is the best designer' (2019: 105). In the final section of the chapter, I want to focus on this 'wild' aspect of consciousness, developing an ecological concept of mind through a reading of the third text in this corpus: *The Wild Robot*.

Going wild: An ecological concept of mind

My reading of *The Wild Robot* moves from probing the figuration of the ghost in the machine to an exploration of the way in which minds as extramaterial phenomena arise from physical matter. The question of how goal-oriented complex systems arise in nature draws interest from across the scientific disciplines and, as Anthony Aguirre et al. suggest, requires thinking 'across traditional subject boundaries' (2018: 4). *The Wild Robot* offers an imaginative intervention in the debate as it traces the evolution of Roz from a computational machine whose goals have been imposed externally by her makers to a self-determining, cognitive organism. This transformation cannot be accounted for by eliminative materialism and computational theories of mind. Rather, what is required is an extramaterialism that locates absential phenomena within living processes. *The Wild Robot* negotiates a complex dichotomy of computation and conscious thought. At first the two are distinct, though computation is suggested to be analogous with what occurs inside animal minds. As Roz develops, however, computation becomes a subvenient dynamic that contributes to the emergence of a higher-order self without determining that self.

The premise of *The Wild Robot* seems to endorse a Cartesian split and, in his coda to the story, Brown suggests that it was inspired by similarities he observed between robots and animals. He notes that animal routines and behaviours seem 'almost robotic' and links animal instincts to computer programmes (2016: 272). In Descartes's *Discourse* neither animals nor machines have the universal faculty of reason, could never declare their thoughts to others, and cannot 'act from knowledge' but only from the 'disposition of their organs, as one sees that a clock, which is made up of only wheels and springs, can count the hours' (1968 [1647]: 100, 99). If *Tin* and *Wildspark* literalized the metaphor of the ghost in the machine, *The Wild Robot* literalizes this Cartesian doctrine of animals as machines. However, Brown's narration, which moves from an external view of Roz as a black box to an internal focalization of her experience, suggests the opposite: animals and machines act with reason, experientiality, and subjectivity. There are two simple points arising from this disjunction, and a third that is more complex. First, is that psychonarration gives the impression of interiority no matter who is being narrated. Second, this mode of storytelling suggests that neither animals nor machines ought not to be placed on the other side of a Cartesian cut. The third point pertains to the cut itself, and the consequences for the concept of information, which is the basis of Roz's existence. Like all organisms, she processes information in order to survive, demonstrating a physical definition of information as inversely proportionate to entropy. Information processing is what prevents living cells and systems from entropic decline, staving off disorder and randomness. A logical consequence of Descartes's doctrine is that this information processing is rendered meaningless, and that the physical world can be reduced to computation. If meaning exists, it does so irreducibly in the individual experience of those subjects with minds. However, *The Wild Robot* denies this Cartesian cut, suggesting that subjectivity emerges from information processing, providing 'a conceptual bridge from mechanistic relationships to [the] end-directed, informational and normative relationships' found in life (Deacon 2011: 33). Roz's adaptations to her environment, in part deriving from her evolutionary programming and in part from the demands of the environment itself, leads to the emergence of a unified mind that generates its own purpose. Paradoxically, this emergence suggests an important distinction between computation and cognition, the former being parasitic on an extrinsic teleology and the latter existing because of consequences that arise internally. While *The Wild Robot* could thus be interpreted as an endorsement of the possibility of full AI at some point in the future, here I take it as demonstrating the reflexive nature of mind, its entanglement not only with the body but with the wider environment and with the other minds that inhabit that environment, and the web of semiotic communication they produce – all of which renders information processing meaningful.

Roz exemplifies emerging theories in systems biology that state 'organisms live and die by the amount of information they acquire about their environment' and that information translates into fitness in an evolutionary sense (Wagner 2007: 1). The robot's first days on the island are a trial: she acquires scrapes and dents because her robot body is not equipped for the terrain and is almost torn apart by a pair of bear cubs. The narrator notes that 'the animals were experts at survival' and describes how Roz begins to observe them, gaining ideas as to how to camouflage herself and ward off predators (Brown 2016: 31, 35). Roz can retrieve information pre-programmed into her 'computer brain', such as key facts about the opossum she encounters, which is 'known for mimicking the appearance and smell of dead animals when threatened' (2016: 66). However, it is only in acquiring new information from an interaction with the opossum itself that Roz improves her chances of survival. This is – echoing cybernetician Gregory Bateson – information as 'a difference that makes a difference' (Bateson 1979: 99). The opossum talks about her 'acting' abilities, suggesting that the robot should try it for herself (Brown 2016: 66). Roz agrees that to 'act less robotic' is a good survival strategy that will help her 'make some friends' and 'help her live longer, and better' (Brown 2016: 67). This is an example of evolutionary programming. Roz is a programme that can change herself instead of having to be rewritten by a programmer, but her criterion of success also transforms in the process. When she first awakens, Roz declares that she will move and communicate and learn in order to find better ways to 'complete tasks', that she will 'stay out of the way and keep myself in good working order' (Brown 2016: 7). After talking with the opossum, she develops a new criteria and goal, that of living 'better'. Roz's observations and interactions process meaningful information in the sense theorized by Carlo Rovelli (2018). Rovelli describes the recursive growth of meaningful information as organisms identify correlations with their external environments that contribute to survival (Rovelli 2018: 18, 21). Though nothing external, no 'wild spark', has entered Roz's body nor transformed her computational states, this information processing loop is nonetheless more than the exchange of physical tokens; it is *about* something, it is intentional.

As an evolutionary programme, Roz reveals something about evolution itself and its relationship to consciousness. As she transforms herself in response to other creatures and environmental stimuli, Roz demonstrates 'Darwinism 2.0' – a set of theories that suggest evolutionary processes are goal-directed. Eschewing the orthodox idea that evolution proceeds from chance mutations, research in epigenetics and cellular biology suggests that mutations might be 'directed towards a useful goal' and that evolution is an 'informational learning curve' (Davies 2019: 123, 126). Roz's learning curve directs her adaptations further and further from her pre-programmed directives. For example, she quickly abandons efforts to keep herself clean and to repair the dents and scrapes on her body, ending up 'smeared' with mud, covered in flowers and leaves such that she resembles 'a great tuft of plants walking through the forest' (Brown 2016: 42–3). Becoming 'part of the landscape' allows Roz to better observe the other animals and gather information, which in turn further adapts the programming (Brown 2016: 43). Roz's early explorations of the island mimic the idea of adaptation as an 'informed search', elaborated in the work of biologists Eva Jablonka and Marion Lamb (2014: 100). Roz's informed searches include observation leading to mimicry, but also seeking out specific expertise: the stick insect for camouflage; the goose, Loudwing, for parenting advice when she adopts an orphaned goose chick; the beavers for advice on building a home in the forest, and so on. Her mutations, including the performance of wildness that helps her fit in and learning the animals' language, are neither mindless nor random, but proceed from her informed searches, themselves the result of, and contributing to, evolving goals and intentions.

Roz's relationship with her adopted son, Brightbill, accords with ideas of epigenetics, another aspect of Darwinism 2.0, the process whereby environmental factors affect how genes are expressed and the heritability of these expressions from one generation to the next. Epigenetics rejects the notion of genes as deterministic blueprints and allows that organisms play an 'active role' in their development, that they 'impose direction on evolution' (Laland 2016: 42). This biological reframing of 'nature versus nurture' find imaginative expression in *The Wild Robot*. When Brightbill hatches, Loudwing suggests 'he must be a runt' and that it will take 'a miracle for him to survive', but Roz adapts her behaviour to become an 'excellent' mother so that he thrives (Brown 2016: 76, 99). My mapping of this relationship to epigenetics is analogous, of course, since there is no biological relationship between Roz and Brightbill. Nonetheless, Roz's adaptations, which include her willingness to work with others and a decisiveness in the face of crisis, impose a direction on Brightbill's development such that he transforms from being the runt to the 'graceful' leader of the migrating flock, taking over from Loudwing when the annual migration goes awry (Brown 2016: 201). Like Roz, Brightbill has developed the capacity to respond adaptively and is resilient to the demands of an unpredictable environment: his becoming is not determined by a fixed genetic inheritance. My reading of Roz as exemplary of the goal-directed nature of evolution is, therefore, analogous, but there is an important sense in which sentience is a micro-evolutionary process in action and that Roz's interconnection with, and impact on, the environment reveals that 'the experience of being sentient is what it feels like to *be* evolution' (Deacon 2011: 782). Bateson makes a similar claim in describing learning and thought as 'fundamentally similar' to evolution; both are probabilistic in nature and emerge from the interaction of sensory systems with events and changes in the external environment (Bateson 1979: 148, 97). Evolution and mind 'fit together into a single ongoing biosphere' (Bateson 1979: 162) just as Roz's mind adapts to the island and in turn shapes the island and the lives of its inhabitants.

The evolution of Roz's mind is entangled with the bigger mind of the island, emerging out of the communicative loops that connect it to other minds. Indeed, Roz's information collection on the island reveals that information is not discrete, but integrated and complex, revealing the entangled ecology of which she is now a part. In one scene, having learned camouflage from the stick insect, Roz hides among the plant-life. Her observations are recorded as follows:

> Spiders spun intricate webs.
> Berries beckoned to hungry mouths.
> Foxes stalked hares.
> Mushrooms rose up from leaf litter.
> Turtle plopped into ponds.
> Moss spread across tree roots.
> Vultures hunched over carcasses.
> Ocean waves beat against the coastline.
> Tadpoles became frogs, caterpillars became butterflies. (Brown 2016: 45)

Roz collects information about predator and prey relationships, which are essentially modes of energy transfer, but these are also nested in other kinds of interactions that suggest meaning and intentionality, including the spreading of moss across tree root as it too gains and responds to information about its environment, allowing it to grow, and the semiotic signals instantiated by the berries and the hungry animals looking for food. This scene illustrates Godfrey-Smith's notion that 'sentience is brought into being somehow from the evolution of sense and acting, it involves being as a living system with a point of view on the world around it' (2018: 79). Roz interprets the different points of view and perceptual loops she encounters, noting, for example, that the inclination of the doe's head signals her intentions to her family that they ought to 'look for clovers by the stream' (2016: 48). As Davies suggests, 'the vast and complex web of life on earth is woven from information exchange between individuals and groups at all levels' (2019: 104). Roz enters this network of information exchange by learning the semiotics of this ecology, rather than relying on pre-programmed data. What at first sounds like a meaningless 'screech' becomes to Roz 'animal words' (2016: 39, 48). Immersion in this communicative ecology of the island not only allows Roz to collect more data but entangles her with dynamic relationships of obligation and reciprocity that, in turn, build her cognitive capacities. She becomes nested in a mesh of nature, exchanging favours with other animals, such as the beavers and the doe who help Roz build a home and a garden in exchange for her tree-felling skills and food sharing. It is via such dynamic interrelationships that the animals attempt to maintain what they see as the 'balance' of the island, though they are aware of disruptions beyond their control such as the changing climate and rising sea levels (Brown 2016: 191). The dynamics of this ecology, in which interacting organisms contribute to higher-order population dynamics and equilibrium, are analogous to the way lower-order processes in the brain contribute to the emergence of higher-order sentient activity. Roz's emerging mind mirrors the ecology in which she finds herself and in turn contributes to the dynamic transformation of that ecology.

Roz's adaptations to, and growing interconnection with, the ecology of the island create a bridge from computation to cognition, transforming her from built machine to living organism. Despite alluring descriptions of minds and evolution as computational processes, there is an important distinction. As Deacon notes, designers and users determine the form of a machine to be suited to a task, but this task otherwise has no relation to the machine's existence. In contrast, 'organic forms evolve in the process of accomplishing a task critical to maintaining the capacity to produce this form, so the task space and the form of the organism are essentially inseparable' (Deacon 2011: 192–3). The machine-organism comparison is tempting in biology, suggests Deacon, where researchers try to make sense of the end-directedness of living processes without recourse to non-physical phenomena, but it elides something particular about life (2011: 193). Brown makes the machine-organism comparison in his suggestion that animals are like robots, but his story inverts this logic in its transformation of Roz. She articulates this change herself, addressing the other animals towards the end of the story: 'I was just a machine. I functioned. But you – my friends and family – you have taught me how to live . . . you have also taught me to be wild' (Brown 2016: 217). As already discussed, Roz's adaptations not only make her more fitted to the island but lead to the internal emergence of new goals replacing those imposed by her makers. As Deacon suggests, organisms 'are entirely organized around a central goal-directedness, self-generation, and perpetuation. End-directedness is an intrinsic defining characteristic of an organism, not something only assessed from outside and extrinsically or accidentally imposed' (2011: 726). Over the long winter nights when the animals declare a truce and shelter in Roz's lodge, their discussions turn to their purpose. When Roz declares that she does not think that she has one, having seemingly forgotten her pre-programmed directives, the animals suggest various options: that she is meant to grow gardens, or care for Brightbill. Eventually, Roz decides 'perhaps I am simply meant to help others' (Brown 2016: 192). Functionally, helping others is not unlike her original designation as a ROZZUM unit 7134, destined for a TechLab Industries worksite, but it is qualitatively distinct in that it is a self-directed purpose that has emerged from her growing entanglement with the ecology of the island.

Roz's shift from computation to cognition manifests in her behaviour, the formulation of new goals, and in an increasingly internalized narration that describes her 'wondering', 'worry', and 'thought' (Brown 2016: 172, 189, 212). In this sense, she exemplifies the thesis of 'bio from bit' advanced by Sara Walker in dialogue with Wheeler's original formulation of 'it from bit'. Walker argues that not only is information at the heart of what life does, but that the higher-level complex structures to which it gives rise themselves have causal power to produce further transformations (Walker 2018: 81). As complexity increases, new properties emerge that 'can themselves have causal consequences, allowing agents to have an active say in achieving their own goals' (Walker 2018: 82). In this sense, Roz transforms from bit to bio as her information processing gives rise to an emergent self that is more than the sum of its parts and which, in turn, exerts influence over those parts. 'You move and talk and think, mama. You're definitely alive,' Brightbill tells Roz (Brown 2016: 125). The causal supervenience of the emergent self is most apparent at the end of the story, however, after Roz's encounter with the recos. Roz's body is 'ruined' – she is little more than a head and a torso (Brown 2016: 262). Nonetheless, she maintains her sense of self, asking the animals to help her into the recos' ship so that she can seek out her makers, get repairs, and somehow find her way back to the island. She declares a series of intentions, a purpose, and 'command' over the other animals to bring this about (Brown 2016: 263). This is not because her artificial consciousness – her computer brain – is housed inside her undamaged head, but because the self that is Roz persists despite the damage to her components. As Deacon argues, in the case of living organisms, 'wholes precede parts, integration is intrinsic' (2011: 74). The machine metaphor no longer adequately describes Roz, then, and the logical necessity for *telos ex machina* has become redundant in the process.

I also read Roz's becoming wild through Luciana Parisi's elucidation of Gilbert Simondon's conception of the technical object. Parisi's reading of Simondon emphasizes the ability of the technical object to 'aggregate and change over time' through its responsive to the environment (2017: 156). She argues that Simondon's is a 'counterintuitive theory' that presents the technical object at its most concrete when it is able to act as a 'natural' object (2017: 158). Roz embodies this, at first mimicking the form of plants for survival and information gathering, but later donning natural camouflage as a 'party dress' so she can 'celebrate life and wildness' with the other animals (Brown 2016: 216–17). Parisi suggests that the 'concretization' of the technical object occurs in phases so that it becomes successively independent from the external regulatory environment in which it was ideated (the factory) – achieving an internal coherence and losing its artificial character (2017: 158). These phases are represented in Brown's narrative in the short chapters titled for the significant events to which Roz responds and, in turn, which transform her: 'the camouflaged insect' chapter precedes 'the camouflaged robot', for example, while 'the fight' with the young bears leads to 'the new foot' and so on. Through such encounters Roz becomes an 'energetic accumulation of being' (Parisi 2017: 159). This accumulation is rendered most obvious in her encounters with the recos, who have come to the island to reclaim lost property for TechLab Industries – including Roz. The 'cold' 'flat' voices of the new robots are unable to communicate with the islanders (Brown 2016: 226). Roz bombards them with questions that they cannot answer, their stock responses useless against such enquiries as 'What is my purpose?' and 'Why can I not ask questions?' (Brown 2016: 227). They compute that Roz must be 'defective' and attempt to 'commence deactivation' as the animals come to Roz's rescue (Brown 2016: 227). In the face of this 'forest assault', the recos' computational processes are inadequate. Reco 3 ends up sunk waist deep in mud, covered in bird droppings and Reco 2 is swept away down the waterfall after being bombarded with logs by the bear cubs. While Roz has adapted to the fluctuations of the environment as opportunities for transformation, the recos, as mere machines, can only attempt to defend.

This reading of Roz as technical object re-establishes a connection between humans (and other organisms) and machines maintained by cybernetics, though not in a way that mechanistically reduces either. In this reading, Roz's experiences echo Latour's insistence that we misunderstand machines. Also drawing on Simondon, Latour suggests that machines in 'no way obey the principles of mechanics, which remain a form of idealism' (2018: 121). Latour expounds his non-machinic account of machines in *Aramis*, a text that strives to return the 'souls of machines' into techno-social discourse (1996: vii). Latour's aim is to turn a technical object into the 'central character of a narrative', which is also what Brown attempts (Latour 1996: vii). Both texts are in dialogue with Mary Shelley's archetypal machine-organism fable, *Frankenstein* (1818). In *The Wild Robot*, Roz is repeatedly identified as a 'monster' before being accepted by the islanders. Recalling her awakening on the beach, the seal 'Shelly' tells the others that 'we thought she was dead, but when we reached into the box, she came to life and climbed out looking like a sparkling monster' (Brown 2016: 137). Latour insists that it is Victor who is the real monster, seemingly unable to understand what he has created (1996: 83). Brown's reading of Shelley's novel is more allusive and elusive, but that the humans intervene only to reclaim their lost property suggests a similar interpretation. *The Wild Robot* positively reimagines Victor's monster in Roz's transformation, which also exemplifies the hybridity Latour asserts in *Aramis* and elsewhere. There is, in fact, no cut between 'technical things' and 'natural things' – as Roz at first insists – but an interpenetration in which organisms are extended into and through objects and vice versa. Roz, then, is a post*humous* subject, not only because she walks out of the robot gravesite, but because she transforms into a new and 'strange' kind of life beyond the externally imposed ideations of her human creators (Brown 2016: 126).

Conclusion: The entanglement of mind, brain, and world

My readings of *The Wild Robot*, *Wildspark*, and *Tin* have explored the ways in which contemporary philosophy, science, and other disciplines such as biosemiotics, are seeking to undo a persistent Cartesian dualism that constrains understandings of life and mind. I have argued that the imaginative rendering of a Cartesian 'ghost in the machine' in children's Fantastika reveals the tensions in dualist formulations of mind and body, gesturing to alternative ontologies that emphasize a mind-body continuum without recourse to eliminative materialism or transcendental posthumanism. Unravelling the paradoxes of the ghost in the machine and reading these texts alongside extramaterial theories of life and mind, especially those that accord a central role to information in the emergence of consciousness, point to alternative configurations of mind and matter that emphasize the embeddedness of thought in the physical environment. Rather than endorsing a Cartesian cut, then, Fantastika imagines a conceptual bridge, the emergence of mind and life from non-mental processes and inorganic matter. Such processes are entangled and irreducible to mereological analysis. That is, neither life nor mind can be reduced to constituent parts as though they were merely the product of a complex mechanism. Instead, the depictions of machine consciousness in these texts suggest the reverse: an ecological concept of mind that accords causality both to bottom-up, or subvenient, processes, and to top-down supervenient wholes, including the larger mind that is the environment itself. In Chapter 4, I continue to think about the strangeness of other minds that comprise the environment of which humans are a part, delving further into evolutionary narratives that unsettle our feelings of earthly belonging and instead emphasize our interdependence with more-than-human beings.

4

Precarious interdependence

The oceans of the ecoweird

Introduction: Ecological belonging as interdependence

In *Deeplight* by Frances Hardinge, a priest of the 'old religion' tells one of the characters what it was like to speak to the gods: vast, aquatic beings who once terrorized the ocean. He tells of their 'complex minds', of the lack of warmth and kinship in their eyes, of the ways in which their consciousness started to 'gutter' as their bodies swelled to gargantuan proportions (2019: 276–7). Whereas the science fiction novels discussed in Chapter 3 were concerned with exploring the mystery of consciousness, the contact with 'alien' minds in *Deeplight* is a prompt for questioning ecological belonging. Building on the ecological and evolutionary themes explored in my reading of *The Wild Robot*, here I turn to contemporary weird fiction to explore relationships of interdependence between humans and their environment. In so doing, I develop an account of the 'ecoweird' that emphasizes the precarious ethical relations that inhere in ecological belonging. Like the concept of entanglement, interdependence requires a conceptual shift from considering things in isolation to things as mutually constituted. As Jonathan Beever argues, 'interdependence' is a dark term that eschews the easier concept of 'interconnection' that circulates in ecological thought and that preserves the autonomy of human being (2020: 2). As dark matter, interdependence emphasizes both the contingency and the precarity of ecological relationships, an uneasiness akin to that disclosed by Hardinge's characters when they encounter their oceanic gods.

The weird is a slippery mode that manifests across multiple genres, and, although it is most often associated with horror, its recent emergence in fiction for children and young adults reveals that the weird provokes a range of affects, including humour and pleasure (Germaine Buckley 2017: 29). In this chapter I suggest that the aesthetics, affects, and story moves – to use John Clute's term for the architecture of Fantastika – can do more than imagine a mind-shattering confrontation with 'outer unknown forces' and a 'defeat of those fixed laws of Nature which are our only safeguard against the assaults of chaos and the daemons of unplumbed space' (Lovecraft 2012: 57). Lovecraft's description of the weird, which is often quoted by horror critics, offers scant resources for developing eco-ethical propositions. The imagined obliteration of self in the face of the 'chaos' of the Outside, the radical ontological alienation, is hardly conducive to ecological thought. Happily, Lovecraft is not the last word on the weird and there are possibilities in the mode, apparent in contemporary children's and YA fiction, for thinking about human interdependence with a more-than-human world. These possibilities emerge from the way the weird attends to the 'gaps' that puncture anthropocentric modes of access to the world, a key aesthetic element identified in Graham Harman's work on Lovecraft (2012), though the ethical ramifications of the 'gaps' are not considered there. I build on existing theorizations of the weird, particularly those that emphasize a phenomenological dimension, to elaborate on how the gaps of the weird disclose the precarious interdependencies that sustain human subjectivity. My reading of two contemporary ecoweird novels written for older children and young adults argues that the weird provides sutures for the gaps that puncture anthropocentric phenomenological experience even as it exposes those gaps.

I present *The Last Zoo* (2019) by Sam Gayton and *Deeplight* (2019) by Frances Hardinge as ecoweird novels because they enweird human interrelationships with other beings and with the ecologies in which they are embedded, revealing gaps and wounds at the heart of human experiences of the world. As Roger Luckhurst suggests, the weird 'dissolves generic glue' and is 'a category that defies categorisation' (2017: 1041–2). These two novels attest to this disruptive character of the weird and draw on multiple genres to suggest that the mode, sitting within the umbrella of Fantastika, is not so easy to define as others such as science fiction, fantasy, and horror. I am also interested in the uncanny and the gothic, modes which sit under the umbrella of Fantastika in their own right, but which I incorporate here into a definition of the ecoweird because of their use in these novels. Hardinge and Gayton also draw on the genres of science fiction, speculative fiction, and climate fiction, as well as making specific intertextual references to a range of novels across genres such as *Alice in Wonderland* (1865) and *Frankenstein* (1818). Such generic entanglements are key to the ethics they elaborate as they explore the storyable dark matter of ecological belonging.

The Last Zoo by Sam Gayton is set in the near future and depicts a group of early adolescent children. These children are the self-styled 'rekkers' who live on a rag-tag fleet of ships known as the Ark, which is moored next to a gaping hole in reality, 'the Seam', located fifty miles off the coast of California. The rekkers are named for the now-abandoned 'recreation' vessel on which they spend their free time, though the word 'rekke' also has sailing and mining connotations pertinent to the setting of the story. The Seam, which appears to human eyes as a mountain of darkness, is the result of a reality bomb detonated by scientists searching for a solution to the climate crisis. Initial explorations into the Seam resulted in 'mind-fray' and the disappearance of most of the (adult) research team in 'glitches' that circulate around ground zero. Since children are at less risk from mind-fray, they are recruited to enter the Seam and extract its resources. This involves contacting the mysterious Seamstress, a ten-legged creature whose clacking limbs weave new species from the imaginations of those who enter. The new species, called 'voilà', are housed in enclosures on the Ark and cared for by the children, hence the title of the novel, which institutes a tension between the biblical idea of the 'ark' as a vessel for the salvation of all creatures, and a zoo, which exhibits other animals for the viewing pleasure of human visitors, albeit often with the justification of conservation. There are, however, no visitors allowed into this 'zoo' to view its hybrid mythological-theological-fantastical creatures: smellephants, hummingbird dragons, unicorns, genies, angels, and devils. Also, as one of the rekkers comments, the ARK is a poor conservation experiment since the sixty new species extracted from the seam hardly make up for the mass extinctions caused by anthropogenic global heating and habitat destruction. Nonetheless, the humans hope that their bizarre zoo holds the solution to the climate crisis. They keep the creatures they deem to be useful, and the others are allowed to go extinct. As doomsday cults sweep the planet and 'ohtwo' factories fail in overcrowded cities, humans need a miracle, with hopes pinned on the 'angels' in the care of Pia, an orphan who looks after the 'celestial' voilà. The zoo is a bizarre experiment of biological engineering, (un)natural selection and weirdly accelerated evolution. It is a laboratory, a quarantine zone, and an ark. In their role as 'seamers', the kids in *The Last Zoo* perform a similar role to the explorers in Jeff Vandermeer's novel, *Annihilation* (2014), a novel that has become central to an emerging canon of contemporary ecoweird fiction. Like the explorers entering 'Area X' in Vandermeer's novel, the children in *The Last Zoo* enter a zone at the very edge of human epistemic and phenomenological limits. At the same time, the book explicitly draws on classic children's portal fantasy, referring to the wardrobe into Narnia and the rabbit hole in *Alice in Wonderland* (1865). There is power in childish imagination, then, though, as the word 'Seam' suggests, *The Last Zoo* is interested in using this imagination to (re)suture its punctured reality. The story works to a conclusion that returns the children in the sprawling mesh of relationships that comprise their dying planet, gesturing towards a precarious hope for the future.

Deeplight by Frances Hardinge draws more overtly on the tradition of Lovecraftian horror than *The Last Zoo*, mingling this genre with elements of fantasy. The novel is not directly concerned with the climate crisis, though it explores human-ecological relationships in other ways. *Deeplight* is a secondary world fantasy set within 'The Myriad', a group of islands whose inhabitants live in fearful memory of the oceanic 'gods' they once worshipped. The gods were a bizarre amalgamation of humanoid, cephalopodic, tentacular, and inorganic bodies, vast, unfathomable beings to whom regular sacrifices were made in exchange (supposedly) for the protection of the islands. Like *The Last Zoo*, the novel focuses on early adolescent children: Hark and Jelt are orphans who scratch a living on the island of Lady's Crave (named after its god, the Hidden Lady) by means of cons and petty crime. Remains of the old gods occasionally come ashore and are sold as 'godware', valuable material for use in strange technologies, or worshipped as relics by those who still remember the gods with awe. When Hark is caught helping a smuggling gang illegally procure such relics, he is sold into indentured servitude and sent to the remote island of Nest to care for the elderly priests of the old religion. His new master, Dr Vyne, tasks him with ferreting out the priests' secrets to further her classified scientific project: the creation of a new (biomechanical) god that might be controlled by humans to serve their political interests. Hark's loyalties to Jelt, an abusive friend, become strained by his new position and, further, when Jelt is injured in a foolish dive into the 'Undersea', a layer of the ocean that is composed of liquid human fear and was once the domain of the gods. While rescuing Jelt, Hark finds a pulsating godware 'heart', which heals the sick and injured and begins to transform Jelt into something monstrous. As Hark becomes tangled in the consequences of Jelt's metamorphosis, Vyne's experiment, and the revelations of the old priest, Quest, he must confront the reality of what the gods once were and enter the Undersea to prevent a new one from rising. Like *The Last Zoo*, *Deeplight* develops its weird ecology in and around the ocean, exploring the ways in which its characters are severed from, but also intimately connected to, the blue depths – an ecological zone that prompts both fear and desire.

The oceans of the ecoweird

As these summaries suggest, the weird is concerned with the dark matter that is human belonging in environments that are frightening and beyond human control, yet intimately connected to them. In both novels these environments are interstitial sites that border the ocean or reside below it: the Seam and the Undersea. The ocean has been a frequent setting for evoking feelings and anxieties critics now identify as 'ecohorror' since at least the eighteenth century. Emily Alder reveals multiple synergies between the gothic, for example, and writing about the sea from the late eighteenth century to the present, which she identifies as 'nautical gothic' (2017: 1). Focusing on nineteenth-century literature, Keri Stevenson notes that the sea often figures as a kind of 'monster' in ecohorror texts. Elsewhere, Jonathan Newell considers William Hope Hodgson's ocean stories from the early twentieth century as key to the development of the aesthetics of the weird (2020: 131–44). Unlike conventional ecohorror texts that pit humans against the ocean, however, the weird provokes a paradoxical rupture-suture in fundamental ontological categories, a cutting-together-apart, to borrow Barad's terminology, of the human with-and-from myriad ecological others that comprise the oceanic environment. Newell recognizes this potential in the weird, reading Hope Hodgson's ocean tale 'The Voice in the Night' (1907) against its ecophobic grain to discuss the ways in which the stories represent humans as 'porous beings drawn into a pulsating universe of human and non-human agents' (Newell 2020: 133). However, where Hodgson writes about a weird ocean in ways that 'tend to foreclose the full ethical, political, and environmental obligations that new materialism implies' (Newell 2020: 136), I contend that Gayton and Hardinge's fiction eschews fears of contamination and the obliteration of individual selfhood seemingly threatened by ocean environments. Instead, they evoke an ambivalence about the ocean that is identified by Steve Mentz, in his survey of the oceanic imaginary in literature, science, and philosophy: 'Poised on the sea's edge, we balance between kinship with and alienation from the watery part of the world' (2020: 4). This precarious position on the border of the ocean is generative for ecological ethics, particularly through a focus on kinship. Just as the witches in the novels discussed in Chapter 2 looked to the sky gods and not just the soil, to understand their earthly belonging, here our characters exchange 'solid ground for liquid sea' (Mentz 2020: 4). The ocean is not romanticized in these ecoweird stories, but nor is it only a site of phobia and ontological alienation. Rather, it is the catalyst for a precarious reconfiguration of relationships of interdependence that comprise life on earth, which is rendered urgent in a time of climate crisis.

Deeplight and *The Last Zoo* describe Anthropocene oceans that suggest that the human is intimately connected to myriad ecological others and that human actions impact those ecological relations in destructive ways. The philosopher Stacy Alaimo develops her theory of transcorporeality, which is a 'sense of the human as substantially and perpetually interconnected with the flows of substances and the agency of environments', in the context of just such oceanic environmental crises (2012: 476). Reading Alaimo's work alongside these ecoweird texts makes clear their particular figurations of transcorporeality in the context of polluted ocean flows that carry with them the histories of human violence. This violence is, in *The Last Zoo*, what Rob Nixon calls 'slow violence': 'a violence of delayed destruction that is dispersed across time and space, an attritional violence that is typically not viewed as violence at all' (Nixon 2011: 2). Pia echoes Nixon's concept when she reflects that the end of the world has not come about in 'the flash of fire and fury' people imagined, but that it has been 'almost unnoticeable, like the winding down of a clock' (Gayton 2019: 51). Pia lives among the evidence of environmental slow violence. Inside her ark lie 'hundreds upon hundreds' of crates containing 'pointless junk' that will never be delivered to customers (Gayton 2019: 18). Pia looks at the crates as 'so much garbage. No wonder the world was a mess' (2019: 19). On deck, the mess is even more apparent. The wind tastes of 'salt and burning plastic. The sun burns like a reactor fire over the irradiated sea' (Gayton 2019: 177). Mired in this toxicity, Pia must search for the missing angels as the Zoo begins to fall apart. The voilà disappear one by one from the ships, and the human inhabitants are taken over by a virus that spreads paranoia and fear.

Human fear is also prevalent in *Deeplight*, where it forms a different kind of Anthropocene ocean, one that is literally awash with terror that contains the power to create gods. The inhabitants of the Myriad look upon the ocean with terror and awe, as an alien realm, but it is *their* fear that pools to form the Undersea, which turns out to be a thoroughly human zone. Where the environmental crisis of *The Last Zoo* evokes the slow violence of anthropogenic climate change, the 'cataclysm' of *Deeplight*, which figures in the characters' memories as the final wrath of the gods before they were all destroyed beneath the waves, is a more fantastical oceanic apocalypse. However, despite the fantasy elements favoured in *Deeplight*, the novel is also interested in showing how humans are intimately connected with and by oceanic flows. In his journey to the Undersea, Hark sees the 'submarine graveyard' in which lie hundreds of 'vast salvage vessels' rusting on the sea bed after having been 'chewed' up and 'spat' out by a zone of the ocean they call 'the Embrace', a word suggesting both intimacy and violence. He notices that life has regained a 'sucker-hold' on the metal bones of the ships, transforming them into new habitats for the creatures of the deep. In the absence of the gods, new oceanic flows and exchanges have sprung up in the Myriad, too, as competition for 'godware' fuels economic violence among the islanders. The old priest Pale Soul recognizes this violence in Dr Vyne, warning Hark against the consuming desire to 'sell everything, [. . .] cut apart everything, [. . .] know everything' (Hardinge 2019: 196). The violence of the trade in godware is not just apparent in the brutal marketplace of Lady's Crave, but also figures as an objectification of the natural world, which is 'carved up, weighed, scraped, sold, or boiled for glue' (Hardinge 2019: 10). The crises that play out on the ecoweird oceans in both texts are, however, not simply warnings about environmental catastrophe or human hubris. They are generative of new ethical engagements that might arise from the ambivalent relationships, or embrace, between humans and the ocean.

To explore these ambivalent relationships the ecoweird draws on estranging and discomforting aesthetics to figure the ocean as a contact zone with other modes of consciousness than the human. Newell identifies the aesthetics of disgust, for example, as central to the ways the weird facilitates 'normally foreclosed modes of apprehension, functioning as a cognitive catalyst for thinking of the kind of speculative realism and new materialism urge' (2020: 12). *Deeplight* makes explicit the aesthetics of estrangement in the concept of 'frecht', which characters apply to objects that come from the ocean depths. Frecht, a German word equivalent to the English 'impertinent', names 'a twisted beauty that turned your stomach even while it turned your head [. . .] an ugliness and an otherness that could only be holy, a breach of the rules that echoed those that no rules could bind' (Hardinge 2019: 70). Frecht discloses an ontological shift, experienced by the viewer as a 'knot in your eye, your gut, your mind' and a paradoxical ecological relationship between humans and the ocean gods that is at once estranging and intimate. Conflicting emotions characterize experiences of the Seam in *The Last Zoo*, too. Standing on deck, Pia 'shudders' at the island mountain, 'a shard of black volcanic rock that juts out from the sea' (Gayton 2019: 23, 22). The illusion that this is a mountain is not a stable one, and the Seam plays tricks on her imagination as she watches the glitch rage around it like a storm. Just as frecht evokes both fear and awe, 'something inside' the Seam that Pia can only glimpse from the corner of her eye provokes terror and fascination. These experiences of the ocean suggest something of Lovecraft's insistence on the shattering of laws of Nature. *Deeplight*'s gods are bound by no rules and their realm, the Undersea, displays none of the expected material properties of water. In *The Last Zoo*, the Seam is a literal 'tear in reality's fabric where all logic and laws have come loose and lie unstitched' (Gayton 2019: 33). Whilst in Lovecraftian fiction the revelation of shattered laws often ends the weird tale, here the Seam suggests a stitching together as well as a coming apart, as different consciousnesses mingle to weave new realities. Pia can see this weave from the ship, the hanging threads that 'sing', 'weep', 'each one dreaming' (2019: 34). In *Deeplight*, stories of the Undersea also reveal it as a contact zone with other modes of consciousness, however different to the human, from the high-pitched scream of the Glass Cardinal to the pulsating vibrations emanating from the Hidden Lady's heart. These oceans are not some radical Outside, then, but ecological sites that, following Morton's *Dark Ecology*, 'evoke melancholy and negativity concerning inextricable coexistence with a host of entities that surround and penetrate us' (2016: 298). The estranging aesthetics of the ocean as a contact zone evoke the 'idea that the nonhuman has validity and power and significance all on its own without us', but the paradoxical intimacies that also emerge from this contact also suggest that the human is part of the nonhuman (Morton 2016: 159–60).

As dark ecologies, the oceans in *The Last Zoo* and *Deeplight* provide a setting for enweirded stories of kinship and bodily exchange. I turn to feminist phenomenologist Astrida Neimanis and ecocritic Alaimo to explore these aspects of the ecoweird further. For both thinkers the waters of the ocean evoke the permeability of human subjectivity and embodiment, and function as metaphors for understanding the ways in which humans emerge from, and are enmeshed in, a more-than-human world. Neimanis's phenomenology of the human as 'bodies of water' troubles 'dominant Western and humanist understandings of embodiment, where bodies are figured as discrete and coherent individual subjects, and as fundamentally autonomous' (2017: 2). This project does not aim at a wholly positive vision of interconnection but is about the ways that bodies 'leak and seethe, our borders always vulnerable to rupture and renegotiation' (Neimanis 2017: 2). *Deeplight* offers visceral images of bodies of water in its account of Jelt's transformation by the heart of the Hidden Lady, which moulds the flesh of his body into something inhumanly aquatic and hungrily violent. Jelt welcomes the transformation, but those around him believe the heart emanates a kind of 'poison' (Hardinge 2019: 190). Encounters with godware reveal that human bodies can be 'persuaded to return to old shapes or adopt new ones' and even 'taught to accept something alien' (Hardinge 2019: 272, 295). Neimanis evokes Alaimo's concept of transcorporeality as a lexicon for this kind of 'uncanny mode of being' that is both human and more-than-human at the same time (2017: 41). For Alaimo, thinking transcorporeality 'at sea' involves thinking about human bodies in their environments, tracing substantial interchanges that render the human permeable, and dissolving stable outlines to counteract fantasies of 'transcendence and imperviousness' that confound environmental thought and action (2012: 477). *Deeplight*'s transcorporeal exchanges may be monstrous, especially in the case of Jelt, but they prompt ethical questions about the ways that human fears, consumption, and violence shape the environments in which they are embedded.

The Last Zoo is less visceral in its depictions of transcorporeal exchange, but it is more explicit about its environmental implications. Alaimo's argument about substantial interchanges rendering the human permeable is concretized in Pia's relationship with the angels. The celestial creatures epitomize fantasies of human transcendence and autonomy, with the zoo's director placing all his hopes on them reaching maturity and providing a miracle to solve the climate crisis. His fantasy is disrupted by a predatory worm, or virus, which has been produced in the Seam by another rekker, Zugzwang. Zugzwang's invisible worm literally punctures the Angels, making holes in the celestial light that forms their bodies before wounding the Seamstress and unravelling the Seam. Outside, on the ocean, the worm functions like a microscopic virus, infecting the human inhabitants of the Ark and contaminating them with fear and paranoia. Though she fears that the Angels have been killed, Pia unknowingly carries the remains of one of them around on her body, nurturing its light as it heals from the attack. However, at the end of the story, the angels elect to leave the Ark, insisting that the humans return to their sprawling cities and find a solution to the crisis for themselves, refusing to provide a 'miracle'. In both novels, the ongoing trouble emanating from ecoweird oceans make clear that human becomings are determined by '*myriad* forces', or 'caught up in and transformed by *myriad*, often unpredictable agencies' (Neimanis 2017: 45; Alaimo 2010: 146. My emphasis). Being a rekker, or, more aptly, a Myriaddan, makes clear the ways in which human being is permeable to the churning, flowing, and exchange of always already weird ecologies and that, as Bruno Latour suggests, there is 'no cure' for such a condition (2017: 13).

Deeplight and *The Last Zoo* are also evolution stories that insist upon co-worldings that stretch across space, time, and species. Neimanis's phenomenology depends on the idea that all bodies of water 'owe their corporeal existence to gestation in a watery milieu', and she examines various speculative and scientific stories about the evolutionary origins of human beings in the ocean (2017: 106, 110). Thinking evolution in watery terms challenges a popular account of Darwinism, 'that ruthless teleological process of linear, filial descent', a Hobbesian sense of nature as a 'war of all against all', and Herbert Spencer's notion of 'survival of the fittest' (1864), with symbiosis, transfer, cross-species contamination, and viroid life (Neimanis 2017: 115). Alaimo also considers oceanic evolutionary stories as exposing humans as corporeal amalgams rather than as an exceptional product of evolutionary progression (2012: 480). *Deeplight* and *The Last Zoo* explore the evolution of more-than-human creatures in watery milieus to implicate the human in such amalgams, placing humans within a more-than-human evolutionary history and tracing the relationships of kinship and care this history contains. Though the fishy origins of humans may seem too distant and too alien to provoke recognition of kinship, the gods of *Deeplight* are revealed to be intimately bound up with humans, containing at their core human hearts and souls transformed by the waters of the Undersea over vast scales of time. The result is a bodily amalgam of cephalopod, fish, mammal, and inorganic components. The gods are monstrous yet provoke intimate recognition in the characters. The priest Quest, for example, tells of his bond of friendship with the Hidden Lady, of the love he fostered for her even as he intended to destroy her. The gods of *Deeplight* are an apt figuration of Morton's watery metaphor that describes the human as 'woven into the coral reef of actual entities underneath the smoothly gliding submarine of human civilisation' (2017: 74). Rather than sitting above or atop this reef, 'we are one of [its] unspeakable entities' (Morton 2017: 74). In *The Last Zoo*, cross-species kinship is figured through the voilà, which emerge from an exchange between human and inhuman consciousness in the Seam, a process called 'imageration'. The radically hybrid forms of life that emerge do not conform to reductively materialist ontology and confound the experimentations of the Zoo's director, forcing the humans to find new and strange ways of providing care. In turn, the voilà provide medicine, technology, sustenance, and friendship. Transcorporeal tales of evolution, then, suggest a broad 'community of descent' that encourages kinship and punctures the imposition of the idea of 'species' as an impassable division (Alaimo 2012: 483).

The evolution stories in *Deeplight* and *The Last Zoo* are fabulations in which humans can evolve into sea gods with chains for limbs or can co-evolve angels made of celestial light from their imaginations. The point of oceanic evolution stories is not, however, to discover an objective scientific truth about human origins, but to acknowledge an 'abyssal, unknowable depth' (Neimanis 2017: 113). While certain strains of Darwinism and evolutionary biology would seek to bring everything under the objectifying light of the microscope, a praxis aptly captured in the cold hubris of Dr Vyne who dismisses the gods of the Myriad as nothing more than 'savage fish' to be 'carved up' for examination, speculative fabulations about human origins suggest that not all our evolutionary debts are knowable (Hardinge 2019: 212; Neimanis 2017: 143). This appeal to an epistemic limit does not fetishize oceanic origins as radically other but, rather, acknowledges kinship and interdependence without attempting to capture the more-than-human world within a scientific totality that would objectify, categorize, and divide. Neimanis insists that oceanic origins offer an 'unknowability we can learn from' (2017: 147). Elsewhere, Alaimo argues that the trope of the sea as 'alien' suggests that sea life 'hovers at the very limits of what terrestrial humans can comprehend' (2012: 477). For Alaimo this prompts a recognition that pausing on the water's edge is prudent, and that being receptive to other ways of knowing is not a barrier to ethical action (2012: 477). This conception of the sea as epistemic limit contrasts with the epistemology of the old weird, expressed in Lovecraft's oceanic horror tale, 'Call of Cthulhu' (first published in 1928). There, the eruption of something ancient and monstrous from the depths of the ocean prompts the narrator to praise 'the inability of the human mind to correlate all its contents' and express his concern that the 'straining' of the sciences would 'open up such terrifying vistas of reality, and of our frightful position therein, that we shall either go mad from the revelation or flee from the deadly light into the peace and safety of a new dark age' (Lovecraft 1985: 61). No ethical engagement is possible in this conception of epistemic limits. In contrast, ecoweird oceans suggest that '[d]welling in the dissolve where fundamental boundaries have begun to come undone, unravelled by unknown futures, can be a form of ethical engagement' (Alaimo 2016: 2).

An uncanny definition of the ecoweird

Evolutionary tales of the ocean emphasize it as a site that is both an intimate home *and* an alien realm. It is this contradiction that encapsulates the ecoweird and suggests its kinship with other modalities of the dark Fantastic concerned with intimacies and estrangement, especially the gothic and the uncanny. Typically, however, scholars have drawn distinctions between these modes. The predominant argument is that the weird gestures to a radical 'Outside', a noumenal realm beyond human experience. China Miéville's articulation of the 'Weird-as-novum, unprecedented, Event' in contrast to the revenants of the gothic has been taken up by other critics, including in my previous work on children's literature (Miéville 2008: 110; Germaine Buckley 2018: 174–98).

Likewise, following Miéville, Luckhurst argues that the weird is 'not reducible to the gothic's economy of the uncanny', which always leads back 'to the unfamiliar home: the womb' (2017: 1052). The machinery of the gothic 'inherently domesticates', according to Luckhurst, in sharp contrast to the estrangements of the 'really weird', a term he takes from Lovecraft's essay, 'Supernatural Horror in Literature' (1927) (Luckhurst 2017: 1052). Here I problematize these distinctions to advance a new definition of the ecoweird not as a mode that points to the outside of human experience, but as one that discloses the uncanniness of ecological belonging.

The Last Zoo provides a good example of the complication I introduce as the 'ecoweird'. The reality bomb, which in the novel is a technological device invented by scientists attempting to find a solution to climate crisis and used by them to open the Seam, suggests something of the 'Event' Miéville attributes to the weird. However, the resulting tear in the world points not to a radical outside, but to a space that intimately connects human subjectivity and imagination with myriad others. The bomb is, in fact, a profoundly uncanny invention. As Pia climbs down the tunnel into the Seam, she first encounters a 'blacker than black' darkness and a crushing silence she names 'oblivion' (Gayton 2019: 162). Once within the Seam, though, Pia's imagination 'clothes' the space and gives it the appearance of a cluttered glasshouse, with plants, wicker chairs, and scatter cushions: it is 'nothing like what she expected' (Gayton 2019: 162). The Seamstress is briefly visible as something ten-legged and 'glitter-black' but quickly transforms into the smiling Doctor Celeste Lalande, inventor of the reality bomb and the first person to be taken by the glitch (Gayton 2019: 169). As Lalande, the Seamstress wears a faded grey T-shirt that she patches with golden threads taken from the memories of all who have entered her realm, telling Pia that it is good to 'mix imaginations', otherwise 'the realities drift apart' (Gayton 2019: 166). This encounter is both deeply strange and strangely familiar, challenging the idea that the weird is divorced from the uncanny.

My reading of *The Last Zoo* and *Deeplight* suggests that what the ecoweird provides is a puncturing of the anthropocentric bias of the Freudian uncanny, and a corrective to its prohibition against recognizing agency in anything other than the human. Freud's concern with the power of uncanny irruptions to destabilize the bourgeois human male individual takes on a new resonance in a time of climate crisis, which has revealed to Western thought the very thing it has long denied: the animacy of the world, the agency of more-than-humans, and the liveliness of matter. *Deeplight*'s representation of such vibrant matter, to borrow Bennett's term, is most evident in its descriptions of godware, and the ways in which the Heart, for example, 'pumps out' energies that travel through air, rock, and flesh, moulding the bodies around it into new shapes (Hardinge 2019: 106, 190). Amitav Ghosh suggests of the uncanny that 'no other word comes close to expressing the strangeness of what is unfolding around us' as we confront the climate crisis, and that uncanniness is the recognition of 'something we had turned away from . . . the presence and proximity of non-human interlocutors' (2016: 57). Such nonhuman interlocutors are present in *Deeplight*, particularly in the stories told by Quest of his trips to the Undersea to converse with the Hidden Lady. Without someone with whom to share her stories, her mind was in danger of 'guttering out' completely (Hardinge 2019: 277). In *The Last Zoo*, Pia has to master the language of 'Tellish' to communicate with the genies on the Ark, and decode the allusive, metaphorical language of the angels, both of which point to different ways of correlating the world to those of the human. The sea gods of the Myriad and the bizarre creatures on the Ark suggest seemingly alien forms of embodiment and comprehension, disclosing different modes of access to the world. However, in both cases, a sharp distinction between the human and these seemingly inhuman others is dissolved. In *Deeplight*, this dissolution unfolds in a series of revelations that upend Hark's understanding of the gods. His awe of them as preternatural beings is shattered by Dr Vyne's reductive materialism, but this view is later challenged by Quest, who tells Hark that, at their core, all the gods have 'the groaning, maddened remains of a human soul' (Hardinge 2019: 281). Thus, the gods are neither utterly alien nor are they only 'animals', categories that preserve the human as exceptional and autonomous. Rather, the gods are intimately connected to humans, both in terms of their origins and in the way they continue to shape life in the Myriad.

This insistence upon the uncanny as essential to the ecoweird reveals the mesh of ecological relationships in which humans are embedded. The uncanny continues to name relationships of intimacy in this new context, but it is through the nonhuman that intra- and inter-subjectivity emerges, rather than via a Freudian family drama. Here my elaboration of the ecoweird is further indebted to Morton's 'dark ecology', which he describes as both uncanny and weird because of its defamiliarizing effects (2016: 26). Elsewhere, Morton suggests the need to embrace a 'haunting, uncanny, spectral dimension' that he names the 'symbiotic real' in order to sustain cross-species solidarity (2017: 93). The symbiotic real is fractured, damaged, messy: dark ecology isn't a biophilic fantasy of symbiosis but raggedly intimate and horrifyingly meaningless. The symbiotic real is the mesh of more-than-human interrelations that comprise the biosphere, and it is to this realm that the uncanny gestures, Morton suggests, ridiculing Freud's reduction of the problem to a fear of the human vagina (2017: 27, 94). I read Morton's disavowal of the Freudian uncanny in favour of the symbiotic real as part of his ongoing challenge to the taboos of Western metaphysics and his insistence on intimacy rather than division, something that finds sympathy in these ecoweird tales. Emily Alder and Jenny Bavidge also draw on Morton's 'dark ecology' in their defence of the gothic as one mode of the dark fantastic suited to negotiating the climate crisis. They evoke his description of dark ecology as 'a vast, sprawling mesh of interconnection', as 'radical intimacy', and coexistence with other beings (2016: 42). Alder and Bavidge suggest, without using the word 'uncanny', that 'some variety of radical intimacy, then, rather than repression, disavowal, elision, or hyperseparation, emerges consistently' from the work of ecocritics such as Morton, and they argue for the 'essential' role the gothic might play in elaborating such theories (2020: 231).

The definition of the ecoweird I am developing through *The Last Zoo* and *Deeplight* problematizes the inside/outside distinctions often upheld in extant accounts of the weird as a literary mode. As discussed in Chapter 1, Fisher also defines the weird in contrast to other modes of the dark fantastic, especially the eerie, by evoking Lovecraft's description of the mode as 'real externality' (Lovecraft qtd in Fisher 2016: 16). Fisher uses this idea to suggest that the weird is ontological, that it perturbs the world and intimates that the 'cosmos must [. . .] be stranger than our ordinary experience can comprehend' (2016: 15). Just such a perturbation appears in *Deeplight*, too. Quest tells Hark that talking to the Hidden Lady 'was like accepting an invitation to someone else's house, only to find that the walls are made of teeth and all the doors lead to the moon' (Hardinge 2019: 276). The image of a house made strange also figures in *The Last Zoo*, when Pia enters the angels' dwelling on the deck of her Ark. The house has 'billions of rooms', though she can only access the hallway and even this makes her 'sick and dazzled' as the 'bending and pinning and stitching of light' within scrambles her vision (Gayton 2019: 9). These unfathomable houses disclose a reality beyond human experience, but this reality is not a radical externality. It is an imaginative contact zone that welcomes even as it estranges; it extends an invitation as it disrupts expectations. Encounters in such spaces prompt a remaking of the characters' relationships, values, and dispositions that recognizes the (inter)dependencies on which the human self is built. This remaking evokes a final aspect of the weird present in Fisher's taxonomy, which he connects to the etymological root of the word (meaning 'fate'), pointing to the 'twisted forms of time and causality that are alien to ordinary perception' (2016: 12). Again, this aspect of the weird manifests in *The Last Zoo* through the figure of the Seamstress. As she sews her 'spiralled pattern', she speaks to Pia of the threads that comprise 'realities', emphasizing an entangled, looping multiplicity (Gayton 2019: 169). The texts provide evocative images of the weird, then, that echo extant critical work on the mode, but that eschew the emphasis on absolute alterity. Instead, the texts suggest that the weird is a phenomenological mode. That is, it is to do with human situatedness within, and the emergence of perception from, a more-than-human world.

Negotiating belonging: Severing and suture

My definition of the ecoweird emerges from the texts' negotiation of the theme of ecological belonging. This theme is also apparent in new accounts of the weird that are concerned with the climate crisis. The geographer Jonathan Turnbull identifies the weird as the paradigmatic modality of the Anthropocene because 'recent scientific discoveries are changing how we envision ourselves in relation to the environment, making visible interconnections between humans and nonhumans across micro and macro scales' (2021: 275). Drawing on Fisher, Turnbull suggests that the weird evokes (un)earthly belonging (Turnbull 2021: 275). The ambivalence of the weird, its evocation of simultaneous estrangement from and connection to our planetary home is also central to Brian Onishi's concept of 'weird ecology', which he likewise develops in response to climate crisis (2020: 158). Onishi argues that weird fiction evokes feelings of uncanniness that expose the cycles of self-harm perpetuated by humans and the concomitant transformation of other entities into 'hostile forces' (2020: 158). Following Onishi, the ecoweird uproots feelings of homeliness, 'leaving us anxious in our own home with an ecology (remembering the etymological relation between eco and home) that is hostile and strange' (Onishi 2020: 158). Onishi relies on Lovecraft to elaborate how 'weird ecology' inaugurates a 'newly realized foreign world' but in so doing he does not preclude the uncanny (2020: 159). Indeed, Onishi yokes the weird to the uncanny to reveal the relationships of interdependence that constitute ecological reality and that ground human phenomenological experiences of that reality. The ecoweird discloses a contingentism that insists on the non-separation of perceivers and perceived phenomenon, on the entanglement of subjects and objects (Onishi 2020: 166). That is, the ecoweird figures nature 'as an uncanny irruption' within human perception (Onishi 2020: 166), rather than as something external, pointing not to radical alterity or ecological estrangement, but to an uneasy belonging.

I also develop the idea of the ecoweird in dialogue with figurations in *The Last Zoo* and *Deeplight* of wounds and tears, seams and sutures. These figurations render stark the trauma inherent in anthropocentric thought, which is identified by Morton as the 'severing'. The severing is a 'foundational traumatic fissure' between the human-correlated world and the symbiotic real (Morton 2017: 13). Morton's account of the severing describes a 'walling off' of human space from the contingent relationships and uncanny affiliations on which it depends, giving rise to metaphysical dualism and the privileging of anthropocentric modes of 'access' to reality as the sole form of consciousness (Morton 2017: 23, 16). It is an act of violence, a trauma that is constantly replayed at the level of human sociality and politics, especially through racism and fascism (Morton 2017: 23). Morton's theory echoes that of the Great Divide developed by Bruno Latour. Other ecological writers use similar language of trauma, violence, and pain to describe a self-imposed human/ecological divide. Botanist Monica Gagliano, for example, describes it as a 'rift' and the source of 'humanity's pain' (2018: 129). Her work restores plants as communicative subjects within the Western scientific practice, seeking to challenge the 'fictional walls' that science has created in its project to control a 'natural' world it has divided from the human (2018: 86). The consequences of the Anthropocene make stark the illusory nature of any such 'control' promised by science, but also reveals the gaps that puncture anthropocentric experience. More-than-human beings experience, act, and correlate the world, pushing back against a perceived human autonomy and mastery, revealing the holes that were already in the wall. *The Last Zoo* makes clear that the climate crisis is, in part, the human world 'malfunctioning' (Morton 2017: 74). Malfunction engulfs the Ark as Zugzwang's virus unravels the seamstress' creations and infects the human keepers with fear and paranoia.

Fear, pain, and trauma characterize the severings and sutures that are central to *Deeplight*, too. Old wounds that fester from the days when the Myriad lived in fear of the gods are opened when Vyne's creation and Jelt meet in the Undersea. For Quest, the trauma of his own part in causing the cataclysm that claimed thousands of lives is rekindled as he urges the other characters to prevent the emergence of a new god. For Jelt, the experience promises a kind of healing, both of his physical wounds and of the trauma of his violent childhood, through being sutured into an invulnerable aquatic body and becoming a god. The climactic scenes in the Undersea evoke ecophobic terrors of the loss of an individual human self to an inhuman void, but they also provide a way for characters to reconcile their feelings of (un)earthly belonging and to preserve the contingent relationships that comprise the symbiotic real in the face of a threatened and violent totality. The transformation scene involves a fusing of Jelt's warped body into Vyne's biomechanical creation, and of this amalgamation with the heart of the Hidden Lady. Jelt is 'mangled' and 'rotten', covered in leprous scales and gaping wounds. He grabs the heart and forces it into his flesh 'with a rictus of effort and pain', cracking open his chest. Immediately, the flesh closes over the hole, and the other wounds on his body begin to heal: 'the relic had found its home' (Hardinge 2019: 385). Here the novel evokes the gothic aesthetic of the 'abhuman' and Alaimo's concept of transcorporeality to ambiguous effect. In part, Jelt's transformation is figured as monstrous, a scene of horror. As Newell points out, the abhuman comes from the weird stories of William Hope Hodgson and denotes figurations of monstrosity and degeneration (2020: 131). Kelly Hurley's appropriation of the term for the analysis of fin de siècle gothic develops it into a theory of the human self as 'fragmented and permeable' and always on the edge of becoming other than itself (Hurley 1996: 4). Hodgson and other weird writers offer anxious representations of such becoming other that perpetuate various forms of racism, classism, and misogyny. However, while Hardinge's portrayal of the abhuman retains elements of gothic horror, it relocates the source of that horror. Rather than anxieties about bodily exchange and relationships of interdependence threatening some fantasy of (white, male) human autonomy, here the threat is the end of all relations: the god is a monstrous totality that seeks to consume and incorporate everything in the surrounding environment.

Jelt's scales, tentacles, and the pearls of flesh that erupt along his wounds make clear that the environment is not 'out there' but already within the very substance of human being. His transformation is also reliant on the Hidden Lady's heart and on Dr Vyne's biomechanical creation, both of which reveal that matter is not a substance but a doing, a 'congealing of agency' (Alaimo 2010: 154). Borrowing Barad's language, Alaimo elaborates agency as emerging not from within a subject (such as Jelt himself, or even from Dr Vyne's designs), but from intra-actions in a web of relations in which bodies and environments are co-constituted. The Undersea is as agentic as the other elements at play in the transformation: the heart uses the water to pump its energy through Jelt's body and complete the metamorphosis from human to god. In its visceral portrayal of opening and closing wounds, the scene also illustrates the ways that matter as transcorporeality complicates distinctions of inside and outside, which I have suggested is also a key element of the ecoweird. As Alaimo states, the 'outside' is already within,

> inhabiting and transforming what may or may not still be 'human' through continual intra-actions. In this dynamic scenario, matter – nature, if you will – is

> always an agent of change and always already within and without the permeable membrane of the human. (Alaimo 2010: 154)

The added complication in *Deeplight* is that the heart that acts as such an agent of change is revealed to have been human all along. Indeed, it was 'torn' from the Hidden Lady by Quest himself in an act of violent betrayal of their former intimacy. The merger with Jelt, then, is a (re)suturing in which the subject enfolds, and is enfolded by, a congealing of agency that is both profoundly inhuman and intimately human at the same time.

If the transformation of Jelt, his becoming-god, figures matter as transcorporeality, the end result, being-god, renders matter a brute substance, a horrific totality. In this turn, *Deeplight* captures the ambivalences of the ecoweird. The horror of the scene inheres in the threat of a violence represented by the god, rather than in racist, classist, or misogynist fears of bodily exchange and interdependence. As Vyne confesses, she built the god to be 'hungry' and Quest warns that once the transformation is complete the Jelt-thing will eat and expand, threatening all life in the Myriad. Appropriately, the god's first desire is to 'swallow' his former friend, Hark, so he 'won't have to stretch as far' in his new body (2019: 400). The Jelt-thing threatens to obliterate all ongoing interrelationships and future congealing of agencies, offering an effective end to the transcorporeal exchanges that comprise life in the ocean. There is a critique here that is applicable to interpretations of relationality that revel in becoming overwhelmed by an expanse of vibrant matter such that the difficult, messy business of subjectivity is given over for a fantasy of total participation. Such fantasies eschew the ethical engagement demanded by maintaining relationality. At the same time, there is also a critique of another response to relationality that finds refuge in an old fantasy of mastery. The Jelt-thing ascends briefly to the status of god, flexing its invulnerability and power as it boasts of obliterating its enemies. Though the pattern of Jelt and Hark's friendship has suggested it to be so, intimacy is not mastery. Accordingly, Jelt's dominance is short-lived, and he is destroyed by Hark's new companion, Selphin, who manages to rip the heart from the god as it attempts to consume Hark. This is a re-severing that leaves the god a 'thing of patches and tatters' once again, with no sign of the original Jelt in the wreckage (Hardinge 2019: 409). In *Deeplight*, then, severing and suture play out over and again with different ethical implications each time. On the one hand, severing and suture suggest the intra-activity and lively agency of matter, that the human is always enfolded within the more-than-human. On the other hand, processes of severing and suture critique fantasies of consumption, power and totality, forms of being in which ongoing relationality is foreclosed. Those who survive this encounter in the Undersea return to the surface, nursing new intimacies with the ocean, figured on their bodies as 'marks' whose shapes recall the more-than-human creatures of oceanic depths. The destruction of Jelt makes clear Neimanis's ethical proposition that we ought not to try to 'solve' the paradoxical problems of embodiment, but to live with them (2017: 18).

Beyond ecophobia: From ethics to politics

Thus far I have argued that the ecoweird reveals the severings and sutures that comprise human being in a more-than-human world, and that, in so doing, it makes clear ethical implications. The texts are explicit in their ethical agenda, expressing a need for characters to account for their responsibilities to humans and nonhumans alike. They do this while negotiating a pervasive aesthetic of the dark fantastic: ecophobia. Simon Estok defines ecophobia as a 'uniquely human psychological condition that prompts antipathy towards nature' and suggests that it pervades representations of the environment (2018: 1; 2016). *Deeplight* and *The Last Zoo* evoke ecophobia but suggest ways for the characters to move beyond its paralysing and destructive effects by emphasizing the representations of fear itself, rather than on the creatures or the environments that prompt fear. In place of passively ecophobic representations, the texts give voice to an ethical demand that hails human subjectivity from a more-than-human world. Some of the critical framework for this has already been discussed: the uncanny and transcorporeality. However, in this section I make explicit an ethics of separation and demand that is the structure of what Morton calls the 'symbiotic real'. The uncanny remains important in this elaboration of a foundational ethical structure to human subjectivity, and, accordingly, I turn to Spivak's concept of 'planetarity' (2003) to show how the ecoweird implicates humans in relationships of responsibility at scale, refusing the ethically impoverished politics of both globalization and nationalism. Thinking the ecoweird through planetarity makes evident the social and political force of the mode, something that is often missed in critical accounts of the weird. *Deeplight* and *The Last Zoo* are both explicit about the ways in which human sociality and politics are subtended by ecological ethics.

Ecophobia has become an important concept in discussions of ecohorror and ecogothic that aim to show how such texts address human fears of the environment and of impending environmental collapse. *Deeplight* and *The Last Zoo* enter the conversation, providing explicit examples of ecophobia that have devastating consequences. For Estok, ecophobia is a maladaptive human survival strategy that is nurtured by the horrific depictions of nature that persist in fiction and other forms of media (2018: 23, 8). Ecophobia is not only a response to the natural world; it is also what 'allows humanity to do bad things to the natural world' (2018: 11). That is, ecophobia is as much a cause of the climate crisis as a response to it. For Estok, ecophobia centres on human agency, on a perceived loss of control by the human over the nonhuman, especially when the more-than-human world reveals its agency and intentionality (2018: 32). In their staging of nightmares of loss of control, such genres as ecohorror and the ecogothic are, according to Estok, 'always ecophobic' (2019: 48). *Deeplight* seems to concur with Estok in its revelation that the monstrous gods are themselves products of human fear. The Undersea is itself a repository of fear, 'a dark womb where monsters are born and thrive' (Hardinge 2019: 273). Where other critics suggest that the ecogothic demands a perceptual shift from anthropocentrism to ecocentrism, Estok points out that 'it is ultimately the human world that matters most . . . in the perceived threats of the environments represented in such texts' (2019: 48). Again, *Deeplight* illustrates Estok's argument: the threat of a new god rising from the Undersea is a threat to human life in the archipelago: there is no ecocentric turn here, though there is an exhortation for human characters to reconsider their relationship with the ocean. Such reconsiderations may well be prompted by texts that evoke ecophobia and Estok admits that theorizing ecophobia through gothic texts might 'help bring to light social and environmental injustices and perhaps help to curb violence against people and the environment' (2019: 42). Again, this is the case in *Deeplight*, which also stages an explicit critique of the ways in which the gods have been mutilated, dissected, and turned into commodities that fuel violence and inequality in the Myriad. Hark's indentured servitude is one aspect of the violence perpetrated by humans against their environment, and each other.

The Last Zoo also offers representations of fear that respond to debates about how useful ecohorror representations are in a time of climate crisis. Writing about ecohorror more broadly, Christy Tidwell and Carter Soles admit that the mode 'runs the risk of reinforcing fearful responses to the nonhuman or – equally dangerous – leading to a feeling of hopelessness' (2021: 4). *The Last Zoo* makes clear this problem of hopelessness in the face of ecohorrific events through its portrayal of 'doomsickness', an attitude of nihilism that pervades life in the collapsing cities of the mainland. The word 'sickness' also suggests that this is a pathological psychology, which accords with Estok's account of ecophobia. The problem of doomsickness is so bad that governments have outlawed 'doomsay', 'obsessive talk related to the end of the world', though to no avail (Gayton 2019: 130). Indeed, Zugzwang's doomsickness is what leads to his infiltrating the Seam and giving the Seamstress the 'threads' to create the viral worm, turning the adults on the Ark into a violent mob. As discussed, the worm also physically wounds the Seamstress and the angels, effectively destroying the Seam and ending the experiment. Through such concrete representations of fear as Zugzwang's worm, which is an entity borne of fear and despair, and the Undersea, an environment composed of liquid terror, *Deeplight* and *The Last Zoo* thematize and materialize the problem of ecophobia. In so doing, they signal a desire to move beyond the ecophobic idea of nature as a threat to humans, and of paralysing images of climate chaos, and to examine the problem of human fear itself.

The ecoweird offers a unique perspective on ecophobia because of its emphasis on phenomenological experience; it locates human fear in the ruptures within perception, suggesting that fear emerges from a relational encounter between body and world, rather than arises either because of an external cause, on the one hand, or an internal psychological phenomenon on the other. In other words, as ecoweird texts, *Deeplight* and *The Last Zoo* complicate a distinction between psychology and world, mind and environment, materially situating the horrifying ruptures within the environments in which humans are embedded and also in embodied experiences of those environments. The texts thematize ecophobia as materially constitutive of the weird ecologies they imagine and examine ways of resolving its disruptive effects. In *Deeplight*, fear is an 'essence, as real as oil or blood' (2019: 64). Fear flows from the islands into the ocean, pooling in the Undersea, where it takes on the power to change bodies and distort minds. When Hark breathes Undersea water for the first time he experiences it as a contaminant, convulsing in pain and panic as he receives memories of countless people who drowned at sea: 'These terrors were not his, but they were in his eyes and throat and lungs. He was full of them, choking on them' (Hardinge 2019: 382). The Undersea is a material contaminant and yet something profoundly human and psychological, containing the power to warp the environment. The Seam, too, makes material the fears of humans; every Seamer must be assessed so that their 'nightmares, phobias, buried traumas' do not emerge in the form of some monstrous voilà (Gayton 2019: 159). Ecophobia is concretized further in the form of the predatory worm made by Zugzwang, a figuration that suggests that the risk to human and more-than-human life comes not from the external environment, but from within humans themselves.

Through their representations of fear as a material and embodied relation, the texts also find ways to ameliorate its catastrophic effects. In *The Last Zoo*, the danger of the worm originates in Zugzwang's feelings of loss of control and despair, pathologies bound up in an ecophobic cycle in which fear breeds further destruction. However, even though the catastrophic effects of the worm cannot be reversed, and the Seam is abandoned, the humans are healed from the virus and able to return to the mainland. The cure comes from antibodies that inhere in the secretions of the 'gargantulas', the Ark's most terrifying voilà. That such nightmarish creatures provide a physical remedy for contagious human fear is an irony the novel is keen to emphasize. Moreover, the ending nurtures a precarious kind of hope in the aftermath of the doomsickness that has swept through the Ark. Pia recognizes that Zugzwang was right to name humans as the 'problem' but rejects his ecophobic solution of accelerating the end of the world. Instead, she cultivates a hope that humans can be changed as she apprehensively returns to the mainland to make a life there, reassured that many of the voilà were saved by the angels and reside somewhere beyond the reach of their human captors. In *Deeplight*, the destructive cycle whereby human fear feeds the Undersea and produces monstrous threats that in turn breed more fear is not resolved by the characters at the end of the story: the Undersea remains a part of the ecology of the Myriad. However, Hark, Selphin, and Quest do prevent the birth of a new god and manage to rekindle their love for the ocean, which they treat with a renewed and precarious respect. Selphin's transformation is the most dramatic. Throughout the novel she has been terrified by the ocean, imagining it is determined to take her life. The last scene of the novel sees her swimming in the shallows having reached an uneasy compact with the ocean. She tells the waves, 'you can't make me live in fear of you' (Hardinge 2019: 430).

Moving beyond ecophobia requires listening to an ethical demand that hails humans from a more-than-human world. Ecoweird texts like *Deeplight* and *The Last Zoo* disclose this demand, but also make clear the difficulties of the ethics of response-ability entailed in their ecological entanglements. Ecophobia is a response to the paradoxical condition of life in the Anthropocene, which is that humans are simultaneously part of, and alienated from, something we have called 'nature'. The sudden sense of no longer feeling at home, the uncanniness of the ecoweird, emerges in a rupture of anthropocentric mastery and autonomy, prompting ecophobic responses and making monsters such as Jelt and the worm. However, the rupture is also the site of an ethical demand that hails the human from an ecological milieu, a milieu from which the human is estranged but upon which it remains dependent. The strange, discomfiting nature of the demand is made clear in *Deeplight* through Hark's ambivalent relationship with the heart of the Hidden Lady, which he both fears and yet is fiercely protective of. He knows that the heart is reaching out and wants to mould itself a new body, but he recognizes its vulnerability. Pia also struggles with the demands for help left by the angels in the form of halos of numinous light. The halos communicate in dreams, symbols, and allusions that intimate an ethical responsibility that directly contravenes Pia's duties as a keeper on the Ark. As texts written for and about older children, *Deeplight* and *The Last Zoo* make clear that response-ability is about rendering one another capable and finding ways to respond differentially and with accountability (Despret 2004; Barad 2007: 380). The authors do not reject the long-standing task of children's literature to inculcate values, though instead of learning the tenets of a normative moral framework, the characters face the difficult task of cultivating response-ability in themselves and others. For Pia, this involves the rejection of any 'magical solution' to the climate crisis in favour of the messy task of changing people (Gayton 2019: 298). No moral programme to bring about this change is offered, but Pia is nonetheless rendered capable through the hopefulness that emerges through her relationships with the voilà and the Seamstress. For Hark, the events of *Deeplight* offer a series of ethical choices, and a call for him to 'pay attention' to the way he is shaped by, and in turn shapes, others (Hardinge 2019: 235). These ethical ideas are related through conversations and internal dialogue. Underlying such moments of reflection is a constitutive connection between ethics and subjectivity, between response-ability and becoming, made clear in Quest's lesson to Hark that 'we are what we do and what we allow to be done' (Hardinge 2019: 233). The ecoweird locates this lesson in a more-than-human world, suggesting that if subjectivity emerges through an ethical demand from the Other, as per Levinas, then it is the other as multiple others, made up of the myriad beings that compose the symbiotic real.

The ecoweird offers an imaginative rendering of the paradoxes and difficulties entailed in thinking Levinasian ethics in a more-than-human world. Though Levinas's writings maintain 'the centrality of the human other' and deny the ethical alterity of nature, eco-philosophers find his themes of responsibility, alterity, and the vulnerability of the body useful for exploring pressing environmental question (Edelglass, Hatley and Diehm 2012: 3, 9). For example, Ted Toadvine's phenomenological interpretation of ethics suggests that Levinas's insistence on the emergence of human subjectivity in a foundational separation from nature, which Levinas names the *il y a*, is antithetical to 'the shibboleth of contemporary environmentalism, namely that human beings are part of nature' (2012: 163).

Yet, as discussed, the idea of the human having been alienated from nature also abounds in environmental writing. As Toadvine notes, this is 'an ambiguous situation by which we find ourselves simultaneously immersed in yet separated from [nature]' (2012: 163). As I have already suggested, this is an apt description for the condition of life in the Anthropocene and is precisely the situation thematized by ecoweird texts. Thus, a synergy between Levinas and the ecoweird becomes apparent when reading both alongside Toadvine's writing, which emphasizes a phenomenological, or embodied, engagement with the world. He finds in Levinas's account of the separation of human subjectivity from the *il ya a* paradoxical 'independence within dependence' that echoes the precarious belongings cultivated by *Deeplight* and *The Last Zoo* (Toadvine 2012: 172). The ecoweird dramatizes Toadvine's assertion that the environment from which we live is 'non-possessable', to use Levinas' term, yet it conditions existence even across the divide (Toadvine 2012: 172). Human needs emerge from a rupture within the environment that produces distance between human beings and the elements on which they depend, which in turn produces the world of sociality and politics, all of which are subtended by those environmental needs. However, this process does not entirely sever the human body from its natural milieu and such bodies remain, for Toadvine, an ambiguous site of (in)dependence.

Ambiguous (in)dependence figures in *Deeplight* and *The Last Zoo* as bodily and worldly 'wounds' that never fully heal. The Seam is described as one such 'wound', and Pia describes it as having become 'infected' by Zugzwang's worm. In *Deeplight*, Jelt's body is a tissue of wounds, a site where suture and severing play out multiple times, though other characters also carry 'marks' of the Undersea that inscribe the traces of more-than-human beings on their skin. Following Toadvine, these are images of an embodied experience that pull human subjects in contrary directions at once, revealing their enrootedness in, and separation from, the environment. Toadvine draws on Merleau-Ponty to develop 'an alternative description of our emergence from nature' to counter Levinas's insistence on separation over and against participation as the condition for ethics (2012: 166, 178). This emergence produces an anonymous, natural self, 'which the personal subject, the "I", finds already engaged with the world' (Toadvine 2012: 182). This is an anonymity within, a lived body that sides with the world, an alterity 'at the heart of [. . .] putative self-givenness' (Toadvine 2012: 184). The heart of the hidden lady figures as an apt image of just such an 'anonymity within', and Selphin warns her friends against its silent transfigurations of their inner selves, fearing that they will never know they have 'been made into somebody new' (Hardinge 2019: 221). *Deeplight* expresses a fear of this anonymous, natural self, but also encourages intimacy with it, to which Hark's fierce care of the Lady's heart attests. Here the *il y a*, the natural ground of being, is not an irreducible alterity that threatens the dissolution of the human. Instead, it is an anonymity that inheres within, intimate and vulnerable, and which makes its own set of ethical demands for care and sustenance. The heart is a wound, too, delicate, and exposed. Wounds offer an image of ethical responsibility, then, of a separation from nature that is never quite complete, but that requires ongoing relationships of care and accountability. Toadvine describes this mutual becoming of human and nature as 'dehiscence', that is, the (re)opening or separation of a wound that has partially healed (2012: 188). Through the idea of dehiscence, and a phenomenological articulation of environmental ethics, Toadvine contests that there is no 'Other' as such, no pure alterity, but a profusion of others, including humans, who are all an expression of the 'dehiscence' that is nature (2012: 189). As ecoweird texts, *Deeplight* and *The Last Zoo* suggest a similar ontoethical proposition, keeping wounds open and insisting on the difficult ethical relationships on which human existence and perception are founded. The wounds in both texts offer ways of imagining Toadvine's notion that humans and other animals are 'variant folds within the world's flesh' (2007: 52).

The wounded bodies and environments of *Deeplight* and *The Last Zoo* also point to problems of human politics that emerge from our ongoing separation from nature. As Latour suggests, faced with the climate crisis, 'all forms of belonging are undergoing metamorphosis', and he points to the contradictory trajectories in contemporary politics towards ever more rampant globalization, on the one hand, and exclusive nationalisms on the other (2018: 16). Where *The Last Zoo* offers a criticism of the flows of global capital, *Deeplight* is concerned with the way in which crisis leads to violent forms of nationalism. Both are political projects aimed at solving the problem of (un)earthly belonging, but which perpetuate the violence, racism, and inequalities that emerge from foundational divides. *The Last Zoo* offers stark images of economic globalization, including the piles of mouldering crates in Pia's Ark. They are branded for an internet supermarket called 'dib$' and feature a smiley face logo holding its thumbs up next to a dollar sign: 'A happy little logo, speaking the simple language of money and bargains' called Dibsy (2019: 18). Smiley faces are also implicated in the economic collapse that figures as the background to the story. The events on the Ark occur thirty years after a computer virus, called Megalolz, has decimated the internet and turned all connected devices to junk. The collapse of the internet and the ensuing economic crisis prompted dirty and dangerous wars, hastening the effect of climate change, resulting in the destruction of national governments as well as the drowning of major cities. Pia looks upon relics of the i-era with disgust; the smiling face of Dibsy is a reminder of the arrogance and wastefulness that has precipitated catastrophic environmental, social, and economic crises. That the collapse was caused by a computer virus echoes one of Gayatri Spivak's key criticisms of globalization. She says that 'the globe is on our computers. No one lives there. It allows us to think that we can control it' (2003: 72).

Fantasies of control also shape politics in the Myriad, though in the inverse direction to the trajectory of globalization. Pragmatic but avaricious island governors are under pressure from a populist group called the League to adopt exclusionary military policies to protect the archipelago from a feared invasion by the people of the continent. The League Captain, a zealous man who moulds his recruits after the fashion of an army, secretly funds Vyne's project in hopes she will build a new god to serve the Myriad and vanquish its enemies. 'Fear of foreigners', 'fear of change', and fear of otherness in many forms are rife on the islands, prompting the narrator to reflect that 'a god could thrive in these times' (2019: 274). As Latour suggests, one response to the failure of globalization, and to the inequalities it has perpetrated, is a 'new affinity for borders' (2018: 4). Though couched within a fantasy setting, Hardinge's representations of populist nationalism suggest a critique of real-word conditions when read in the context of the book's writing and publication, a period which has seen far-right populism surge in Britain and the UK. In both texts, then, the ecoweird and its uncanny elaborations of belonging, interdependence, and response-ability allow for strident critiques of globalization and nationalism alike as untenable, destructive, and unethical forms of political organization. The destruction wrought by Megalolz creates the debris in which Pia must attempt to remake her society, while the fantasies of the League Captain come to a violent end when he is torn asunder by the hungry Jelt-god.

The alternative to globalist and nationalist conceptions of belonging is planetarity, a concept that has been articulated by Spivak through a Levinasian ethical framework, drawing on the uncanny in ways that inform my reading of the ecoweird. Spivak first articulates 'planetarity' in contradistinction to other notions of planetary belonging, such as the earth, the world, the globe, and, especially, globalization (2015: 290). Following her rejection of the idea of the 'globe' as a totalizing fantasy, a 'neat ball crisscrossed by latitudes and longitudes', Spivak turns to the planet as 'the species of alterity, belonging to another system', evoking Levinas's idea of precarious separation from nature as she suggests that our habitation of the planet is 'on loan' (2003: 1). Just as Morton reconfigures the Freudian uncanny to theorize the symbiotic real, so does Spivak jettison the family drama of the unheimlich in a shift 'from vagina to planet as the signifier of the uncanny' (2003: 74). For Spivak, the uncanny has more to do with Levinas's ethics of alterity, his insistence upon a constitutive responsibility to the other. As she notes, life on the planet must be 'lived as the call of the wholly other' and to be human is 'to be intended toward the other' (Spivak 1999: 427; 2003: 73). For Spivak, then, the uncanny offers a way to think of humans as 'planetary subjects rather than global agents' and her work echoes the paradoxes of belonging explored in these ecoweird texts: planetarity 'contains us as much as it flings us away' (2003: 73). Though Spivak is not directly concerned with environmental issues, others have taken up planetarity as a way of thinking of the planet as a world ecology. Amy Elias and Christian Moraru describe the planet as a relational structure of awareness and a 'non-negotiable ecological ground for life' (2015: xii). As a structure of awareness, a thickening of the web of relations that comprise human and nonhuman being, the planet is key to non-totalizing, non-homogenizing, and anti-hegemonic modes of interrelation (Elias and Moraru 2015: xxiii). My ethical reading of *Deeplight* and *The Last Zoo* suggests a similar awareness evoked by the ecoweird, which balks at attempts to totalize, master, and objectify so-called natural as well as human beings. Similarly, the setting of these stories on ecoweird oceans provides an apt figuration of the flows of planetarity, which Min Young Song describes as forming a 'different order of connection, an interrelatedness that runs along smooth surfaces, comprises multitudes, and manifests movement' (2011: 568). The ethics of ecoweird as elaborated here echo those of planetarity, while the oceanic settings of the novels point to the temporal and spatial scales over which such ethics operate. In the thickening of relations that comprise planetarity in the Anthropocene, however, there is no easy resolution to the problems of belonging and response-ability. In the final section, therefore, I consider the ways in which the narrative structure of the ecoweird negotiates such a thickening and examine the resolutions it provides.

Ecoweird endings: Following the threads of ongoingness

The ecoweird is one mode of what Donna Haraway (2016) calls 'speculative fabulation' and it is good at 'staying with the trouble' of ecological belonging in a time of climate crisis. The ecoweird offers 'stories in which multispecies players, who are enmeshed in partial and flawed translations across difference, redo ways of living and dying attuned to still possible finite flourishing, still possible recuperation' (Haraway 2016: 10). It is this dimension of the 'still possible' that Pia aims for as the ships take her back to the mainland: 'the world might be dying, but there's hope. I can feel it. Not a foolish or deluded thing, but fierce and real' (Gayton 2019: 417). The endings of these novels provide a precarious sense of recovery from the traumas endured, echoing Anna Tsing's assertion that precarity is the condition of life for all in the Anthropocene. Moreover, precarity is, specifically, a condition of 'being vulnerable to others' and of being 'thrown into shifting assemblages, which remake us as well as our others' (Tsing 2015: 49). My reading of *Deeplight* and *The Last Zoo* has suggested that the ecoweird concerns itself precisely with just such precarious and co-constitutive becomings. It is fitting that, at the end of *Deeplight*, Hark is given a new name by his new friend Selphin, a sign-name that translates as 'eel-over-head' and points to the ongoing multispecies, transcorporeal co-worldings of which Hark continues to be a part. The name 'made him feel more real' (Hardinge 2019: 429).

The ecoweird is also self-aware of its status as fabulation and is explicit about its figuration of ecological belonging as 'storied matter' (Iovino and Opperman 2014: 1). As discussed in the introduction, the phrase storied matter points to the signifying force, narratives, and meanings produced by materiality. In ecoweird tales, storied matter also manifests as a response to ecological belonging and storytelling is offered as one way of responding to the ethical demand that hails the characters from a more-than-human world. Pia navigates her way through the Ark and the Seam with the help of the genies, speaking to them in their own language, Tellish, which 'sees the whole world as one great interweaving epic they called the Tale' (Gayton 2019: 15). The Tale is an imaginative rendering of the mesh of storied matter that Iovino and Opperman argue interweave human and nonhumans (2014: 2). Storytelling has an ethical function in *Deeplight*, too. Quest relates his experience of being the Hidden Lady's 'storykeeper', venturing into the Embrace to listen to her memories in an attempt to slow her descent into mindlessness. In the same way, Hark becomes Jelt's storykeeper, vowing that he will tell Jelt's stories throughout the Myriad both to keep Jelt's memory alive and to take responsibility for the violence that Hark allowed to take place out of misplaced loyalty to his friend. Hark advances the role of storykeeper from that of listener, which is implied in his name, to something more active. In this way, *Deeplight* is in sympathy with Haraway's work on how to cultivate 'ongoingness' in a time of climate crisis (2016). She argues that telling stories is a 'method of tracing, of following a thread in the dark', that 'a dangerous tale of adventure' concerned with who lives and who dies and how is a means for cultivating multispecies justice (Haraway 2016: 3). *The Last Zoo* echoes the metaphors of strings, threads, and tangles that litter Haraway's account of ongoingness. At the end of the novel, Pia is heartened to think about the voilà, now somewhere beyond the reach of the humans, imagining the genies 'talking in Tellish about new beginnings; about hope-not-lost; and about the threads of life, running endless and stubborn, through the ever-weaving tapestry of the Tale' (Gayton 2019: 302). Here, the ending of the novel keeps open the act of speculative fabulation, of string figuring, new ways of becoming not yet foreclosed despite the acknowledgement that the world is 'dying'.

Cultivating ongoingness in a dying world is a challenge for storytelling. As Tsing notes, '[we] are stuck with the problem of living despite economic and ecological ruination. Neither tales of progress nor of ruin tell us how to think about collaborative survival' (2015: 47). For Sarah Dillon, whose focus is on the horror fiction of the Anthropocene, the problem of storytelling pertains to narrative structure. She critiques much horror fiction for 'end-of-the-road' narratives that lead nowhere (2018: 20). Dillon states, drawing on Haraway, that 'the world has not ended yet; we are not yet living in the dust of this planet; our story is not over' (2018: 20). The challenge to literature is to recognize the 'thickening' affect of horror that pervades life in the Anthropocene, while conceiving of story modes 'that will transit all us critters into a future present in which the dust does not lie thickly over this planet' (Dillon 2018: 22). Here, Dillon evokes John Clute's structural account of Fantastika, and the story moves of 'thickening' and 'aftermath' that characterize horror stories. In Clute's taxonomy of fantastic fiction there are two poles, the 'bound' and the 'free', which describe opposing relationships with planetary belonging (2016: loc 5799). Clute argues that genres such as horror, and some science fiction, tend to the bound fantastic in their move towards 'bondage', whereas fantasy gestures towards an escape and so typifies the free fantastic (2016: loc 5799). At each end of the spectrum there are specific story 'moves' that elaborate on the relationship between humans and the planet. On the one hand, there is the 'vastation' of horror, which 'contagiously joins the world [. . .] to the sentient creatures (almost always humans) tethered to its disintegrating and/or newly exposed frame' (Clute 2016: loc 6751). This tendency to bondage is explored in both *Deeplight* and *The Last Zoo*, with the latter most explicitly considering a kind of contagion ('doomsay') that suggests no exit from impending climate collapse. What both novels resist, however, is the final move of horror: 'aftermath'. This is an awareness that the story is done, and that the world is 'incapable of change', that 'there is no cure to hand, no more story to tell' (Clute 2016: loc 5666). While both novels concur with this lack of a 'cure' for earthly belonging, they resist the nihilism of the aftermath. Again, *The Last Zoo* is most explicit about this aspect of its structure. The architect of the doomsay virus is Zugzwang, a boy named for a situation in chess wherein all moves will worsen the player's situation and defeat is inevitable. Zugzwang performs the most destructive of responses to climate change, which Haraway describes as the 'position that the game is over, it's too late, there's no sense in trying to make anything better' (2016: 4). Zugzwang's nihilism, and the aftermath it threatens, is thwarted by multispecies cooperation, and by Pia, whose name is short for 'Cornucopia' and gestures to a lost, yet hoped for, abundance.

Even though *Deeplight* and *The Last Zoo* explore the thickening affects of horror, the threat of contagion and disintegration, they also refuse the narrative resolution of the free fantastic. Cornucopia is not, after all, able to bring about a miracle, nor heal the planet such that abundance flourishes. This contrasts with the story moves of fantasy where worlds threatened by a 'thinning', a sense of wrongness and lessening, are saved through a recovery, a healing, or a 'return' that also represents an escape from the bondage of planetary belonging (Clute 2016: loc 6252). Indeed, both *Deeplight* and *The Last Zoo* suggest that the weird occupies an interstitial space between the free and the bound fantastic, turning from the story moves of horror to those of fantasy and, often, back again, without capitulating to either 'return' or 'aftermath'. Thus, they do not turn away from ecological disaster and the slow violence of the Anthropocene, recognizing the need to cultivate ethical response-ability in the present. The emphasis is on continued conditions of precarity, a recognition of vulnerability but also of possibilities. For Pia and the other rekkers, the 'deluded' hopes of the Ark come to nothing, but their experiences reconnect them with life on the mainland, forcing them to make a life in the ruins that makes a difference (Gayton 2019: 191). A similar narrative pattern emerges in *Deeplight*. While the selfish Jelt is 'twisted and trapped' inside the monstrous god body before being ripped apart, Hark survives his encounter in the Undersea. Though scarred, he returns to the Myriad, having forged new relationships of care and companionship. Pia and Hark fail to find answers that would make their worlds safe, but they successfully overcome 'game over' fantasies and threats of oblivion. The precarious interdependencies and belonging figured through the ecoweird are sustained at the close of the stories, with wounds and seams remaining open as a sign that relationships of care and response-ability are ongoing. In the final chapter of the book, I turn to speculative fiction for young adults that grapple more explicitly with the future of the climate crisis, shifting focus from the need to cultivate ongoingness to the urgency of somehow making a future that is otherwise to the present.

5

Speak for the trees?

The material politics of climate futures

Introduction: Plant-thinking and climate fiction

In the previous chapter I discussed the ways in which weird fiction negotiates the uncanny relations that comprise ecological belonging. This uncanniness exposes the tensions that subtend the concept of ecology, which in mainstream environmentalism conjures the myths of balance and holism, promoting a fantasy of stable interconnections between organisms (Kricher 2009). Such an idea of ecology is indebted both to mechanism and cybernetics and is influenced by imperial ideologies of the nineteenth century, which sought to naturalize the social hierarchies imposed on indigenous people. However, 'nature' is not a hierarchical order, a complex machine, nor a computer programme; it does not tend towards balance and the whole is not, ontically, more significant than the parts and relations that comprise it. The climate crisis, and the disruptions that now characterize life on Earth, make this stark. Eschewing the image of a self-regulating system that unfolds deterministically, ecology figured as entanglement emphasizes the contingent, evolving, and a-symmetrical nature of the relationality that comprises organic life and environments. This entangled ecology has important implications for climate futures. In this final chapter I further interrogate the climate futures of Fantastika, exploring imaginings of what the mycologist and science writer Merlin Sheldrake describes as the 'fraught' relations of interspecies symbiosis and intimacy that form a planetary web of life (2020: 234).

Inspired by Sheldrake and other contemporary science writers, my approach draws on plant studies, which I find apt for elaborating relational ethics in a time of climate crisis. As Gibson and Brits suggest, plant-thinking is rooted in being-as-relation (2018: 17). Botanist Monica Gagliano (2018) makes a similar claim in her exploration of the relational ethics of care demonstrated by plant life, as do the philosophers Michael Marder (2013) and Emmanuel Coccia (2019), whose descriptions of the radical openness of plant life inform my analysis in this chapter. These thinkers promote the idea of vegetal life not as a lower order of life that plays a mechanical role in the stable running of the biosphere but as lively, intentional, agentic, and collaborative being. The turn to plant studies in this chapter is also inspired by the youth-led climate justice movement, which aims to establish solidarity between humans across the globe and advocates for better relationships between humans and nonhumans. One such relationship is that between vegetal and human life, which is the subject of the song 'Speak for the Trees' (2014) by young activist, Xiuhtezcatl Roske-Martinez, director of the conservation organization Earth Guardians. Roske-Martinez's song calls for listeners to imagine themselves as trees native to his home state of Colorado whose habitats are being destroyed. As the song develops, the singer exhorts the listener not only to speak on behalf of the trees but to identify as one: 'Your body is a tree like gardenia Your heart is the seed and it beats for love! You are the Baobab, Redwood, & Pine: You are the future in present time' (Roske-Martinez and Earth Guardians 2014). This shift in identification that occurs in the song draws focus away from the mainstream environmentalist posterity narratives that imagine plants as objects to be protected and the environment more broadly as a space that ought to be preserved for future generations of humans. Such posterity narratives objectify both plants and children in service of an imagined future stability, in which 'nature' has been returned to a state of balance. Instead, the shift to imagining oneself as a tree explores the potential for an unknown nonhuman future through a bodily engagement with the land itself. This engagement is creative, imagining an entanglement between self and tree as the starting point for action in the 'present time', decentring human concerns about the future.

Imbricated in the material turn, plant studies' focus on the subjectivity, agency, and personhood of vegetal life supports the philosophies and approaches explored in the preceding chapters, which aim at dismantling the anthropocentrism that underpins environmentally destructive behaviours (Coccia 2019; Gibson and Brits 2018; Hall 2011; Laist 2013; Marder 2013; Miller 2002; Nealon 2015; and Woodward and Lemmer 2019). Plant studies is related to the new animisms discussed in Chapter 2 through its conferral of personhood to the more-than-human world and in its dialogue with knowledge about plants that abound in indigenous life-worlds (Gagliano 2018; Kimmerer 2013). The vegetal turn in philosophy also echoes similar sentiments to those developed through speculative realism, discussed in Chapter 1. Plants are dark matter and occulted beings. As Marder suggests, 'to get in touch with the existence of plants one must acquire a taste for the concealed and the withdrawn, including the various meanings of this existence that are equally elusive and inexhaustible' (2013: 28). This respect for plant being as always partially withdrawn from human engagement counteracts anthropocentric exceptionalism and instrumentalist attitudes towards plant life, resisting the ways in which vegetal life has been valued only for the external ends it serves (Marder 2013: 25). Vegetal beings escape the scope of human understanding and so retain something of their subjectivities even when seemingly exhausted by capitalist agroscientific processes.

A more generous attitude to plant-life is spreading beyond the academy, too. The vegetal turn in philosophy is accompanied by a burgeoning interest in trees, plants, and fungi in popular science and nature writing (Beerling 2007; Pollan 2013). Such writing tends to confer, as a rhetorical strategy, personhood, and sociality onto plant life as in Peter Wohlleben's popular work on woodland ecology (2016, 2021). In this chapter, I suggest that contemporary YA Fantastika joins these other modes of plant-thinking in its speculations about vegetal life and better modes of living with communities of plants. I examine such figurations of plants to explore the metaphysics, ethics, and politics of entanglement in writing that directly engages the future of the climate emergency: climate fiction.

The sympathy between plant-thinking and climate fiction, or cli fi, is evident in much of the contemporary science and academic writing already referenced. This contemporary (re)consideration of vegetal life aims at new ways of understanding plants, their ecological being and subjectivities, and even their politics. It is also interested in challenging the subordination of plant life in Western scientific and philosophical schemas, which has fuelled environmental destruction and contributed to the climate emergency. In this chapter, I put plant studies in dialogue with examples of young adult fiction that uses the imaginative horizon of future climate crisis events to explore human uses of vegetal life and our ecological embeddedness. Cli fi, a distinct modality of Fantastika popular for young audiences since the turn of this century, is a recent literary term, made popular by the writer Dan Bloom and typically applied to describe near- or post-apocalyptic fictions about climate change (Glass 2013). Cli fi tends to imagine the future through the thematic of catastrophe, providing explicit sociopolitical commentary on the present climate emergency, the global lack of action, and warnings of impending crisis if the status quo persists. As Rebekah Sheldon points out, catastrophe is an important theme in ecological thought since, on the one hand, it might be made to serve rhetoric that would delimit the future in terms of its continuity with the present, warning of future harm that might be forestalled. On the other hand, catastrophe can function as a signifier of the dynamism inherent in the system, of the possibility of a 'system-wide transformation' (Sheldon 2016: 41). As I will show, YA climate fiction mobilizes catastrophe to explore temporality in this way, recognizing that – as Sheldon contends – 'all systems are unstable and groundless' (2016: 41). This follows work by Alice Curry on YA dystopia, which she contends envisages climate change 'as an immediate and devastating shattering of cultural norms' (2013: 18). Plant-thinking, in its appeal to the eruptive growth of plant life, the rhizomatic openness and proliferation of vegetal being, is a productive partner in these disruptive imaginings of the future.

Where the River Runs Gold and *Green Rising*

The cli fi novels discussed in this chapter are *Where the River Runs Gold* (2019) by Sita Brahmachari and *Green Rising* (2021) by Lauren James, both of which explore climate futures, young people's agency, and human interdependence with plant and fungal life. Like other contemporary climate fiction, the novels imagine anthropogenic climate catastrophes unfolding in near-future societies suggested to be continuous with the neoliberal, and neocolonial, capitalist regimes of present-day North America and Europe. *Where the River Runs Gold* draws on the popular YA genre of dystopian fiction, which, as Curry (2013) has argued, is also concerned with environmental themes. The novel imagines an oppressive future society in which climate disaster has intensified the conditions produced by the neoliberal economics, nationalist politics, and technocratic societies of the present day. The ARK government of the novel is not, as its nomenclature suggests, a life raft for the survivors of climate catastrophe, but a totalitarian regime run for the benefit of corporations in which young people are exploited as resources as those in charge scrabble to maintain power and capital in an era of massive food insecurity. The ARK's age-based discrimination intersects with racial and class-based segregation and the oppressive world of the novel is one towards which, Brahmachari suggests, we might be headed if climate justice is not enacted in the present. In short, the novel advocates for the position held by young climate strikers: political change to create social and economic equality is necessary for climate action. Dystopia is used here to provoke hope as well as a warning, however, since ecological regeneration and social transformation are imagined to be possible through the actions of a young heroine, Shifa, a figure the writer has stated was inspired by Greta Thunberg and other young climate activists (Brahmachari 2019b: n.p.).

Green Rising is similarly hopeful in terms of imagining a future beyond the present realities of climate crisis. It also centres on the figure of the agentic child common to contemporary YA fiction and imagines a near-future society more like that of the present. James adapts the epistolary narrative form for a science fiction story, interspersing chapters of narration focalized variously through its two main protagonists, Hester and Theo, with excerpts from online media, news feeds, legal documents, text messages, and so on. The focus on network technologies in the novel emphasizes the mass mobilization of youth culture and politics in a time of climate crisis. This is accompanied by an interest in the positive and negative effects of speculative bio- and geo-engineering technologies. James's young protagonists are entangled with both nature and technology and seek to use their relationships within these phenomena to mitigate and reverse climate breakdown and prompt political transformation. Their action puts them in direct conflict with vested corporate (adult) interests in such technologies and pits them against antagonists who would co-opt youth action back into the colonial-capitalist system. This representation of intergenerational conflict notwithstanding, James's stated aims were to write a hopeful novel about the future of climate change, suggesting that action on the crisis is most likely to be supported by 'inspiring optimistic stories that show a future where we've done things right' (2021b: n.p.).

In both novels the imagined agency of young people on which these hopeful climate futures rely is made possible through characters' interrelationship with plants, trees, and fungi. These child–plant connections are underpinned by the fact that plants have functioned in Western philosophy as 'synechdoches of nature as a whole' (Marder 2013: 31), and on a Romantic-era construction of childhood as synonymous with 'nature', two rhetorical strategies that function to place both vegetal life and children outside of society and politics. However, as the two novels demonstrate, such a rhetorical strategy cannot hold given that the very designation of 'nature' is in such crisis, its meaning more obviously unstable than in the Romantic period. Climate change reveals that the political order now includes everything that once belonged to 'nature' (Latour 2017: 3), and, equally, that 'nature' now contains the political. This is clear in the ways in which the novels also draw on a more contemporary construction of the child as a social agent whose action will bring about transformative political change, as well as a more generous account of the agency inherent in vegetal life. My reading of the novels follows these shifting rhetorical strategies in environmentalism, dis- and then re-entangling the concepts of 'nature' and childhood to do better service to both plants and children in speculating about the climate futures. I argue that the novels offer a critically informed interrogation of the notion of plants and children as 'nature' and that they narrativize the themes of contemporary plant studies.

Where the River Runs Gold figures trees, flowers, and seeds as vital (if mute) actors in Shifa's struggle against the ARK regime. Shifa is a custodian of seeds and bulbs nurturing a dream of one day restoring nature to the barren city. Escaping incarceration by her government and its corporate partners, Shifa finds an ecologically diverse wilderness beyond the bounds of the city, which provides the material for ecosystem rewilding and social revolution at the end of the novel. The material that Shifa brings back to human society includes seeds thought to be extinct and the discovery of the survival of keystone species: pollinators. Vegetal life is also an extramaterial agent in the novel, which links the power of imagination and storytelling to the latent generative power contained within the seeds that Shifa carries. In this, *Where the River Runs Gold* echoes Coccia's insistence that the seed is a metaphysical space of imagination, a natural form that 'allows one to transform the world' (2019: 32). Shifa's discovery of a wildlife haven on Meteore Mountain far outside the oppressive walls of Kairos City perpetuates an association of children with the 'natural' that has persisted in Western culture since the Romantic period. This association is mobilized in the novel in a complex way, suggesting the child as an agent of ecological restoration and social transformation, an agent located simultaneously within and without the systems in need of change. The novel closes at an unspecified time in the future, in a society populated by flourishing humans and more-than-humans. Thanks to Shifa's rebellion and discovery, young citizens are no longer exploited, but work happily in conservation sanctuaries learning about ecology, collecting fruit, tending hives, and climbing trees. Brahmachari thus ends the novel with an image of socially responsible and liberated young people, and a call for rewilding that echoes that being made by ecologists, climate scientists and activists in the present time (Monbiot 2013; Dennis 2021; Strassburg et al. 2020).

Green Rising also depicts young protagonists as materially entangled with vegetal life. In the world of the novel many adolescents discover they have developed a genetic symbiosis that allows them to spontaneously generate plants, fungi, and algae from within their bodies and out of the earth. These powers are revealed to be the result of horizontal genetic transfer from chemical compounds released by the Dalex Energy corporation in an ill-advised geo-engineering scheme. During this scheme, plant DNA transferred to human embryos across an entire generation, creating a symbiotic cellular connection between various plant species, the effects of which manifest during human adolescence. This is a different figuration of the child–nature connection derived from Romanticism to that deployed in *Where the River Runs Gold*, since instead of being relegated to a lush, green idyll beyond society, as Shifa is at the close of that novel, the young people of *Green Rising* are endowed with new bodily capacities that lend them political power they can wield in the intergenerational conflict over climate change, and they find themselves engaging in direct action at toxic waste sites and oil pipelines. Through the science fiction conceit of horizontal gene transfer and human–vegetal symbiosis, the young people – known as 'greenfingers' in the world of the novel – embody the slogan often exclaimed by young climate activists: 'we are nature defending itself' (James 2021: 336). While many greenfingers engage in 'guerrilla' rewilding tactics, others are co-opted by corporations seeking to capitalize on the new 'technology', or else have their rights curtailed by hastily written laws. The conflict over whether greenfingers will serve or disrupt the status quo centres on three young people, Gabrielle, a climate activist, Hester, the heir of Dalex Energy, and Theo, the son of a fisherman. Despite their different social backgrounds, the three characters come together to lead a movement against corporate environmental destruction, mobilizing the greenfingers to rewild vast areas of the globe and reverse GHG emissions. In different ways, then, both novels suggest the need for an alliance between vegetal and human life, and, in equating young activism with the propagation of vegetal life itself, they imagine the continuity between the materiality of plant life and human culture and politics. They imbricate human and plants in intimate partnerships, and advocate cultivating respect for, and allowing the proliferation of, plant life in bringing about hopeful climate futures that do not rely on continuity with the present (which is implied by the concept of sustainability), nor on the restoration of an imagined past (which tends to persist in Romantic ecological imaginaries). Instead, they imagine a future that might emerge out of the unpredictable mutations and unrealized potentials that persist in materiality.

Vegetal subjectivity: Beyond anthropocentrism

While plant studies represent a development in the academy during the late twentieth and early twenty-first centuries, the personhood of plants has been a feature of children's literature since at least the early twentieth century. *Green Rising* and *Where the River Runs Gold* develop this trope of the child–plant partnership from children's literature, which has often been used to communicate environmentalist messages. Zoe Jacques notes, for example, that writing for children and young audiences 'grants subject status and makes trees worthy of protection' (2015: 115–16). She cites J. R. R Tolkien's *The Hobbit* (1936) and *Lord of the Rings* (1954) in which trees speak for themselves and voice their interests, and *The Lorax* (1971) by Dr Seuss, in which others speak on their behalf. In both texts forests are at risk because of destructive human activities. Jacques's other examples, such as *The Giving Tree* by Shel Silverstein (1964), the publication of which coincided with the burgeoning environmental movement, rely on sentimentalized depictions of trees as servile and 'hierarchically inscribed under man' (Jacques 2015: 139). Lydia Kokkola concurs with this assessment of the status of plants in the history of children's literature, suggesting that neither the didactic environmental message of *The Lorax* nor the depiction of sentient trees in the *Harry Potter* novels challenges the prevailing human-plant hierarchy nor recognize, as does contemporary plant studies, that 'plants – not humans – hold the balance of power over the future of the earth' (2017: 277, 279). There is a tension in climate fiction, then, between anthropocentrism, on the one hand, and ecocentrism, on the other hand, where perspectives that centre human agency and interests coincide with perspectives that suggest the intrinsic value of more-than-human beings. This is especially the case in texts that focus on the political development of young human agents as key to ecological restoration. This anthropocentric formulation of agency on which young adult fiction tends to rely requires further interrogation that this chapter will develop.

Where the River Runs Gold and *Green Rising* negotiate existing tensions in the representation of plants and trees from fiction, considering the radical reconfiguration of human behaviour and attitudes necessitated by the climate crisis. The explicit aim of the texts is to communicate the transformative political aims of the contemporary climate action movement and, in so doing, push beyond anthropocentric representations of 'nature' in which plants are accorded instrumental value or else subordinated to an environmental background. At the same time, the novels cannot avoid repeating the anthropocentric tropes that have come before. In *Where the River Runs Gold*, Shifa finds 'comfort' and succour as she shelters in the hollow trunk of the 'survivor tree' on Pollination Farm, a forced labour camp for children run by the ironically named 'Freedom Fields' corporation (2019: 156). She approaches the tree in a way that recognizes its personhood, asking permission to climb its 'ancient' and 'majestic' branches (2019: 181). Enveloped within the canopy of the tree, Shifa communes with other creatures, feeling the beetles and hearing birdsong, which lend her strength and inspiration to save her brother Themba and escape the farm. Though Shifa approaches the tree as a fellow subject from whom permission must be sought for this interaction, it primarily functions as a resource for the development of a human child's agency. Shifa's actions following her communion with the tree bring about her own escape from the farm, along with her bother and 'Freedom' ward, Luca, and, eventually, transformative change for the rest of society, while the tree remains mute and rooted in place. However, there is a shift in perspective at the close of the novel that tempers this hierarchy that would seemingly favour human voice and movement over mute and enrooted plant-being. In the final pages, when the story shifts forward into the future, the narration refocuses on the Survivor Tree itself, now thriving as part of a woodland conservation sanctuary. A nameless child climbs the branches of the tree and finds within abandoned and anonymous pages from Shifa's story, described as a 'riddle from another time' (2019: 340). The temporal persistence of the tree in Shifa's absence reframes the earlier encounter between tree and child, suggesting the relative brief nature of human life in contrast to that of the tree. The shift in perspective also suggests that the ethics and politics of climate change must refer to more-than-human lives and temporalities. That is, ethical climate futures must not focus on human genetic survival, but on the proliferation of more-than-human life.

Green Rising also moves from an instrumental representation of plants focused on human concerns to a recognition of vegetal subjectivity, interiority, and agency. The instrumentalist representation of plants in *Green Rising* is most evident in their narrative role in 'empowering' the greenfingers. Here, the symbiotic relationship between human and vegetal life allows children to become heroic agents of change. In this way, the novel rehearses a narrative arc common in YA fiction, one which propels young people from a position of subordination to that of being able to fight back against adult oppressors or overcome barriers imposed on their freedom. In this case, plant life provides the material for such overcoming as young people find themselves able to wield powers that adult politicians cannot ignore. The novel thus exemplifies what Curry has identified as a definitive shift in the discursive construction of childhood away from Romantic developmentalism 'towards the agential political child capable of moral and social action' (2013: 8). In the case of Theo, one of three main protagonists in *Green Rising*, a genetic symbiosis with fungi allows him to join mycelial networks, imagined in the novel as a single interconnected web of fungi, lichen, and plants that extends across the globe. Connecting to this mycelial network enhances the greenfingers' powers and produces a powerful, material solidarity between disparately located activists. In this role, the mycelia are very much conceived of as part of Theo's 'power' rather than as vegetal agents in their own right (2021: 299). This focus on Theo's powers as coordinator of the uprising notwithstanding, the capacities and agency the young characters develop in the novel emerge from the capacities of vegetal life, including their networked, non-individualistic, and heteronomous modes of being in the world. This accords with Kokkola's insistence that plant-thinking must recognize that the future is contingent on plants, not humans.

Green Rising further moves away from an anthropocentric framing of the young people's powers when it focuses on the subjectivity of plants. When Theo is searching for plant life in the soil, he detects intentionality in the roots, seeds, and fungal hyphae that live there, interpreting the 'vibrations' he senses as a vegetal 'desperation' to grow (2021: 69). Vegetal life is described as having emotional qualities that connects human and plant-being. As the children become more attuned, they begin to recognize when the plants are 'contented', exhibit cravings to consume 'mulch and compost', and start to find pollination 'sexy' (James 2021: 204, 224). At the same time as human bodies increasingly express vegetal desires, the plants come to express human emotions, seeping from Hester's fingers and pores whenever she is stressed, or bursting into flower when she finds contentment in Theo's company. Growing into these emotional relationships with plants, the children accept the vegetal beings as a 'real part' of themselves (James 2021: 88). This acknowledgement echoes Marder's hypothesis that 'vegetal life is coextensive with a distinct subjectivity with which we might engage, and which engages with us more frequently than we imagine' (2013: 8). The plants make Hester 'actually pay attention to all the feelings she usually suppressed' (James 2021: 250). At the same time, it becomes 'impossible not to care' for the plants now the greenfingers can 'feel' vegetal their emotions, such as the 'contented vibrations' of plants soaking up sunlight (James 2021: 193). Thus, the symbiotic relationships imagined in *Green Rising* not only aid the empowerment of youth; they represent an emotional phenomenon that is inclusive of human and vegetal subjectivities and makes porous the border between them.

Vegetal politics: Planthropocene and Symbiocene

As the plant–child partnerships discussed so far suggest, both *Green Rising* and *Where the River Runs Gold* imagine plant-being and young people's subjectivities as an entangled phenomenon and, in so doing, evoke a more-than-human dimension in their explorations of climate futures. Exploring a vegetal perspective on the crisis complicates the idea of the Anthropocene. The importance accorded vegetal life in both novels gestures to alternative formulations of the current epoch of climatic change. One such alternative is Natasha Myers's concept of the 'Planthropocene', which seeks to counteract the focus on human agency in the idea of Anthropocene along with its elision of the fact that 'we are not one and we are not alone' (2017: 299). The expansion of Theo's subjectivity in *Green Rising* echoes this idea. When he connects to the network of fungi teeming in the soil, Theo feels 'part of something greater than himself' (James 2021: 113). Myers suggests that 'Planthropocene' names 'a way of doing life in which people come to recognize their profound interimplication with plants . . . to make alliances with these green beings' (2017: 300). Such alliances are genetic and political in *Green Rising*, which Theo recognizes when he reaches out to the mycelial network and understands how it might help them put a stop to the environmental destruction being wrought by the Dalex corporation: 'it's connecting us together!' (James 2021: 169). Here humans and plants together perform what Marder calls the 'vegetal democracy', 'an inherently political space of conviviality' in which divisibility and participation are 'paramount' (Marder 2013: 51). The young people involved in the movement proliferate across the globe, dividing into non-hierarchically organized groups to plan and carry out their uprising. Physically, the plant life produced by the activists pushes up through their skin, releasing spores and seeds into the air, and, also, emerges from the earth itself, suggesting it is both an extension of their bodies and divisible from it, and that their participation leaves traces of their now more-than-human bodies across the surface of the globe. Vegetal democracy in *Green Rising* entails, as Marder suggests, an 'opening' to the other for life to flourish (2013: 69). Theo's discovery of the mycelial network unfolds at the same time as the uprising expands through online social networks, represented by forum posts, message threads, and other fragments that intersperse the narration. Here James underscores a material continuity that extends from the participation that comprises networked organic life through to the online networks of activists.

Although the alliance between plants and humans in *Where the River Runs Gold* is less intimate than in *Green Rising*, it also suggests the necessity of mutuality between vegetal and human life. Here, too, the connection between plants and children is material and political, imagining plants and trees as vital actors in the biosphere and in bringing about social transformation. Shifa collects new seeds, bulbs, and roots from the secret garden she finds hidden at Pollination Farm, realizing that she needs to escape not only to report the atrocities of the work camp to the wider world, but to share her seed store and begin the vital process of rewilding. At the same time as Shifa aids the proliferation of vegetal life with her custodianship of their seeds, the plants aid her by sharing stories and memories. Travelling down the river away from the farm, Shifa encounters a willow that seems to beckon with its branches and brushes her with its 'feeling' leaves (2019: 258). Shifa is drawn to initials carved on the branches left there by the old owner of the farm, Lona, whose story 'map' to Meteore Mountain is the one Shifa must decipher to escape Freedom Fields. Shifa realizes that the tree is 'sharing a message' and that she is on the right path (2019: 258). The willow and the Survivor Tree both function as social analogues of what forest ecologist Suzanne Simard calls 'mother trees', nodal points in the woodland network that transfer information and energy to other plants (Simard 2021). Here the information and energy shared take the form of fragments of Lona's story map and a concomitant nurturance of the children's courage.

The presence of nurturing trees in *Where the River Runs Gold* gestures to the idea now emerging in ecological thought of the vegetal world as one of mutual aid, as it is in Albrecht and Van Horn's concept of the 'Symbiocene' (2016). This names an era in which human life replicates the 'mutually reinforcing' processes found in other living systems, enhancing interdependence and benefit 'for all living beings' and ecosystems (2016: n.p.). The Symbiocene is another way of thinking about vegetal politics since it equates the life-sustaining processes of woodland and mycorrhizal networks with collectivist politics. In this analogy between vegetal life and human politics Albrecht makes explicit a latent ideology of mutuality present in popular contemporary science writing. Sheldrake, for example, tells his readers that the history of evolution is 'full of intimate collaborations', a fact that James's novel explores through its supposition of a genetic exchange between plants and human embryos (Sheldrake 2020: 12). Elsewhere, Wohlleben describes forests as 'communities' in which exchange and mutual aid, not competition, is the rule, a feature of forests that Shifa and Theo both discover as they alternatively give and take from the plants with which they become entangled (Wohlleben 2016: 4). Wohlleben also evokes Coccia's plant philosophy when he refuses the metaphor of nature as a 'war zone' and instead claims it is 'characterized by solidarity' (2021: 105–6). The uprisings against environmental destruction and climate injustices precipitated by Shifa in *Where the River Runs Gold* and the Greenfingers in *Green Rising* evoke these descriptions of vegetal life, and, therefore, suggest the same material continuity between the 'natural world' and young people's politics as expressed in Albrecht's elaboration of the Symbiocene. As Pickard, Bowman, and Arya suggest, in real-world climate action led by young people, young people 'show dedication to what they consider "radical" peaceful protest actions rooted in their concept of kindness' and emphasize the need for 'interconnected approaches to human endeavour' (2020: 273). Likewise, the acts of radical kindness undertaken by young people in both novels, which includes risking their lives for humans, animals, and plant-life, is a distinct turn from the representation of nature in the anthropocentric *The Giving Tree* or J. K. Rowling's *Harry Potter* novels, where plant-life serves human needs. Instead, plants and young people are mutually implicated in material entanglements that suggest 'radical' (that is kind, participatory, and communal) approaches to society and politics.

Immersion in the phytocene

The vegetal–human connections that are, in the novels, variously represented as material and genetic, social and political, and imaginative and cultural suggest alternative ways of thinking through relationality to those which have preceded this chapter. Reading the novels alongside critical plant studies I consider entanglement as analogous with 'immersion', which is a concept developed in Coccia's plant-thinking, and, also, related to the political idea of the 'collective', a term taken from Bruno Latour, and central to the 'common worlds' described in Affrica Taylor's work on childhood. Each of these ideas, when brought into dialogue with the ontoethical concept of entanglement, offers ways to rethink the vexed concept of agency, the tensions and limitations of which have been brought to the fore by the climate crisis. Climate crisis, as discussed previously, brings human agency into focus as a global force at the very same moment as that agency disintegrates into a complex web of organic, chemical, social, and political systems. The immersive common worlds and collectives constructed by vegetal life in these novels are instructive in reconsidering agency in the face of this paradox.

Of course, human agency as a discrete and unique force in the world is a fiction. The vegetal–human phenomenon imagined by Brahmachari and James reveal this to be the case because they are not new amalgams but emerge from the already enmeshed common worlds of plants and people across which agency is shared. Here my reading of the novels differs from Curry's analysis of YA dystopias, which emphasizes the crumbling of old societies and ideologies, and the emergence of 'new, and different world orders' (2013: 42, 60). Eschewing the idea that vegetal democracy is a new world order, I turn to Coccia, who emphasizes the ancient interdependencies between humans and plants. Coccia writes that 'it was the plants that, millions of years ago, transformed the world by producing the conditions of possibility of animal life' (2019: 71). Theo's connection to seaweed in *Green Rising* echoes Coccia's point when he reflects that the seaweed and algae that fall from his fingers are 'the original plant[s] that everything else had evolved from' (James 2021: 160). Coccia extends his claim, emphasizing the continuity between the biological and the political, when he states that 'the human sphere – culture, history, the life of the mind – is not autonomous, it has a foundation in what is not human' (Coccia 2019: 62). He calls this foundation the 'climate', drawing attention to the fact that plants produce the air humans breathe and, therefore, the conditions for the growth of ostensibly 'human' phenomena.

Green Rising emphasizes just such ancient nonhuman origins in the supposition of genetic interrelationships between plants and humans, including the 'spontaneous endosymbiosis through horizontal gene transfer' that seems to be the source of the greenfingers' power (James 2021: 147). This horizontal gene transfer leads to the emergence of 'new properties' in the human genome that give rise to the powers displayed by the characters in the novel (James 2021: 147). The conceit recalls Margulis's theory of symbiogenesis (1998), discussed in the introduction, and underscores the latent potential in materiality distributed between species and that might emerge in their collaboration. The characters' encounter of this symbiogenetic legacy is also uncanny, as the greenfingers discover through their changing bodies: Gabrielle's forearms become embedded with tiny seeds and Hester's eczema peels away from her skin in flakes of bark. The greenfingers find it harder and harder to 'stop the plants encroaching' onto their bodies, engaging in intimate negotiations between 'the absolute familiarity of plants' and 'their sheer strangeness' (James 2021: 224; Marder 2013: 4).

The figuration of vegetal–human symbiosis as an embodied and evolutionary possibility emphasizes the continuity between the material and the political apparent in Albrecht and Van Horn's claim that humans are embedded in an 'evolutionary matrix' (2016: n.p.). They argue that the material for making the Symbiocene lies within humans as 'latent potential' (2016: n.p.). In other words, political transformation is a material possibility that persists within our genetic heritage. Again, *Green Rising* dramatizes this claim in its descriptions of the greenfingers activating and developing their vegetal powers. During training, Daisy, one of the activists, exhorts the others to 'focus on the potential' inside the seedlings, on their wish to grow, a potential that Theo then feels both externally, within the seed, and, internally, within his own body (James 2021: 66). The transformative potential of latent possibilities in materiality is also stressed throughout *Where the River Runs Gold*, in which vegetal metaphors for political change abound. Thinking about her escape from Pollination Farm, Shifa imagines the possibility of rebellion as a 'seed' 'planted' inside the recruits, the growth of which the farm guardians attempt 'to stamp out' before it 'spread[s] like wildflowers' (Brahmachari 2019: 152). Brahmachari's recourse to metaphors of organic growth in her images of political and social transformation emphasize the material-political continuity underscored by the concept of the Symbiocene and make clear its exhortation to draw on possibilities that already persist in material being. In advancing such ideas, both the concept of the Symbiocene and *Where the River Runs Gold* echo the ethics sketched by environmental philosopher Aldo Leopold, in which he claims that 'politics and economics are advanced symbioses in which the original free-for-all competition has been replaced . . . by co-operative mechanisms with an ethical content' (1949: 172).

The ancient connections between plants and humans, and the formation of what Coccia calls the 'phytocene', a geological era produced by plants, conceive of reality as a space of immersion rather than embeddedness. That is, humans are not embedded in an earthly environment, which is a common rhetoric in mainstream environmentalism and ecocriticism, but immersed in an atmosphere first created by plants, which facilitates organic exchange and hybrid modes of being (Coccia 2019: 132). The phytocene is not only a biospheric term; it has cultural and political implications because plant-life created the conditions for human history and culture. Immersion differs ontologically and ethically from Curry's elaboration of the 'poetics of earth' in YA dystopia because it emphasizes a less enrooted notion of being. Curry's discussion of embeddedness begins with a critique of the 'planetary consciousness' inculcated in mainstream environmental rhetoric, often figured via the 'transcendent imaged of a dematerialised planet', noting that it engenders dislocation and disengagement (2013: 19). She traces in YA novels a counter impulse that seeks to promote a 'responsible place-based engagement with the earth', an earthly sense of belonging (Curry 2013: 20). This sense of belonging emerges in Curry's corpus through local, place-situatedness engagement with landscape (2013: 192). *Green Rising* and *Where the River Runs Gold* sustain this reading to an extent, exploring the specific place-based attachments of their characters. For example, Theo assumes that the reason his body produces seaweed and algae is because of his connection to his coastal home, and, in the early portions of the book, he only manifests seaweed of the kind that grew in the harbour where he grew up. Equally, in *Where the River Runs Gold*, Lona's connection to her home around Pollination Farm allows Shifa to find Meteore Mountain and escape the devastation of a second storm that occurs during the climax of the novel. However, in both cases, a place-based engagement becomes more expansive as the temporal and spatial focus of the narrative extends, forward in time in the case of *Where the River Runs Gold*, and, in *Green Rising*, zooming out to the international space station from where Theo and Hester coordinate their global uprising. Drawing on Coccia, I suggest that a too-narrow focus on earthly embeddedness risks, in its enrooted conception of ecological belonging, eliding the openness and mobility available in an immersive concept of plant-being and atmospheric exchange, which are paradigmatic of the ways in which, as Coccia states, 'that every being of the world is in the world with the same intensity with which the world is in it' (2019: 132). This is made evident when Theo recognizes his affinity lies not with seaweed as he first assumes, but with fungi and lichen, beings whose 'boundary-stretching' promiscuity has prompted ecologists to question the concept of the individual organism and consider, instead, being as a continual process of exchange and merger (Sheldrake 2020: 13, 124).

Coccia develops the concept of immersion by thinking through plant-being not as enrooted in the earth, but as ecologically hybrid, situated between land and air. Theo's fungi are paradigmatic of such hybridity, occupying their own Kingdom of classification, defying the distinction between organism and environment, individual and ecosystem. Like plants, fungi live their life both above and below the ground, a mode of being *Green Rising* continually explores in its descriptions of branches rising into the air as well as the murky depths of the root network under the ground. In its exploration of the hybridity of plants, *Green Rising* follows Marder in situating vegetal beings 'at the intersection of the physical elements' and as 'decentred in their milieu, which they neither organize nor oppose' (2013: 63). This decentred being provides a stark contrast to the environmental attitudes displayed by adults in both novels. Dalex, Edgar Warren, the ARK government, and Freedom Fields all deny their immersion in the environment and, instead, attempt to both organize and oppose it, configuring ecology as a space of zero-sum competition in which others must lose in order for them to win. In contrast, atmospheric biochemical processes of plant-being reveal the world not as 'a space of competition or mutual exclusion' but as 'the most radical form of mixture . . . in which everything seems to be able to change its nature, to pass from the organic into the inorganic' (Coccia 2019: 80–1). Here Coccia echoes Margulis's theories of symbiogenesis, insisting that the immersive nature of plant being is the engine of species cooperation and evolution 'because each living being lives already, at once, in the life of others' (Margulis and Sagan 2003: 27; Coccia 2019: 81). The citizens of Kairos City feel the effect of this mutual compenetration acutely in the wake of climate devastation, which appears to have destroyed pollinators. Without these keystone species ensuring the mixing and exchange that guarantees life on earth, children are recruited to do the work of pollination. As she works in the polytunnels, Shifa imagines herself as 'a little hummingbird, balancing at an angle' on the delicate petals of the flower, seeking the secret space inside its centre the right moment to insert her 'beak' (2019: 166). Despite the ways in which Shifa as a child is exploited by the ARK government in its attempt to organize the devastated environment according to an instrumentalist attitude to plant-life, this intimate description of child-as-pollinator emphasizes the ethical idea that life is always life *with*, and so dependent on, myriad others.

The greenfingers' immersion in the world as atmospheric mixture is even more explicit, dramatizing Coccia's argument that plant-being reveals 'there is no material distinction between us and the rest of the world' and that life is the action of 'mutual compenetration between subject and environment, body and space, life and medium' (2019: 32, 37). That immersion is material and begins under the skin is dramatized in the opening pages of the novel when Gabrielle first notices the green shoots emerging from under her fingernail, writhing upward searching for the light, eventually covering her arm in 'a green, seething mass of vegetation' (Coccia 2019: 39; James 2021: 10). These bodily connections soon expand, particularly after Theo develops his connection to the mycelial network and feels the 'immensity' of interconnected vegetal life under the soil (James 2021: 170). The expansion of the greenfingers as a collective through mycelial collaboration ensures that the novel moves beyond a place-based engagement with eco-politics. Theo ends up coordinating the global rising from a space station in orbit around the earth, a position from which he is better able to work with the mycelia, and from which he experiences vegetal life at the scale of the biosphere. This implies a planetary consciousness, though it is neither transcendent nor dislocated. The children's sense of immersion in the earth is emphasized throughout. Even from his planetary vantage point, Theo puts down multiple 'roots' into the areas of vegetation springing up all over the planet, feeling himself 'sinking into the land' and oceans as he connects with emergent patches of vegetal life in myriad locations (2021: 323). These descriptions also echo Gagliano's claim that 'the plant exists in a state of open communion in which the fiction of personalized boundaries collapse' (2018: 16). Indeed, at the height of the uprising, Theo feels his skin turn 'soft and collapsing' as nature begins to 'claim' him (James 2021: 344). The recurring image of the collapse of bodily boundaries between human, plant, and environment provide pertinent dramatizations of immersion throughout the novel without limiting ecological belonging to place-based embeddedness.

The concept of ecological immersion rather than embeddedness suggests a radical openness between environment and organisms that eschews any hierarchy between the two. As Coccia states, plant life 'demonstrate[s] that living beings produce the space in which they live rather than being forced to adapt to it' (2019: 25). This ontoethical proposition is dramatized in both novels by disastrous agroscientific or geo-engineering management of the environment as well as attempts to restore ecosystems changed by climate catastrophe. In each case there is a failed attempt to force the environment to adapt to human needs, such as in Dalex's toxic geo-engineering project, or the ARK government's disastrous food production policy. Coccia's point is not that beings can either shape their environment or else find themselves shaped by it, but that there is a continuity between atmosphere and organism that agroscientific practices, geo-engineering, and environmental management misunderstand. In attempting to manage the environment, Dalex unwittingly transform a complex network of biochemical processes, catalysing unseen actants. This leads to an unintended adaptation in the form of the greenfingers. The greenfingers subsequently join in with the (re)making of the environment. First, they approach this in the same way as Dalex and their early attempts at cleaning up the environment at the site of an oil spill create a disastrous algae bloom. The activists fail to understand the complexity of the marine ecosystem and their own place within it: there is no possibility of restoring the site to a state of purity that existed prior to human intervention. This point is made again when the narrator describes the piles of plastic that remain intact beneath the newly 'rewilded' garbage dumps. The greenfingers must move beyond the idea of organizing their environment, instead engaging in ecological practices that allow a deepening entanglement and intimacy between vegetal and human life. Immersion thus eschews ontological purity since it is 'impossible to purify the environment of our presence' or to cordon off being from its surroundings (Coccia 2019: 66; Marder 2013: 69). This is immersion as adaptation, which is not simply the result of the environment acting on organisms, but a two-way process in which living beings modify the atmosphere and so create a 'new world' to hand down to future generations (Coccia 2019: 42). Landscapes dramatically change due to the actions of young people in both novels. At the end of *Where the River Runs Gold*, for example, Shifa squeezes open her flower-shaped seed packet she has protected through the novel, watching as 'hundreds of seeds and specimens [that] she'd collected fly out, spreading far and wide across the Kairos Lands' (2019: 329). The epilogue that narrates the result of this from the vantage point of the Survivor Tree demonstrates that Shifa's actions do precipitate a major rewilding of the landscape and that this also transforms relationships between humans and the environment. Shifa's action of letting the seeds proliferate on the wind, however, is not an act of deliberate land management, but demonstrates the openness, exposure, and communion that are key to ecological immersion.

Agency in the collective

Where *Green Rising* and *Where the River Runs Gold* capitulate to the lure of the child–nature dyad as a symbol of ontological purity rather than paradigmatic of ecological immersion, it is because of a Western construction of both nature and childhood that has persisted since at least the eighteenth century and has tended to function, as Affrica Taylor suggests, as a 'reassuring fact of life' (2013: xiii). Of course, nature and childhood can only be idealized by being separated from, and valorized as the exotic other of, degenerative adult society. As Taylor points out, this has the unfortunate effect of denying 'real children's real-world relationships and it positions them in the paradoxical situation of needing protection from the world in which they actually reside' (2013: 87). This also has the effect of denying childhood agency. Where agency is imputed to youth, in contemporary discussions of climate activism for example, the Romantic legacy often persists. Even Curry's analysis, which acknowledges the constructedness of both 'childhood' and 'nature' within a 'romantic framework of shared ontological purity' (2013: 7), capitulates to an association that burdens young people with the responsibility of environmental restoration when she states that her corpus promotes hopeful images of 'ecological growth and renewal: the image of a bud, flower, or weed blooming' (2013: 21, 32). *Green Rising* literalizes this Romantic imaginary with its descriptions of green shoots emerging from the bodies of the children. In the case of *Where the River Runs Gold*, the connection between children and nature is one of custodianship, but also rehearses the 'secret garden' pastoral image, in its use of spaces such as the Flower Tracks and Lona's walled meadow, in which characters hide from ARK surveillance, and in the untouched landscape of Meteore Mountain, in which Shifa shelters at the end of the novel. In these separated sites, however, real-world relationships are not ignored, and children only linger there for a brief time before returning to the messy and heterogeneous common worlds composed of biological, social, and political relationships and symbiosis between humans and plants.

The refusal to quarantine plants and children in an idealized sphere of life in both novels, along with the descriptions of their entangled being and collaboration, recalls Latour's political notion of the collective. For Latour, the collective functions as an alternative designation to both 'nature' and 'society', refusing any binary division between these two imagined sites, naming a 'residence of humans and nonhumans' (1999: 193). The collective is a continually evolving architecture of ecological belonging, of social and political exchange, an open network made up of 'actants' of all types (Latour 1999: 194–5; Latour 1993: 4–5). Over time, the collective unfolds ever-deepening intimacies between actants, echoing the comments on the immersive nature of plant-being discussed above. Indeed, Latour's conception of the collective draws on evolutionary terminology, using the genetic terms 'translation' and 'crossover' to describe the exchange of properties between humans and nonhumans. Like vegetal being, the collective requires an alternative understanding of agency to that which designates it as the property of an individual. Agency is, rather, the result of an association of actants and, so, the 'property of the whole association' (Latour 1999: 183). In the collective, 'responsibility for action must be shared' (Latour 1999: 180). The reason, then, that the clean-up efforts of the greenfingers fail at the oil spill is that they conceive of themselves as human agents imposing action onto an environmental background. It is only when Theo connects the greenfingers to the mycelial network that they begin to function as a collective. Collectives emerge through *Where the River Runs Gold*, too, as Brahmachari emphasizes the interdependence between humans from different sections of the segregated society, including Shifa's family who are indentured citizens, 'Freedom' ward, Luca, who is afforded special privileges, those who work for Freedom Fields, such as the house-carers, 'outlanders' who are forcibly relocated from the city, one of whom Shifa shelters, animals such as the stray cat Daisy, the plants Shifa and Nabil nurture on the Flower Tracks, the Survivor Tree, the Willow and the Ore River. All these actants exchange properties and resources with one another, enacting a transformation of the collective as a whole.

The actants that comprise the collective of which Shifa is part might also be described as forming a 'common world', a term Taylor uses to counter the idea that childhood is 'sanctified, pure and innocent' (2013: 87). Common worlds are not occupied solely by children, separate from the rest of society, but are shared with 'all manner of others' and 'full of inherited messy conditions . . . of entangled and uneven historical and geographical relations, political tensions, ethical dilemmas and unending possibilities' (Taylor 2013: 87). Like Latour's collective, common worlds include more-than-humans and continually unfold via 'an ongoing process of collecting' (Taylor 2013: 87). This act of collection is apparent in Shifa's custodianship of the seeds and bulbs she finds on her travels through Kairos Lands, which she keeps safe from ARK surveillance in a hidden seed packet, as well as the ways in which her resistance to the ARK regime draws in multiple participants, including house carer Hannah, who is moved to speak out about the abuse perpetrated at Pollination Farm, and Freedom Ward Luca, who gives up his privileges to travel with Shifa. While Shifa shelters in the wilderness of Meteore Mountain with Luca and Themba, other members of an emerging and makeshift collective engage in protests that successfully bring down the ARK government. A new politics is formed 'with representatives of all people in the Lands', addressing the lack of solidarity Shifa identifies when she wonders why 'humans could not have worked together to prevent Hurricane Chronos' (Brahmachari 2019: 335, 74). Despite Shifa's reference to 'humans' here, it is clear from the common world she 'collects' that solidarity requires the participation of nonhumans too. Indeed, Nabil describes the protesters painting 'too many Graffitrees to remove' as a sign of their identification with the more-than-human world and their desire to disrupt the sterile streets of Kairos City (Brahmachari 2019: 335). Shifa's care for seeds and plants, for the cat Daisy, and for her brother – to whom she turns out not to be biologically related – demonstrates childhood as a space in which to develop an ethics of care for self, other, and environment, rather than a protected, Edenic space. Echoing Leopold's 'Land Ethic' (1949), which advances a 'moral code of conduct that grows out of interconnected caring relationships' and that 'changes the role of homo sapiens from conqueror of the land-community to citizen of it', the new ARK government promises not to visit the atrocities of the past neither on future 'generations' nor on 'lands' (Leopold 1949: 174; Brahmachari 2019: 335). Here the people and the land form one community, or common world, and care for one cannot be separated from the other.

As common worlds, vegetal–human phenomena demonstrate that notions of the autonomous self and autonomous agency are anthropocentric fictions. Vegetal life leads the way in rethinking agency because of its 'autotelic' nature. As Marder contends, vegetal life does not contain its 'cause' in itself and so necessitates a 're-conceptualisation of being in terms of heteronomy' (2013: 68). The greenfingers are the most obvious example of being as heteronomy in that their 'cause' is evidently external: they result from a process involving industrial chemical toxins and cross-species genetic transfer. On the one hand, the greenfingers are victims of a corporate mass poisoning scandal, like those from real history in which unborn babies have been affected by industrial detritus, notably lead poisoning and, more recently, dangerous levels of air pollution, or by the reckless dispensation of drugs such as thalidomide. On the other hand, the greenfingers are empowered by the resulting genetic symbiosis with vegetal life, which confers new bodily capacities and political power. In either reading, the greenfingers exemplify a mode of hybrid characterization identified by Curry in her corpus of dystopian novels. The hybrid identities of protagonists in those novels have the effect of 'wedding the material needs of earth to those of the young adult' because the 'personal growth or maturation of the young adult arises through, and is occasioned by, his or her ecological embeddedness' (2013: 195). To an extent this is the case for both the greenfingers and Shifa in *Where the River Runs Gold* because both novels explicitly wed the protagonists' maturation to the fate of the ecosystems in which they are embedded.

However, a plant-thinking approach makes clear that Curry's theory of hybrid identities does not go far enough. *Where the River Runs Gold* and *Green Rising* emphasize the heteronomy of being and their stories are as much about vegetal as human becoming. For example, although the greenfingers experience their hybrid identities as empowering, asserting their desires and demands in the face of attempted suppression, their powers require a concurrent process of what Coccia calls 'disapropriation', or 'becoming a stranger to oneself', as they confront their vegetal natures and the origins of their powers. Also, the powers experienced by the greenfingers function primarily to aid the proliferation of vegetal life rather than human flourishing. If *Green Rising* does not mobilize plants to serve human ends, then, their growth might better be described as parasitic on maturing human bodies. This is the suggestion in scenes in which greenfingers feel their bodily resources being depleted by the plants. Theo can feel the vegetal network 'taking what it needed' as he lends his power to the other activists to grow new biomes (James 2021: 326). As the uprising reaches its peak, Theo realizes that there might be nothing left of his human self at the end of the process. The notion of the collective, or common world, however, complicates a binary conception of either symbiosis or parasitism as the basis for cooperation. The participation of both humans and plants in vegetal democracy necessitates the collapse of boundaries that parasitism implies and locates agency throughout a collective of heteronomous beings, enacted in the processes of exchange, reciprocation, feedback, and deepening entanglements, rather than in the push and pull of cause and effect, as one autonomous body acts upon another. The shift from autotelic being to being as heteronomy in Theo's experience of the uprising echoes an entangled conception of causality as always in process, such that no boundary between parasite and host can be drawn. Though Theo becomes almost entirely plant during the uprising, diving into the 'deep pit' of fungal being, he is pulled out by Hester whose kiss forces his lungs to 'remember their form' (2021: 348). This experience does not reinstate Theo's autotelic human being, however, but leads him into a new entanglement with Hester as the two of them resolve to use their powers in concert at the end of the novel to tackle other urgent problems faced by society.

Beyond worlds' end: Climate futures in mainstream environmentalism

In complicating causality, vegetal being suggests very different ideas of futurity to those which tend to circulate in mainstream environmentalism. Environmental discourses are not homogeneous, of course, but in the main, the conception of the future they offer feature young people as resources, both in the form of biological descendants for whom the future must be made safe, and as a guarantee of ecological salvation. These discourses make use of the sentimentalized dyad of children and nature already discussed. The dyad works to foreclose the future through notions of biological inheritance that rely on continuity with the present, through pastoral and nostalgic imaginings of Edenic restoration, and by deploying the child-in-nature as an a-temporal figure whose timelessness serves stasis and deferral. As climate fiction, *Where the River Runs Gold* and *Green Rising* negotiate figurations of this child–nature dyad inherited from environmentalism and children's literature. They also engage with the troubling issue of climate futures via the theme of catastrophe, which look to worlds' ending, as Curry points out, via the 'devastating shattering' of norms (2013: 8). As is demonstrated by both authors' comments, their aim in imagining such catastrophes is to generate hope. This works in two ways. The first uses the catastrophe, as Curry argues in her reading of dystopia, to make room for alternative modes of human-earth interaction (2013: 18). The second aims at forestalling climate anxiety by providing positive imaginings about where the future might head. Both impulses aim to counter game over narratives that provide little motivation for action in the present. However laudable such aims, they also capitulate, at least in part, to the need for epistemological certainties central to popular environmentalism, and so constrain conceptions of the future. Despite this, such constraints are partially undone in the turn to vegetal life. The vegetal–human collectives forged in both books demonstrate that both 'nature' and 'children', if they are to be coupled together, demonstrate multiplicity and openness rather than foreclosure and certainty. The future cannot be predicted and so cannot be made safe, but this uncertainty is a source of potential rather than disaster. In their hybrid and heteronomous becoming, the children–plant alliances figure the future as emergent from organic growth and evolution, the ends of which cannot be known in advance.

Climate futures in mainstream environmentalism tend to focus on making safe a threatened future or ensuring some form of continuity with the present via human survival. As Rebekah Sheldon notes, popular environmental rhetoric 'relies on and activates a series of epistemological certainties', urging for action so that 'things will remain unchanged enough to provide a stable background against which to chart the changes those ramifications we then call the future' (2016: 28). Both Sheldon and Adeline Johns-Putra identify the figure of the child as key to this concept of futurity in environmentalism. Examining contemporary climate fiction, Johns-Putra argues that the image of the child functions as a guarantee, a signifier of future generations, serving an ethics of posterity that collapses the web of obligation between species into 'a single intergenerational strand of time' between (human) parent and child (2019: 4). Sheldon also identifies the child as a figure of biological descendance in climate imaginaries, which 'binds the realisation of nonhuman vitality back into the charmed circle of the human, encircling the future in the promise of generationality' (2016: 5). The future conceived of in terms of future generations of humans implies anthropocentric, rather than ecocentric, ethics, eliding the future nonhuman beings to whom we are responsible, as well as the unknowability of that future (Johns-Putra 2019: 24). It also constructs the child as the 'self-similar issue of the present', suggesting the future will be a continuation of present conditions (Sheldon 2016: 5). Bound up in these notions of the future as posterity is the figure of the child as an object of parental care, who replaces the 'terror' of the future with the sentimentality of parental sheltering, and nurturing (Johns-Putra 2019: 4). Whether the child appears in mainstream environmentalism as a guarantee of human survival, or a comforting object of parental care, its objectification goes hand in hand with impoverished anthropocentric visions of climate futures.

Critiquing the ethics of posterity in mainstream environmentalism, Johns-Putra further contends that such ethics are not, after all, about the future, but aim at a sense of 'transcendence and timelessness' (2019: 5). Children's literature provides an apt partner in this work, since it has tended to locate childhood in fantasy sites, many of which are pastoral or Romantic idylls, to which adults cannot gain entry and to which children who cross the threshold to adulthood cannot return. As Paul Wake contends in his work on childhood spaces in literature, children are constructed as existing in an 'a-temporal present' (2009: 31). The child's entry into temporality ensues its disintegration, a pattern repeated from *Alice in Wonderland*, through Peter Pan, Christopher Robin, and the children who discover Narnia, to name a few. In environmental terms, the secret gardens of children's literature promote the 'innocence and plenitude' that promise, following Johns-Putra's elaboration of environmentalism, an 'idealisation of posterity' (2019: 10). Certainly, this construction of the child as natural and timeless offers little resource for imagining radical climate futures. A rather different figuration of the child is, therefore, becoming more common in environmentalism. Sheldon identifies a shift in the rhetoric in recent years from 'a child in need of saving to the child who saves' (Sheldon 2016: 2). This is a rhetorical move mirrored by developments in children's literature, as Curry's analysis of YA fiction suggests. Curry argues that such novels place young people 'in a more agential and empowered position to meet the challenges of climate crisis' and that climate change operates as a 'brink', or threshold, that inculcates responsibility (2013: 192, 22). This reading of the child as salvific figure for humanity on the brink functions in the obverse to that of the innocent who sits outside of time. However, it is no less an 'attempt to fix the future – to heal it and to immobilise it', as Sheldon argues, and it still relies on an ontologically pure child–nature dyad who can recover the future from the detritus of the present (Sheldon 2016: 29).

Where the River Runs Gold and *Green Rising* rehearse and problematize these ideas about the child and climate futures. The most pertinent image is that of the child as object of parental care, and, therefore, a promise of generationality. Both novels explore parent–child relationships and trace a trajectory for their protagonists from being a child in need of saving to a child who saves. In the opening pages of *Where the River Runs Gold*, Nabil races to rescue infants from the devastation of the storm, Chronos, wondering if it might be 'the end of time' (2019: 5). Baby Shifa looks at Nabil, seeming to ask, 'will you keep me safe?' and Nabil responds by naming her 'Shifa – the one who heals' (2019: 7). The scene evokes the danger posed to future generations by adults in the present, recalling the story of the Titan Cronus, who devoured his children, and presents Shifa as an innocent in need of care. Although Shifa is not Nabil's biological child, she functions as a promise of generationality and a guarantee of a more hopeful future. Later, during her journey down the Ore, Shifa dreams of being given a skep heart by Nabil's father, Baba Suli, whom she has never met. When he says, 'it's in your hands now', Baba Suli refers to Shifa's duty to survive, to pass on the family's stories and traditions, and to bring about ecological restoration, interpolating her from the vantage point of the past, addressing her as a salvific figure whose actions will ensure posterity (Brahmachari 2019: 292). The idea of the child as an image of human descent, however, is complicated by Shifa and Nabil's non-biological relationship, the discovery of which causes a rift between them that is only healed when they acknowledge that families 'are made, not born' (Brahmachari 2019: 80). Their family grows to include many others outside their immediate circle of concern, including the nonhumans Shifa assembles in her collective.

The idea of the child as self-same issue of the present is critiqued more obviously in *Green Rising* through Hester's father, who seeks to make Hester in his own image as an attempt to legitimize Dalex Energy in the face of increased political pressure over climate change. Hester rejects his coercive care by joining the green uprising and coordinating a lawsuit against Dalex to hold them responsible for poisoning an entire generation with their failed geo-engineering scheme, and for other acts of environmental destruction. The lawsuit, which accuses Dalex of having 'stolen' the future from young people, deploys the language of mainstream environmentalism in its evocation of the future as a site of intergenerational conflict (James 2021: 334). The conflict is resolved only when young people enter institutions of power, as they do at the close of the novel when Gabrielle runs for election. The description of political, social, and economic changes that occur because of the uprising promise some radical transformations in terms of disrupting the capitalist status quo, such as faming co-ops and a carbon tax, but the suggested changes also constrain the future in terms of anthropocentric concerns, with reference to technological and health innovations promised by the greenfingers, and a new 'economic boom' (2021: 355, 358). Though they shift in the novel from being objects of care to activists determined to bring about change, Hester and Shifa continue to function to make the future safe, albeit in altered terms than those set out by the older generation.

The planetary factory: Children and plants in reproductive futurism

In exploring the tensions inherent in a rhetoric of parental care both *Green Rising* and *Where the River Runs Gold* expose a reproductive futurism that serves the capitalist status quo. 'Reproductive futurism' is a term Lee Edelman gives to a pervasive cultural imaginary in which children signify wholeness, serving an impulse towards teleology easily fooled by invocations of a never achievable future (Edelman 2004: 22). In ecocriticism, Edelman's ideas offer a critique of the narrow 'genetic survivalism' that abounds in environmentalism (Johns-Putra 2019: 59) and of the rhetoric of deferral that stave off a 'messy' future that is neither 'a descendant nor a salvific redemption of the present' with the idea of replicating the future through children (Sheldon 2016: 35). Here the 're' in '*re*production' points to the repetition of the conditions of past and present into the future, rather than to the production of change. The novels join this critique by revealing how a salvific image of the child, especially the child of nature, turns on its exploitation and control in a heterosexist reproductive futurism. Parental care as exploitation is made overt in *Where the River Runs Gold* when Nabil is forced to sign a 'contract of care' and turn over 'in loco parentis' rights to Freedom Fields (Brahmachari 2019: 90). The Freedom Fields brochure boasts of its 'Youth Recruit-Led Food Production and Pollination Service . . . proving an invaluable pillar in our portfolio to rebuild our great Kairos Lands', but its upbeat, corporate language exposes its aim to exploit the bodies of the children: their 'delicate fingers' are necessary for the pollination process (2019: 46, 50). The novel makes explicit that children and plants alike are seen as mutable resources in what Marder calls the 'capitalist agroscientific complex' (2013: xv). This complex enacts its control of children through bodily modification and coercion. Shifa is forced to undergo laser eye surgery so she can spend hours in the polytunnels, and, in *Green Rising*, Dalex attempt to utilize the greenfingers as an 'unlimited resource', greedily hoping for 'huge rewards if the powers can be manipulated successfully' (James 2021: 40). Just as Shifa and the others are exploited by Freedom Fields in their disastrous agricultural regime, Hester is manipulated by her father and the technocrat Edgar Warren to train greenfingers 'recruits' as part of their devastating plan to melt the ice caps and divert the plundered resources to a terraforming Mars project.

Both novels dramatize the ways in which children in the twenty-first-century imagination continue to play a role in what Nick Lee calls a pervasive adult survival fantasy in which children serve as the material from which the future will be built (2013: 4). Environmental management and parental care alike align in these scenarios, making the future into a control society. Evoking Deleuze's concept of the 'control society' (1992), Morton suggests that environmental politics that aim at eradicating uncertainty and ensuring stability would create a 'monstrous situation' that prioritized predictability and efficiency (2018: 11). This is enacted by the ARK government through their creation of a surveillance state to control resources – the young citizens – allocating them into strict social categories and monitoring their daily behaviours with 'optical surveillance' and 'security and boundary controls' (Brahmachari 2019: 51). The greenfingers recruits are also subject to surveillance and must find ways to organize their uprising without alerting Dalex and Warren. This exposure of the management of the future as aiming at a control society chimes in with queer critiques of mainstream environmentalism's affective tendencies, in particular the critique of the sentimental appeal to the future through the image of a child, which Nicole Seymour states 'play[s] right into the hands of a corporate consortium' (Seymour 2018: 15). Elsewhere, she notes that concern for 'future generations' is common among the conservative right, expressed through a heterosexist reproductive rhetoric, suggesting that concern for the future can only emerge from family reproductivity (2013: 7). However, this same political agenda supports corporate and governmental disregard for the future and allows environmental degradation in the name of capital accumulation. The Freedom Fields Family, which is how it describes itself to recruits, exemplifies this situation, leveraging the heterosexist language of family (re)productivity at the same time as depleting natural resources. Fittingly, Freedom Fields is revealed to be the subsidiary of a bank, a 'technical services' company', and its promise of the 'very best future' for its recruits is merely a cover for the exploitation of young bodies in labour camps. Thus, Brahmachari reveals how, through reproductive futurism, the environmentalist objectification of children as objects of care coincides with a capitalist objectification of children and the land.

In both novels, reproductive futurism is shown to be capable of producing only impoverished climate futures that belie the flourishing embodied by plant life. Despite its mass conscription of child labour and the appropriation of land, the ARK government is only able to offer basic nutrition to its citizens, distributing paltry food parcel to 'Freedoms' like Nabil and his family. In *Green Rising*, the plan to use young people's vegetal power to melt the ice caps and divert the energy to Warren's Martian colony requires indentured labour and the impoverishment of many for the survival of a few. The control societies that emerge from reproductive futurism, then, figure the future as bare survival for most beings, with vegetal and human life alike subsisting only to ensure the smooth running what Marder calls the 'planetary factory' that is imagined by agroscientific regimes of extraction and exploitation (2013: 46). The exploitation of one resource – plants – via 'slavery as crops in production lines', neatly exemplified by Freedom Field's polytunnels, is already evident in contemporary attitudes and uses of vegetal life (Gagliano 2018: 25). *Green Rising* and *Where the River Runs Gold* make plain that these attitudes go hand in hand with a reproductive futurism that would put the imagined plenitude of the child into service, too, seeking to manage, control, and limit the growth of the future in one direction. This deliberately misunderstands the 'nutritional commonality' (Marder 2013: 46) of plant being, which Shifa's care for seeds and the greenfingers' symbiosis with various plant species represent. The agroscientific regimes of the novels thus reveal the 'ontic mistranslation of the ontological principles of infinite vegetal giving', extracting and impoverishing plant and human life alike (Marder 2013: 46).

The novels dramatize the urgent need to counter the impoverishment threatened by reproductive futurism with alternative relationships of care. Queering relationships of care, *Where the River Runs Gold* and *Green Rising* gesture to futures that develop more expansive ethics than those of the present. They first stage a disruption of reproductive futurism through the protagonists' refusal to play their part in the systems of production into which they are co-opted. Shifa defies the 'carers' at Pollination Farm and breaks the 'contract of care' signed by Nabil by leaving. Hester, too, realizes her father's 'care' is really a form of control, and she defies him by diverting Dalex resources to the uprising and initiating the lawsuit to expose his crimes. The disruption does not end with defiance, however, but involves the children remaking relationships of care and forging new, makeshift families as they eschew the ethics of care and posterity deployed by Dalex and Freedom Fields, a care that rewards individualism and self-advancement. The relationships formed in the novels are queer in multiple ways, resisting dominant constructions of the natural world as white and heterosexual as vegetal–human connections allow young people to explore new gender and sexual identities in *Green Rising*, or, else, forge alliances across racial and social boundaries in both novels. The relationships of care that emerge in these alliances are queer especially in the ways they cross-species boundaries and embrace the nutritional commonality of vegetal life in the sharing of empathies and bodily resources. In so doing they follow Seymour's description of queer environmentalism by 'transport[ing] the human closer to the nonhuman' (2013: 28). This commonality enacts a relational social ontology for a more-than-human world, echoing Maria Puig de la Bellacasa's elaboration of the 'disruptive' matter of care not as 'normative moral obligations but . . . about thick, impure, involvement in a world . . .a hands-on, ongoing process of re-creation of "as well as possible" relations and therefore one that requires a speculative opening about what a possible involves' (2017: 6). Puig de la Bellacasa's more-than-human care ethics make explicit how relationships of care pertain to the future as a site of possibility. The relationships of care forged by mycelial and root networks, by the alliances between humans, seeds, and trees, in both novels create space for possibility and for the unknowability of the future, leaving open the capacity for forming new connections and relationships of care with yet unknown beings. In reproductive futurism care is privatized, literally in the case of Freedom Fields, serving a constrained and tightly delineated future trajectory. In contrast, queer care is open and radically entangling as it proliferates in multiple directions towards the future.

Time as growth

Where the River Runs Gold and *Green Rising* play out future catastrophe scenarios not as game over narratives, then, but to speculate horizons of possibility and explore entangled temporalities in place of the notion of time as an arrow. This latter metaphor, which has dominated Western conceptions of temporality due to the idea of 'progress' that has attended thought since the seventeenth century (Jay Gould 1988: 12), is revealed by the novels as a failed myth. This is because, as discussed above, the promised progress is, really, the reproduction of the self-same conditions of the present, or, else, a telos that leads to disaster. Futurity as either stasis or eschatology is forestalled in both novels and, as in *The Last Zoo* and *Deeplight*, a precarious ongoingness emerges instead. Although Nabil fears Hurricane Chronos portends the end of time, a second hurricane at the end of the novel provides the opportunity for change implied in the name of the land he inhabits: 'Kairos'. Where Chronos is the name for the classical Greek personification of time both as cycle and sequence, Kairos designates time as rupture, the time for action. That 'Chronos' has become confused, from Renaissance depictions onwards with the Titan Cronus, who devoured his children, underscores the contrast evoked by Brahmachari between these modes of temporality. Chronos is time as progression, marked by clocks and seasons, or, else as the cycle of begetting and devouring to which all life is subject. Kairos names time as disruption, as Event, in Alain Badiou's sense of the word. That is, the Event emerges out of an intervention, a change in the rules, a revolution that recasts the situation anew (Badiou 2005: 202). Kairos thus implies that the future can be otherwise to the present and offers a vision of time as ontoethics.

Green Rising also emphasizes this modality of time as action, refusing the inevitability of game over climate futures. Reflecting on the uprising, the activists realize 'how close they had been to disaster' and the 'terrible' ramifications if they hadn't 'acted just in time' (James 2021: 369). These are stories about what could happen, of course, and so conceive of the future as the realm of the conditional. They do so by working backward from extrapolation, explicitly commenting on present-day political and material realities. This disrupts a notion of time as an arrow flowing from the past into the future and accords with a non-deterministic conception of temporality. Latour identifies just such a temporality in his description of the Anthropocene, declaring that materiality is produced by a flow of time that works backwards from the future to the present (2014: 14). This is echoed in Elizabeth Grosz's reading of Darwin, which suggests that temporality just is materiality, that time is instantiated not by the measure of clocks or the turning of the seasons, 'not reducible to the spatial and the countable', but embodied in the dynamic forces of material becoming and evolution (2004: 127). This means that the 'past and the present are rendered provisional in light of the force of the future' (Grosz 2004: 7). The provisionality and contingency of the now is typified by vegetal life, which always occupies a middle rather than a beginning or an end, a middle from which it grows rhizomatically and 'from which it overspills' (Marder 2013: 63; Deleuze 1987: 21). The rhizomatic overspilling of vegetal life allows for the imagining of climate futures via a non-linear, entangled temporality. This flows not from the past, nor does the future emerge ex nihilo to determine the present. Shifa's seeds provide a good example of this idea since they contain within them latent possibilities from an ecological past, as well as carrying historical and ancestral associations. When Shifa scatters the seeds on the wind they enact what Sheldon calls a 'dispersion', an opportunity for the coalescence of new relationships and lines of growth (Sheldon 2016: 51). This is temporality as organic life, a movement of growth and transmutation that activates latent possibilities via creative leaps and ruptures.

Conceiving of time as growth, as does Grosz in her synthesis of Darwin and Nietzsche, implies that temporality entails the transformability of living systems via the dynamic interaction of variation, replication, and adaptation (2004: 19–20). Grosz's elaboration of temporality is also an entangled one, in which the futural direction of growth is not determined by past conditions, though not entirely adrift from them, and in which the force of the future ensures that 'life is always changing, always overcoming itself' (2004: 9). Time as proliferation and profusion rather than mere reproduction is typified in plant life. James offers an image of this in her description of a forest that the greenfingers grow outside the Dalex training centre in Texas. An entire ecosystem appears overnight: 'a real, actual forest where there had only been lawn and scrubland. The building had been swallowed by climbing plants . . . a canopy of oaks, elms and orange trees stretched above lush undergrowth' (2021: 87). Accidentally awakening 'everything lying dormant in the ground', the greenfingers activate the latent potential of material conditions, finding in the past of a living system the resources for what Grosz describes the 'unravelling of the givenness of the present' (James 2021: 87; Grosz 2004: 253). That the forest takes over the Dalex site is particularly apt given how the corporation seeks to use the greenfingers to advance its capitalist agenda. In fact, the conflict between Dalex and the greenfingers points to the ways in which the latter embody temporality in the sense described by Grosz. Carrying a mutation in the human genome, the greenfingers exemplify Darwin's point that 'self-overcoming is incessantly at work in the life of the species' (Grosz 2004: 89). Their activism, which is levelled against Dalex's environmental destruction, likewise dramatizes Grosz's elaboration of Darwin that 'politics is an attempt to mobilize these possibilities for self-overcoming in individuals and groups' (2004: 89).

The forward trajectory induced by growing, living systems ensures a temporality in which 'the pull of the future exerts a primary force' (Grosz 2004: 90). This force of the future is also an openness in that it is 'relatively uncontained by the past' (Grosz 2004: 90). Coccia echoes Grosz's description of temporality, emphasizing the temporal movement of vegetal life towards 'inconceivable' futures (2019: 109). As discussed, this unknowability of the future, as instantiated in vegetal growth, is something that must be cultivated to imagine climate futures beyond the replication of the self-same conditions that have led to destruction in our present. Shifa's dispersal of her seed packet dramatizes this cultivation of openness to the unknown. Unlike the planting that occurs in the regimented polytunnels operated by Freedom Fields, there is no knowing where and how Shifa's seeds will grow, nor what rhizomatic connections they might establish. That Shifa throws the seeds into the wind also demonstrates Grosz's suggestion that time progresses via leaps and events, that time is the production of difference brought about by a change to a system. In Grosz's terminology, events are 'ruptures, nicks, which flow from causal connections in the past but which, in their unique combinations and consequences, generate unpredictability' (2004: 8). Hurricane Chronos is one such event, figured as a catastrophe that, in Curry's terms, radically ruptures cultural norms and leads to the emergence of the oppressive ARK regime (Curry 2013: 20) The second hurricane provides an opportunity to change the system again, and, in its wake, more generous and inclusive modes of society emerge. This is not, as discussed, the emergence of a new world order ex nihilo, of course, but the activation of past and present possibilities, which is precisely how the Darwinian motor of life operates. As Grosz suggests, 'only if the present presents itself as fractured, as cracked by the interventions of the past and the promise of the future, can the new be invented, welcomed and affirmed' (2004: 261). The cracks are already there in Kairos City, figured in the gap in the hording that hides Nabil and Shifa's precious Flower Tracks, where they nurture wildflowers in defiance of ARK policies, and in the partially covered door to Lona's walled orchard, for which Shifa finds the key, and, so, escapes Pollination Farm.

If time moves forward via the unpredictability generated by events, if life grows out of cracks in the ground of the past, evolving through mutations in the system, then fitness, in the sense of survival of the fittest, must be understood, as Grosz insists, 'as an openness to the unknown' (2004: 47). This is precisely what the greenfingers embody in *Green Rising*. The ways in which they develop their powers and capacities in light of the events of the novel demonstrate their 'capacity to withstand the unexpected' and suggest that they represent the self-overcoming that is the movement of life (Grosz 2004: 47). The greenfingers thus offer an imaginative figuration of what Grosz, following Nietzsche, calls the 'untimely'. The untimely goes beyond the human, unhinging both progress and continuity with a leap into the unknown (Grosz 2004: 98). The untimely is not an ultrahuman conception of the future, but a figuration life as 'active enough to withstand the drive of the present to similarity, resemblance, or repetition' (Grosz 2004: 11). Events induce the untimely, represented in the novel by the toxic effects of Dalex's geo-engineering scheme and its transmutation of the human genome. The appearance of the greenfingers via this event accords with Darwin's account of life as 'becoming other'; the greenfingers are, literally, 'a species that does not yet exist' (Grosz 2004: 98). In Sheldon's terms, the greenfingers embody 'the mutational in the reproductive' that is foreclosed by reproductive futurism (2016: 6). While Dalex want to capitalize on this mutation and make the greenfingers 'subservient to the requirements of the present', the greenfingers resist, revealing that 'utility cannot make the new' and that the untimely is the obverse of the useful (Grosz 2004: 104, 105). If the greenfingers' 'powers' offer a vision of Nietzsche's will to power, as it is elaborated in Grosz's work, they do so in a way that reveal the will to power as a chaotic distribution of force, a push towards disequilibrium, which is, as Sheldon contends, the condition for the creativity of life (Sheldon 2016: 46). This disequilibrium aims at biological and political destabilization, enabling the greenfingers to bring about a 'different mode of organization' (Grosz 2004: 127). This begins to emerge in the closing pages of the novel, through descriptions of the changes to social, economic, and political models that occur in the wake of the uprising (Grosz 2004: 127). The greenfingers' transformative effects on the biosphere demonstrate the creativity of life and the impossibility of stasis when time is figured as life. As untimely beings, the greenfingers puncture the idea that ecology, or the state of nature, is that which tends towards balance and stasis.

Conclusion

Throughout this chapter I have explored vegetal being as figured in climate fiction as a mode of entanglement. Vegetal being exemplifies Ingold's notion of life as the 'entwining of lines', instantiated in *Green Rising* and *Where the River Runs Gold* as roots, hyphae, branches, and creepers (Ingold 2015: 3). As Ingold states, 'when everything tangles with everything else, the result is . . . a meshwork' (2015: 3). Entering this meshwork as imagined by the novels, I have traced the lines of growth and interdependencies that emerge from vegetal–human phenomena, including genetic symbiosis between these modes of life, their metaphorical and creative affinities, and their political alliances. As in the other versions of entanglement explored in this study, the result is the dissolution of the myth of a bounded human subjectivity, along with anthropocentric concepts such as selves, organism, and environment. What emerges in their place is a thick web of relations that require radically different conceptions of agency and politics. Foremost, the figurations of vegetal life in these novels are of animate and intentional beings, everything but that which the adjective 'vegetative' describes. As Marder explains, plant being relates 'the fullness and exuberance of life, vigour and brimming energy' (2013: 20). Where Western philosophy has ignored this vigour, YA Fantastika renders it vividly. In so doing, the novels couple the need to emancipate vegetal life from extractive agroscientific capitalist systems of (re)production with the need to reimagine the ways in which children have become freighted with the responsibility of ecological restoration, have become salvific figures in environmentalism, and, so, objectified as a resource out of which the future will be built. The novels also reveal the material continuity between organism and environment, the organic and the social, and the botanical and political. These are dark matters because making porous the boundaries between species, kingdoms, and domains of life entails encountering an uncanny familiarity and a disappropriation of the notion of a human 'self'. Moreover, despite their hopeful and emancipatory messages, *Where the River Runs Gold* and *Green Rising* negotiate the dark matter that is the uncertainty of the future of climate change. Whether we name this era the Anthropocene or the Planthropocene, the future is rendered radically unknowable. Epistemological or moral certainties only serve to impoverish our imaginaries. Time is not a smooth progression from the past through the present and into the future, but instantiated in the eruptions and ruptures of growth, a movement that entangles the lines of life in an ever more intimate meshwork.

6

Postscript

Thoughts on the reading experiment

Throughout this book I have described Fantastika as an explicitly eco-ethical mode of literature. In so doing I have avoided presenting a synoptic selection of the diverse works and genres that might be gathered under the umbrella term, nor have I attempted to make sweeping conclusions about the mode as a whole. Instead, I have explored situated diffractive readings of a necessarily idiosyncratic selection of contemporary novels written for young audiences. In so doing, I do not deny other possible arrangements or readings of texts. Doubtless, the literatures of Fantastika might be deployed to serve other purposes, political uses, and readings. The word 'reading' here refers both to criticism as an interpretive act, which selects its corpus, theoretical coordinates, ideological position, and aims at a conclusion about all three, but also to the act of deciphering the information displayed on apparatus in practical laboratory experiments. In both cases there is a joining-together and cutting apart of materiality, a slicing up of the world to produce some new phenomena from which knowledge might emerge. As I suggest in Chapters 1 and 3, however, the readings provided by the instruments we choose, whether these be critical toolkits or measuring apparatus, (re)produce only a portion of the world and cannot provide a direct window to objective truth.

My diffractive reading of Fantastika acknowledges these onto-epistemic-ethical complexities, and assembles, via a series of inclusions and exclusions, texts, approaches, genres, contexts, and imaginative horizons. The result of the experiment is a phenomenon I call 'dark matter'. Dark matter is the material-semiotic stuff of Fantastika that reveals the ethical difficulties and imperatives that emerge from the entanglements that compose our realities. Dark matter is the storyable stuff of the world that is (re)(con)figured through fiction and feeds speculation both about what is (ontology) and what might be (ontoethics). Dark matter is a way of imagining the complex interdependencies and webs of relation that comprise ecological being, immersion, and embeddedness, a way of tracing the entangled ontogeny (becoming) of more-than-human worlds, which, of course, enfold what we call the human. It is dark because it is difficult, and asks us to confront precarity and vulnerability, both our own, and that which we impose on others. It is dark because it is always partially occluded, as are all things-in-phenomena, and to encounter it requires a degree of negative capability, naivety, and the abandonment of a quest for epistemological certainties which would foreclose the future and constrain possibility within the light of the already known. In this sense, then, dark matter suggests that any experimental arrangement, whether it is carried out in a laboratory or the library, will always be partial and unfinished.

To summarize the conclusions of this study would be to offer a false sense of completion that the ontoethics of entanglement refuse. Instead, I turn back to Fantastika itself, letting one more actant into my experimental arrangement to serve as substitute for a 'final' reading. The passage below is from Juliette Forrest's *Twister* (2019), a children's gothic fantasy novel that draws on folklore influences from Scotland and the Southern United States. It tells the story of a young girl, the eponymous Twister, who embarks on a journey to find her missing father, entering the heart of a dense forest to seek the witch that lives there, and discovers her own shamanic powers. In this scene, Twister channels the soul of the forest as she fights a fire that threatens to destroy it:

> Just as my heart was sinking, a green bubble flew past a wooden beam, zoomed towards me and disappeared straight into my pocket . . . all of a sudden, I smelled soil and fizzy-fruit and warm flowers and rotting leaves and mossy-stone and brown rivers and mud and stagnant puddles. Pain jabbed at my muscles and my bones creaked. I lifted my head up. My body was turning into a mass of green foliage. The necklace must have taken the wrong soul. How could a bunch of leaves put a raging fire out? I was agile. Nimble. Supple. I . . . moved in all different directions at the same time. I held treasures and riches and cures. They were deep, dark secrets locked within me waiting to be discovered. Folks thought I was savage and scary and poisonous and death, but really, I was life itself. (Forrest 2018: 214–15)

As this scene suggests, *Twister* gestures to many of the themes and concerns I have identified throughout this book as germane to the dark matter of Fantastika: an engagement with an animated landscape, which discloses itself through vibrant artefacts, like Twister's necklace; the staging of encounters with the ordinarily occulted natures of reality that gesture not to noumena in its thoroughly Kantian sense, but certainly to the nature of things-in-themselves that escape the totalizing tendency of human perception; the evocation of animist cosmologies, often via syncretic compositions that draw on folklore and myth from different geographical and cultural locations; an explicit acknowledgement of the porous nature of the borders that define and divide human selves from more-than-human others, including animal and vegetal life, and the dark matter of relationships between humans and others, including their destructive legacies and our concomitant feelings of vulnerability when confronted with ecological belonging. The novel is not about climate change, but the consuming fire that threatens Twister's forest serves as an apt reminder of ecological crisis. Like *Akata Witch* and other novels discussed in the study, *Twister* pits its protagonist against those who commit destructive acts of nefarious, selfish, or extractive 'magic', confronting the persistent denial of the relations of reciprocity and interdependence that comprise ecological realities. Here, the fire provides a fitting figuration of the ideologies of colonial and neocolonial capitalism, which continue to slash and burn even as young people rally the opposition. In this reading of *Twister*, I contend that the realities of mass extinction and global heating are fundamental concerns of contemporary Fantastika and, so, echo Mark Bould's claim that the Anthropocene is the unconscious of the art and literature of our time (2021: 15). In repeating Bould's claim, I am not suggesting that Fantastika written for young audiences reveals the return of a repressed for all humanity, but rather that its ontoethical propositions resound with urgency in the present moment, joining other counternarratives from around the globe to provide a rebuke to the status quo that persists in the West. As I have argued, following John Clute, Fantastika as a European literature has, since its earliest days, been a site for the exploration of dark matters that the Enlightenment sought to banish, often to the realm of children's stories where it might be safely quarantined. Now more than ever it is imperative to delve into the murk and examine the destructive legacy of Enlightenment philosophy and science.

Dark matter congeals across diverse strata, suggesting that 'materiality' does not accord with a monist notion of substance; it is not a homogenous lump of background 'stuff'. As Vetlesen argues, the new materialisms all-too-often carry out their investigations in the realm of an unspecified 'materiality' without attending to the tangible materials that comprise the world, thereby unconsciously repeating the mistakes of mechanistic thought (2019: 227). Ingold, too, rejects a 'perverse' academic discussion of 'materiality' in favour of paying attention to the specific material composition of the inhabited world (2011: 20). The novels discussed in this study engage in the kind of close-up encounter with materials Ingold and Vetlesen suggest is necessary, depositing their characters within different strata of dark matter. These include delving into the underside and insides of specific geographical landscapes, being dispersed between earth and sky as hybrid ecological beings, immersed in ocean depths to confront human origins in a more-than-human evolutionary matrix, or, elsewhere, tangled up with vegetal and fungal ecosystems. In all the books considered in this study, the environment, that which has been nominated the realm of 'nature', or, the background and container of human life, is not a spatial designation but, actually, the myriad other beings with which humans make the world. The environment is not a location, but the weave of relationships that produce and reproduce being, and which continually unfold in surprising ways.

Since dark matter materializes in diverse and tangled ways, it requires diverse theoretical paradigms and philosophies to think with. Throughout the book I have turned to different approaches that move beyond philosophical dualism, anthropocentrism, and other modalities that insist on bounded individualism and ontological divides. These include the philosophies grouped under the umbrella term 'speculative realism', which address the 'gap' instituted by Cartesian and Kantian philosophies and aim at accounting for the material being of more-than-human 'objects' such that the distinction between subject and object is radically loosened; a turn to the notion of the 'occult', to that which is hidden in our relationship with, and perceptions of, the world; respect for what has been called 'animism', which names diverse cosmologies that provide an alternative to the extractive metaphysics cultivated by the European Enlightenment; theories of consciousness that complicate mind-body dualism and insist upon the imbrication of mind, brain, and environment; evolutionary biology and related theories of information that accord a causal role to intentionality, meaning, and other extramaterial phenomena in the becoming of the world; the aesthetics and ethics of the weird and the uncanny, which together help elucidate (dis)connecting feelings of ecological belonging; and plant-thinking, which offers an immersive concept of being-in-the-world that might help cultivate collective modes of politics. In different ways, these approaches emphasize being as life lived in open communion with, and responsive to, the call of the other, offering variations on what I have referred to throughout the book as a non-anthropocentric Levinasian ethics. These are ethics as ontology, determining being and becoming from their very inception as always already entangled with, and responsible to, myriad others. Throughout the book I have also explored the problem of climate futures, emphasizing the imbrication of materiality and temporality. Fantastika does the important ontoethical work of imagining the future as otherwise to the present, negotiating the need to account for the past and work from present conditions without capitulating to determinism or game over narratives. Fantastika also makes space for the eruption of the new while countering a tendency to ultrahumanist transcendence or the deferral of action onto future generations, both of which are common in environmental rhetoric. Again, dark matter suggests that the problem of the future is not one that has a ready solution, nor any singular metaphysics or epistemology that will make it easy to comprehend. Indeed, our desire to make the future comprehensible is part of the present problem and the dark matter of Fantastika suggests it ought to be resisted.

Resisting epistemological certainty might seem like a particular challenge for children's literature, which has historically been the site for the inculcation of moral values aimed at socialising young people, or, else, seen as a therapeutic expression of the experience of 'maturation', a very anthropocentric concern. Dark matter eschews these ideas of the value of children's literature, pointing instead to narratives that complicate moral problems, conceive of subjectivity as entangled with more-than-human others, and that resist straightforward endings or lineal conceptions of 'growing up'. This broad assessment notwithstanding, I make no claims here about the whole corpus of children's literature from the past two decades. Nor do I suggest these concerns and narrative impulses find expression only in writing for children and young people. Examples of similar dark matter could no doubt be found in Fantastika written for adult audiences and there are likely numerous children's books which would provide no insights at all. In this sense, I reject any easy division between the modes of writing and, so, the ghettoization of children's and YA literatures in the sense of it having its own set of discrete concerns, ethics, and aesthetics. This is an explicit response to Clute's history of Fantastika: dark matter ought not to be quarantined to children's literature. However, I do contend that the issues I have identified here as dark matter pertain most urgently to young people, and I have sought to find narratives that explore the issue of ecology and the future of climate change in ways that puncture some of the assumptions, values, and rhetoric of mainstream environmentalism and other hegemonic cultural discourses about childhood.

There is, of course, much more work to do and other modes and genres of Fantastika not considered here. I have left out, for example, animal stories, horror, historical fiction, and indigenous futurisms to name but a few of the different genres under the umbrella of Fantastika through which contemporary writers are exploring ecology, climate change, and climate futures. There is also an increasing number of young people writing on these issues for themselves, with creative nonfiction, autobiography, diary, and essay writing becoming popular among young activists and naturalists. Works by Dara McAnulty, whose *Diary of a Young Naturalist* (2020) won the Wainwright prize in 2020, Jamie Margolin, whose book *Youth to Power* (2020) describes her experience of founding the climate action organisation, Zero Hour, Bella Lack, who has collected diverse young voices from the front lines of climate action in *Children of the Anthropocene* (2022), and Vanessa Nakate, whose essays on the African context of climate change in *A Bigger Picture* (2022) offer an important rebuke to contemporary depictions of activism as white and European, should be read by adult critics and understood as part of the ways in which young people are imagining, and bringing into being, the future. Fantastika is not only fiction: it names a plethora of creative engagements with the world. Likewise, young writing on climate change is far from being only a set of policy demands or moralising speeches about the need for action: it is about finding ways to explore better modes of being-with and being-in the world.

Given the ways in which children and young people are finding their own ways of expressing their speculations about dark matter, my contribution here that focuses on adult authored works can only be part of the story. Nonetheless, there are important ethical imperatives that have emerged from my analysis. They concern the intimate matter of dwelling and homeliness, of how to live as part of a more-than-human collective and foster solidarity, and the troubling obligations and vulnerability this entails. It has sought to highlight the provisionality and contingency of entangled lives and subjectivities, to draw attention to the difficulties, but also the possibilities, that occur as a condition of precarity and ongoingness. We are not heading into a safe future, nor into a world where life will be simple, ethical choices easy, and relationships and obligations between people and species smooth, nor even always comprehensible. The positive connotation of the word ecology, which is so often evoked in utopian discussions of ecological embeddedness or environmental connectedness, is derived from its etymological root, found in the Greek word for dwelling, *oikos*. Dark Fantastika, as I have argued throughout this book, reveals, in contrast, earthly dwellings to be shot through with feelings of estrangement, and belonging to be bound up with uncanniness. These tensions are made more urgent by revelations of climate chaos and mass extinction, but they were already a condition of material being. Two of the books I have discussed here have explicitly evoked the biblical image of the ark, a vehicle or vessel that might provide passage to a safe future. In both cases, the figure of the ark has been compromised and disrupted, unable to function as a life raft for the coming deluge. Though it eschews both eschatological and utopian imaginings, I do not think that Fantastika is pessimistic. It does, however, underscore the sense that there are no easy answers and that the ethical propositions I have identified here as dark matter are not road maps for transformative change, even if radical action is taken now. Such is the situation given 'the radically unknowable future conjured up by the Anthropocene' (Johns-Putra 2019: 31). Whatever happens with the present situation of the climate crisis, however, there is ample material to be found in the dark matter of children's Fantastika for reimagining the world and remaking the future. These are ongoing experiments that invite readers, critics, and writers to become part of the entanglement.

Notes

Introduction

1 Wave-particle complementarity insists that complete knowledge of phenomena requires a description of both wave and particle properties. The behaviour of light and electrons, for example, is sometimes wave-like and sometimes particle-like, depending on the experimental arrangement. An observed, or detected, electron is found in its localized particle form, but when not measured it is in its wave-like form. This form is described mathematically by an equation called a 'wave function' that determines the probability of finding the particle at any given point within the system. The uncertainty principle states that exact and simultaneous values cannot be assigned to both the position and momentum of particles in a physical system. As these very short descriptions suggest, the ideas that form the Copenhagen Interpretation of quantum physics insist upon the fact that physical reality neither takes a determinate form outside of its entanglement in observation, nor does it materialize deterministically.

2 A key moment in the confirmation of quantum non-locality is the 1982 Aspect experiment. See: Aspect, Alain, Dalibard, Jean and Roger, Gérard. 1982. 'Experimental Test of Bell's Inequalities Using Time-Varying Analyzers', *Physical Review, Letters* 49 (25): 1804–7. Some of the 'loopholes' of Aspect's experiment have recently been closed, further establishing the principle. See Hensen et al. 2015. 'Loophole-free Bell inequality violation using electron spins separated by 1.3 kilometres', *Nature* 526 (7575): 682–6.

Chapter 3

1 See, for example, the *Black Mirror* special episode, 'White Christmas', which first aired in the UK in 2014 on Channel 4.

2 Cybernetics refers to an interdisciplinary field recognizing as an object of study 'a unified set of problems centring about communication, control, statistical mechanics', or the study of 'control and communication . . . whether in the machine or the animal' (Wiener [1948] 1965: 11).

3 The phrase 'hard problem', also mentioned in Chapter 1, was coined by David Chalmers, who states that 'the emergence of experience goes beyond what can be

derived from physical theory' (1995: 208). Those seeking a unified approach include scholars working in the field of 'biosemiotics', such as Don Favareau and Terrence Deacon already cited here, but also a range of thinkers from philosophical and scientific fields seeking to establish 'consciousness science as a general discipline' (Pereira Jr. and Lehmann 2013: 1).

4 A golem is an animated anthropomorphic being from Jewish folklore. It is typically created from inanimate matter such as clay. Moshe Idel notes that the word 'golem' was used in medieval writing to denote amorphous, unformed material (1990: 296).

References

Abram, D. (2011), *Becoming Animal: An Earthly Cosmology*, London: Vintage.

Adeyemi, T. (2018), *Children of Blood and Bone*, New York: Henry Holt & Co.

Aguirre, Anthony, Brendan Foster and Zeeya Merali (2018), 'Introduction', in A. Aguirre, B. Foster and Z. Merali (eds), *Wandering Towards a Goal: How Can Mindless Mathematical Laws Give Rise to Aims and Intention?*, 1–5, New York: Springer.

Alaimo, S. (2010), *Bodily Natures: Science, Environment and the Material Self*, Bloomington, IN: Indiana University Press.

Alaimo, S. (2012), 'States of Suspension: Trans-Corporeality at Sea', *Interdisciplinary Studies in Literature and Environment*, 19 (3): 476–93.

Alaimo, S. (2016), *Exposed: Environmental Politics and Pleasures in Posthuman Times*, Minneapolis, MN: University of Minnesota Press.

Alam, S. (2008), 'Majority World: Challenging the West's Rhetoric of Democracy', *Amerasia Journal*, 34: 87–98.

Albrecht, G. and G. Van Horn (2016), 'Exiting the Anthropocene and Entering the Symbiocene', *Center for Humans and Nature* (blog). 24 May. Available online: https://humansandnature.org/exiting-the-anthropocene-and-entering-the-symbiocene/ (accessed 12 September 2022).

Alder, E. (2017), 'Through Oceans Darkly: Sea Literature and the Nautical Gothic', *Gothic Studies*, 19 (2): 1–15.

Alder, E. and J. Bavidge (2020), 'Ecocriticism and the Genre', in C. Bloom (ed.), *The Palgrave Handbook of Contemporary Gothic*, 225–42, Cham, Switzerland: Springer.

Al-Khalili, J. and J. McFadden (2014), *Life on the Edge: The Coming of Age of Quantum Biology*, London: Transworld Publishers.

Arnold, P. (2018), 'Foreword', in G. Harvey and M. Astor-Aguilera (eds), *Rethinking Relations and Animism. Personhood and Materiality*, xii–xvi, London and New York: Routledge.

Astor-Aguilera, M. and G. Harvey (2018), 'Introduction: We Have Never Been Individuals', in G. Harvey and M. Astor-Aguilera (eds), *Rethinking Relations and Animism. Personhood and Materiality*, 1–12, London and New York: Routledge.

Badiou, A. (2005), *Being and Event*, translated by Oliver Feltham, London: Continuum.

Ball, P. (2018), *Beyond Weird: Why Everything You Thought You Knew about Quantum Physics is Different*, Chicago, IL: The University of Chicago Press.

Barad, K. (2007), *Meeting the Universe Halfway: Quantum Physics and the Entanglement of Matter and Meaning*, Durham, NC: Duke University Press.

Barad, K. (2014), 'Diffracting Diffraction: Cutting Together-Apart', *parallax*, 20 (3): 168–87.

Bateson, G. (1979), *Mind and Nature: A Necessary Unity*, New York: E. P. Dutton.

Beerling, D. J. (2007), *The Emerald Planet: How Plants Changed Earth's History*, Oxford: Oxford University Press.

Beever, J. (2020), 'Introduction', in J. Beever (ed.), *Philosophy, Film and the Dark Side of Interdependence*, 1–8, Lanham, MD: Lexington Books.

Bennett, J. (2001), *The Enchantment of Modern Life*, Princeton, NJ and Oxford: Princeton University Press.

Bennett, J. (2004), 'The Force of Things: Steps toward an Ecology of Matter', *Political Theory*, 32 (3): 347–72.

Bennett, J. (2010), *Vibrant Matter: A Political Ecology of Things*, Durham, NC: Duke University Press.

Black Mirror: White Christmas. (2014) [TV Programme] Channel 4. 16 December.

Blackmore, S. (2005), *Consciousness: A Very Short Introduction*, Oxford: Oxford University Press.

Boden, M. A. (2018), *Artificial Intelligence. A Very Short Introduction*, Oxford: Oxford University Press.

Bohm, D. (1980), *Wholeness and the Implicate Order*, London: Routledge.

Botting, F. (2012), 'More Things: Horror, Materialism and Speculative Weirdism', *Horror Studies*, 3 (2): 281–303.

Bould, M. (2021), *The Anthropocene Unconscious: Climate Catastrophe Culture*, London: Verso.

Bowman, B. and C. Germaine (2021), 'Not (just) a Protest: The Youth Strike for Climate as Cultural Exchange and Collaborative Text', in M. Mikulewicz and N. J. W. Crawford (eds), *British Council Cultural Relations Collection 2021*. Available online: www.britishcouncil.org/research-policy-insight/researchseries/culturalrelations (accessed 12 September 2022).

Braddock, C. (2017), 'Introduction: Animism and Animacies', in C. Braddock (ed.), *Animism in Art and Performance*, 1–22, Basingstoke: Palgrave Macmillan.

Braddock, C. (2019), 'Entangled Animisms: Whakaaro and Dialogue in the Artwork of Shannon Te Ao', *Performance Research*, 24 (6): 69–78.

Bradford, C., K. Mallan, J. Stephens and R. McCallum (2008), *New World Orders in Contemporary Children's Literature: Utopian Transformations*, Basingstoke: Palgrave Macmillan.

Brahmachari, S. (2019a), *Where the River Runs Gold*, London: Orion.

Brahmachari, S. (2019b), 'Where Does the River Run Gold for Children's Rights?', *Sita Brahmachari* (blog). 17 November. Available online: http://sitabrahmachari.blogspot.com/2019/11/where-does-river-run-gold-for-childrens.html (accessed 12 September 2022).

Braidotti, R. (2002), *Metamorphoses: Towards a Materialist Theory of Becoming*, Cambridge: Polity.

Braidotti, R. (2018), 'A Theoretical Framework for the Critical Posthumanities', *Theory, Culture & Society*, 36 (6): 31–61.

Brassier, R. (2014), 'Postscript', in P. Wolfendale (ed.), *Object Oriented Philosophy: The Noumenon's New Clothes*, 409–21, Falmouth: Urbanomic.

Breu, C. (2016), 'Why Materialisms Matter', *Symplokē*, 24 (1–2): 9–26.

Brown, P. (2016), *The Wild Robot*, London: Piccadilly Press.

Bryant, L., N. Srnicek and G. Harman (2011), The Speculative Turn: Continental Materialism and Realism, Melbourne: re.press.

Burgess, M. (2018), *The Lost Witch*, London: Andersen Press.

Butler, C. (2006), *Four British Fantasists: Place and Culture in the Children's Fantasies of Penelope Lively, Alan Garner, Diana Wynne Jones, and Susan Cooper*, Lanham, ML: The Scarecrow Press.

Butler, J. (2020), *The Force of Nonviolence*, London: Verso.

Byatt, A. S. (2003), 'Harry Potter and the Childish Adult', *The New York Times*, 7 July.

Carroll, J. S. (2011), *Landscape in Children's Literature*, London: Routledge.

Chalmers, D. J. (1996), *The Conscious Mind: In Search of a Fundamental Theory*, Oxford: Oxford University Press.

Chang, A. Y. (2019), *Playing Nature. Ecology in Video Games*, Minneapolis, MN: University of Minnesota Press.

Clegg, B. (2019), *Dark Matter & Dark Energy: The Hidden 95% of the Universe*, London: Icon Books.

Clute, J. (2016a), *Stay*, London: Gollancz.

Clute, J. (2016b), *Pardon This Intrusion*, London: Hachette.

Coccia, E. (2019), *The Life of Plants: A Metaphysics of Mixture*, Cambridge: Polity.

Cohen, J. J. (2015), *Stone. An Ecology of the Inhuman*, Minneapolis, MN: University of Minnesota Press.

Coleman, S. (2009), 'Mind under Matter', in D. Skrbina (ed.), *Mind that Abides: Panpsychism in the New Millennium*, 83–108, Amsterdam: John Benjamins Publishing Company.

Coole, D. and S. Frost (2010), 'Introducing the New Materialisms', in D. Coole and S. Frost (eds), *New Materialisms: Ontology, Agency, Politics*, 1–46, Durham, NC: Duke University Press.

Cooper, S. (1994), *The Dark Is Rising*, London: Random House.

Crutzen, P. J. (2002), 'Geology of Mankind', *Nature*, 415: 23.

Crutzen, P. J. and E. F. Stoermer (2000), 'The Anthropocene', *Global Change Newsletter*, 41: 17–18.

Curry, A. (2013), *Environmental Crisis in Young Adult Fiction: A Poetics of Earth*, Basingstoke: Palgrave Macmillan.

Curry, A. (2014), 'Traitorousness, Invisibility and Animism: An Ecocritical Reading of Nnedi Okorafor's West African Novels for Children', *International Research in Children's Literature*, 7 (1): 37–47.

Curry, A. (2017), 'A Question of Scale: Zooming Out and Zooming In On Feminist Ecocriticism', in C. Beauvais and M. Nikolajeva (eds), *The Edinburgh Companion to Children's Literature*, 70–8, Edinburgh: Edinburgh University Press.

Darwin, C. (2008), *On the Origin of Species*, Oxford: Oxford University Press.

Davies, P. (2019), *The Demon in the Machine. How Hidden Webs of Information are Solving the Mystery of Life*, London: Penguin.

Deacon, T. W. (2011), *Incomplete Nature. How Mind Emerged from Matter*, New York and London: W. W. Norton.

DeLanda, M. (1995), 'The Geology of Morals: A Neomaterialist Interpretation', *Virtual Futures 95 Conference*, Warwick University, UK. 26 May. Available online: http://www.t0.or.at/delanda/geology.htm (accessed 12 September 2022).

DeLanda, M. (1997), *A Thousand Years of Nonlinear History*, New York: Swerve Editions.

DeLanda, M. (2006), *A New Philosophy of Society: Assemblage Theory and Social Complexity*, London: Continuum.

Deleuze, G. (1992), 'Postscript on the Societies of Control', *October*, 59: 3–7.

Deleuze, G. and F. Guattari (1987), *A Thousand Plateaus: Capitalism and Schizophrenia*, translated by Brian Massumi, Minneapolis, MN: University of Minnesota Press.

Deleuze, G. and F. Guattari (1996), *What Is Philosophy?*, New York: Columbia University Press.

Dennett, D. C. (1993), *Consciousness Explained*, London: Penguin.

Dennis, R. (2021), *Restoring the Wild: True Stories of Rewilding Britain's Skies, Woods and Waterways*, London: William Collins.

Descartes, R. (1968), *Discourse on Method and the Meditations*, translated with an introduction by F. E. Sutcliffe, London: Penguin.

Despret, V. (2004), 'The Body We Care for: Figures of Anthropo-zoo-genesis', *Body and Society*, 10 (2–3): 111–34.

Dillon, S. (2018), 'The Horror of the Anthropocene', *C21 Literature: Journal of 21st-Century Writings*, 6 (1): 1–25.

Dukić, V. and E. Morin (2017), 'Introduction: Continental Realism – Picking up the Pieces', in E. Morin (ed.), *Continental Realism and its Discontents*, 1–20, Edinburgh: Edinburgh University Press.

Edelglass, W., J. Hatley and C. Diehm (2012), 'Introduction: Facing Nature after Levinas', in W. Edelglass, J. Hatley and C. Diehm (eds), *Facing Nature. Levinas and Environmental Thought*, 1–10, Pittsburgh, PA: Duquesne University Press.

Edelman, L. (2004), *No Future: Queer Theory and the Death Drive*, Durham, NC: Duke University Press.

Edwards, J. and R. Graulund (2013), *Grotesque*, London: Routledge.

Egoff, S. A. (1981), *Thursday's Child: Trends and Patterns in Contemporary Children's Literature*, Chicago, IL: American Library Association.

Einstein, A., B. Podolsky and N. Rosen (1935), 'Can Quantum-Mechanical Description of Physical Reality be Considered Complete?', *Physical Review*, 47 (10): 777–80.

Elias, A. J. and C. Moraru (2015), 'Introduction: The Planetary Condition', in A. J. Elias and C. Moraru (eds), *The Planetary Turn: Relationality and Geoaesthetics in the Twenty-First Century*, xi–xxxvii, Evanston, IL: Northwestern University Press.

Esmonde, M. P. (1982), 'From Little Buddy to big Brother: The Icon of the Robot in Children's Science Fiction', in T. B. Dunn and R. D. Erlich (eds), *The Mechanical God: Machines in Science Fiction*, 85–100, London: Greenwood Press.

Estok, S. C. (2016), 'Ecomedia and Ecophobia', *Neohelicon*, 43 (1): 127–45.

Estok, S. C. (2018), *The Ecophobia Hypothesis*, New York: Routledge.

Estok, S. C. (2019), 'Theorising the EcoGothic', *Gothic Nature*, 1 (1): 34–53.

Favareau, D. (2010), 'Introduction: An Evolutionary History of Biosemiotics', in D. Favareau (ed.), *Essential Readings in Biosemiotics: Anthology and Commentary*, 1–80, New York: Springer.

Fisher, M. (2016), *The Weird and the Eerie*, London: Repeater Books.

Flanagan, V. (2014), *Technology and Identity in Young Adult Fiction. The Posthuman Subject*, Basingstoke: Palgrave Macmillan.

Flanagan, V. (2017), 'Posthumanism: Rethinking "The Human" in Modern Children's Literature', in C. Beauvais and M. Nikolajeva (eds), *The Edinburgh Companion to Children's Literature*, 29–41, Edinburgh: Edinburgh University Press.

Forrest, J. (2019), *Twister*, London: Scholastic.

Gagliano, M. (2018), *Thus Spoke the Plant*, Berkeley, CA: North Atlantic Books.

Garner, A. (2002), *The Weirdstone of Brisingamen*, London: Harper Collins.

Garner, A. (2006), *The Stone Book Quartet*, London: Harper Collins.

Garuba, H. (2003), 'Explorations in Animist Materialism: Notes on Reading/Writing African Literature, Culture, and Society', *Public Culture*, 15 (2): 261–86.

Gayton, S. (2019), *The Last Zoo*, London: Andersen Press.

Gefter, A. and C. Fuchs (2015), 'A Private View of Quantum Reality', *Quanta Magazine*. Available online: https://www.quantamagazine.org/quantum-bayesianism-explained-by-its-founder-20150604/ (accessed 12 September 2022).

Germaine Buckley, C. (2017), '"Do Panic. They're Coming": Remaking the Weird in Contemporary Children's Fiction', in A. Jackson (ed.), *New Directions in Children's Gothic: Debatable Lands*, 16–31, New York: Routledge.

Germaine Buckley, C. (2018), *Twenty-First-Century Children's Gothic: From the Wanderer to Nomadic Subject*, Edinburgh: Edinburgh University Press.

Germaine Buckley, C. (2020), 'Encounters with the "Hidden" World: Speculative Philosophy and Modern Children's Gothic', in C. Bloom (ed.), *The Palgrave Handbook of Contemporary Gothic*, 589–607, Basingstoke: Palgrave Macmillan.

Ghosh, A. (2016), *The Great Derangement: Climate Change and the Unthinkable*, Gurgaon: Allen Lane.

Gibson, P. and B. Brits (2018), 'Introduction: Covert Plants', in P. Gibson and B. Brits (eds), *Covert Plants: Vegetal Consciousness and Agency in an Anthropocentric World*, 11–21, Punctum Books.

Gilbert, S., J. Sapp and A. Tauber (2012), 'A Symbiotic View of Life: We Have Never Been Individuals', *Quarterly Review of Biology*, 87 (4): 325–41.

Glass, D. (2013), 'Global Warming: The Rise of "cli-fi"', *The Guardian*. 31 May. Available online: https://www.theguardian.com/books/2013/may/31/global-warning-rise-cli-fi (accessed 21 March 2022).

Godfrey-Smith, P. (1996), *Complexity and the Function of Mind in Nature*, Cambridge: Cambridge University Press.

Godfrey-Smith, P. (2016), *Other Minds: The Octopus and the Evolution of Intelligent Life*, London: William Collins.

Gould, S. J. (1988), *Time's Arrow, Time's Cycle. Myth and Metaphor in the Discovery of Geological Time*, London: Penguin.

Graeber, D. (2012), *Debt: The First 5000 Years*, New York: Melville House.

Green, W. H. (2001), 'King Thorin's Mines: The Hobbit as Victorian Adventure Novel', *Extrapolation*, 42 (1): 53–64.

Gribbin, J. (1984), *In Search of Schrödinger's Cat: Quantum Physics and Reality*, London: Black Swan Books.

Grosz, E. (2004), *The Nick of Time: Politics, Evolution and the Untimely*, Crows Nest: Allen and Unwin.

Grosz, E. (2017), *The Incorporeal. Ontology, Ethics, and the Limits of Materialism*, New York: Columbia University Press.

Hall, M. (2011), *Plants as Persons: A Philosophical Botany*, Albany, NY: SUNY Press.

Hallowell, I. (1960), 'Ojibwa Ontology, Behavior, and World View', in S. Diamond (ed), *Culture in History*, 19–52, New York: Columbia University Press.

Haraway, D. J. (1991), *Simians, Cyborgs and Women. The Reinvention of Nature*, New York: Routledge.

Haraway, D. J. (1992), 'The Promises of Monsters: A Regenerative Politics for Inappropriate/d Others', in L. Grossberg, C. Nelson and P. Treichler (eds), *Cultural Studies*, 295–337, New York: Routledge.

Haraway, D. J. (1997), *Modest_Witness@Second_Millennium.FemaleMan©_Meets_OncoMouseTM: Feminism and Technoscience*, New York: Routledge.

Haraway, D. J. (2008), *When Species Meet*, Minneapolis, MN: University of Minnesota Press.

Haraway, D. J. (2016), *Staying with the Trouble. Making Kin in the Chthulhucene*, Durham, NC: Duke University Press.

Hardinge, F. (2019), *Deeplight*, London: Macmillan.

Hardy, V. (2019), *Wildspark*, London: Scholastic.

Harman, G. (2009), *Prince of Networks: Bruno Latour and Metaphysics*, Melbourne: Re .press.

Harman, G. (2012), *Weird Realism: Lovecraft and Philosophy*, Winchester: Zero Books.

Harvey, G. (2014), 'Introduction', in G. Harvey (ed.), *The Handbook of Contemporary Animism*, 11–38, London and New York: Routledge.

Hau de no sau nee (1978) [1977], 'A Basic Call to Consciousness: The Hau de no sau nee Address to the Western World', in Akwesasne Notes (eds), *Basic Call to Consciousness*, Summertown, TN: Book Publishing Company.

Hofstadter, D. (2006), *I am a Strange Loop*, New York: Basic Books.

Hopkinson, N. (2004), 'Introduction', in N. Hopkinson and U. Mehan (eds), *So Long Been Dreaming: Postcolonial Science Fiction and Fantasy*, 10–12, Vancouver, BC: Arsenal Pulp Press.

Hornborg, A. (2006), 'Animism, Fetishism, and Objectivism as Strategies for Knowing (or Not Knowing) the World', *Ethnos*, 71 (1): 21–32.

Hunt, P. (1987), 'Landscapes and Journeys, Metaphors and Maps: The Distinctive Feature of English Fantasy', *Children's Literature Association Quarterly*, 16 (2): 11–14.

Hurley, K. (1996), *The Gothic Body: Sexuality, Materialism, and Degeneration at the Fin de Siècle*, Cambridge: Cambridge University Press.

Hutton, R. (2017), *The Witch*, New Haven, CT: Yale University Press.

Idel, M. (1990), *Golem: Jewish Magical and Mystical Traditions on the Artificial Anthropoid*, Albany, NY: SUNY Press.

Iovino, S. and S. Oppermann (2012), 'Material Ecocriticism: Materiality, Agency, and Models of Narrativity', *Ecozon@*, 3 (1): 75–91.

Iovino, S. and S. Oppermann (2014), 'Introduction: Stories Come to Matter', in S. Iovino and S. Oppermann (eds), *Material Ecocriticism*, 1–20, Bloomington, IN: Indiana University Press.

Ingold, T. (2000), *Perception of the Environment: Essays on Livelihood, Dwelling and Skill*, London: Routledge.

Ingold, T. (2006), 'Rethinking the Animate, Reanimating Thought', *Ethnos*, 71 (1): 9–20.

Ingold, T. (2011), *Being Alive*, London: Routledge.

Ingold, T. (2015), *The Life of Lines*, London: Routledge.

Ingold, T. (2021), *Correspondences*, Cambridge: Polity Press.

Jablonka, E. and M. J. Lamb (2014), *Evolution in Four Dimensions, Revised Edition: Genetic, Epigenetic, Behavioral, and Symbolic Variation in the History of Life*, Cambridge, MA: The MIT Press.

Jacques, Z. (2015), *Children's Literature and the Posthuman: Animal, Environment, Cyborg*, London: Routledge.

Jacques, Z. (2017), 'Animal Studies', in C. Beauvais and M. Nikolajeva (eds), *The Edinburgh Companion to Children's Literature*, 42–54, Edinburgh: Edinburgh University Press.

James, L. (2021a), *Green Rising*, London: Walker Books.

James, L. (2021b), 'Positivity in the Apocalypse: Can a Climate Fiction Novel Be Uplifting?', *Climate Fiction Writers League* (blog). 7 September. Available online: https://climatefictionwritersleague.substack.com/p/positivity-in-the-apocalypse-can (accessed 19 September 2022).

Jardine, R. (2010), *A History of Horror with Mark Gatiss*, BBC.

Johns-Putra, A. (2019), *Climate Change and the Contemporary Novel*, Cambridge: Cambridge University Press.

Jones, T. (2017), '"THIS HILL IS STILL DANGEROUS": Alan Garner's Weirdstone Trilogy—A Hauntology', in A. Jackson (ed.), *New Directions in Children's Gothic: Debatable Lands*, 176–88, London: Routledge.

Kelleher, M. and N. Okorafor (2019), 'Author Nnedi Okorafor Delivers Keynote Speech for HP LitFest 2019', *The Daily Campus*. 27 February. Available online: https://www.smudailycampus.com/ae/author-nnedi-okorafor-delivers-keynote-speech-for-hp-litfest-2019 (accessed 19 September 2022).

Kenny, P. (2018), *Tin*, Frome: Chicken House.

Kohn, E. (2013), *How Forests Think. Towards an Anthropology beyond the Human*, Berkeley and Los Angeles, CA: University of California Press.

Kokkola, L. (2017), 'Critical Plant Studies and Children's Literature', in C. Beauvais and M. Nikolajeva (eds), *The Edinburgh Companion to Children's Literature*, 274–80, Edinburgh: Edinburgh University Press.

Kosky, J. L. (2013), *Arts of Wonder. Enchanting Secularity – Walter de Maria, Diller + Scofidio, James Turrell, Andy Goldsworthy*, Chicago, IL: University of Chicago Press.

Kricher, J. C. (2009), *The Balance of Nature: Ecology's Enduring Myth*, Princeton, NJ: Princeton University Press.

Küppers, B. O. (2016), 'The Nucleation of Semantic Information in Prebiotic Matter', in E. Domingo and P. Schuster (eds), *Quasispecies: From Theory to Experimental Systems*, 23–42, New York: Springer.

Lack, B. (2022), *The Children of the Anthropocene: Stories from the Young People at the Heart of the Climate Crisis*, London: Penguin.

Laist, R. (ed) (2013), *Plants and Literature: Essays in Critical Plant Studies*, Amsterdam: Rodopi.

Laland, K. (2016), 'Evolution Evolves: Beyond the Selfish Gene', *New Scientist*. 21 September. Available online: https://www.newscientist.com/article/mg23130920-600-evolution-evolves-beyond-the-selfish-gene/ (accessed 19 September 2022).

Langer, J. (2011), *Postcolonialism and Science Fiction*, Basingstoke: Palgrave Macmillan.

Large, W. (2015), *Levinas' Totality and Infinity*, London: Bloomsbury.

Latour, B. (1993), *We Have Never Been Modern*, translated by C. Porter, Cambridge, MA: Harvard University Press.

Latour, B. (1996), *Aramis, Or The Love of Technology*, translated by C. Porter, Cambridge, MA: Harvard University Press.

Latour, B. (1999), *Pandora's Hope. Essays on the Reality of Science Studies*, Cambridge, MA: Harvard University Press.

Latour, B. (2014), 'Agency at the Time of the Anthropocene', *New Literary History*, 45 (1): 1–18.

Latour, B. (2017), *Facing Gaia: Eight Lectures on the New Climatic Regime*, translated by C. Porter, Cambridge: Polity Press.

Latour, B. (2018), *Down to Earth. Politics in the New Climatic Regime*, translated by C. Porter, Cambridge: Polity.

Le Guin, U. (2004), 'From Elfland to Poughkeepsie', in D. Sander (ed.), *Fantastic Literature: A Critical Reader*, 144–55, Westport, CT: Praeger.

Lee, N. (2013), Childhood and Biopolitics: Climate Change, Life Processes and Human Futures, London: Palgrave Macmillan.

Leopold, A. (1949), *A Sand County Almanac and Sketches Here and There*, Oxford and London: Oxford University Press.

Levinas, E. (1985), *Ethics and Infinity: Conversations with Philippe Nemo*, translated by Richard Cohen, Pittsburgh: Duquesne University Press.

Levinas, E. (1991), *Totality and Infinity. An Essay on Exteriority*, translated by A. Lingis, Dordrecht, Boston, and London: Kluwer Academic Publishers.

Levy, M. and F. Mendlesohn (2016), *Children's Fantasy Literature: An Introduction*, Cambridge: Cambridge University Press.

Lévy, M. (1988), *Lovecraft: A Study in the Fantastic*, translated by S. T. Joshi, Detroit, MI: Wayne State University Press.

Lillywhite, A. (2017), 'Relational Matters: A Critique of Speculative Realism and a Defence of Non-Reductive Materialism', *Chiasma: A Site for Thought*, 4: 13–39.

Lillywhite, A. (2018), 'Is Posthumanism a Primitivism? Networks, Fetishes, and Race', *Diacritics*, 46 (3): 100–119.

Lovecraft, H. P. (1985), *The H. P. Lovecraft Omnibus 3: The Haunter of the Dark and Other Tale*, edited by A. Derleth and D. Wandrei, London: Grafton Books.

Lovecraft, H. P. (2012), *The Annotated Supernatural Horror in Literature: Revised and Enlarged*, edited by S. T. Joshi, New York: Hippocampus Press.

Lovelock, J. (2000), *Gaia: A New Look at Life on Earth*, Oxford: Oxford University Press.

Luckhurst, R. (2017), 'The Weird: A Dis/Orientation', *Textual Practice*, 31 (6): 1041–61.

Manlove, C. (2003), *From Alice to Harry Potter: Children's Fantasy in England*, Rochester, MN: Cybereditions.

Marder, M. (2013), *Plant-Thinking: A Philosophy of Vegetal Life*, New York: Columbia University Press.

Margolin, J. (2020), *Youth to Power: Your Voice and How to Use It*, New York: Hachette.

Margulis, L. (1998), *The Symbiotic Planet. A New Look at Evolution*, London: Orion Books.

Margulis, L. and D. Sagan (2003), *Acquiring Genomes. A Theory of the Origin of Species*, New York: Basic Books.

Mathews, F. (2003), *For Love of Matter: A Contemporary Panpsychism*, Albany, NY: SUNY Press.

McAnulty, D. (2020), *Diary of a Young Naturalist*, London: Little Toller Books.

McCallum, R. (1999), *Ideologies of Identity in Adolescent Fiction: The Dialogic Construction of Subjectivity*, London: Routledge.

Meillassoux, Q. (2008), 'Time without Becoming', lecture at Middlesex University, 8 May. Available online: https://speculativeheresy.files.wordpress.com/2008/07/3729-time_without_becoming.pdf (accessed 14 March 2019).

Meillassoux, Q. (2009), *After Finitude: An Essay on the Necessity of Contingency*, London: Bloomsbury.

Mentz, S. (2020), *Ocean*, New York: Bloomsbury.

Merchant, C. (1980), *Death of Nature. Women, Ecology and the Scientific Revolution*, San Francisco, CA: Harper and Row.

Merten, K. (2021), 'Diffraction, Reading, and (New) Materialism', in K. Merten (ed.), *Diffractive Reading: New Materialism, Theory, Critique*, 1–28, Lanham, MD: Rowman and Littlefield.

Metzinger, T. (2004), *Being No One: The Self-Model Theory of Subjectivity*, Cambridge, MA: The MIT Press.

Miéville, C. (2008), 'M. R. James and the Quantum Vampire: Weird; Hauntological; Versus And/or and And/ or?', *Collapse*, IV: 105–28.

Miller, E. (2002), *The Vegetative Soul: From Philosophy of Nature to Subjectivity in the Feminine*, Albany, NY: SUNY Press.

Monbiot, G. (2013), *Feral. Rewinding the Land, Sea, and Human Life*, London: Penguin.

Moore, J. W. (2016), 'Introduction. Anthropocene or Capitalocene? Nature, History and the Crisis of Capitalism', in J. W. Moore (ed.), *Anthropocene or Capitalocene?*, 1–13, Oakland, CA: Kairos Books.

Morton, T. (2010), *The Ecological Thought*, Cambridge, MA: Harvard University Press.

Morton, T. (2016), *Dark Ecology. For A Logic of Future Coexistence*, New York: Columbia University Press.

Morton, T. (2017), *Humankind: Solidarity with Nonhuman People*, London: Verso.

Morton, T. (2018), *Being Ecological*, London: Penguin.

Myers, N. (2017), 'From the Anthropocene to the Planthroposcene: Designing Gardens for Plant/People Involution', *History and Anthropology*, 28 (3): 297–301.

Nagel, T. (2012), *Mind and Cosmos: Why the Materialist Neo-Darwinian Conception of Nature is Almost Certainly False*, Oxford: Oxford University Press.

Nakate, V. (2022), *A Bigger Picture: My Fight to Bring a New African Voice to the Climate Crisis*, London: Pan Macmillan.

Nealon, J. (2015), *Plant Theory: Biopower and Vegetable Life*, New York: Columbia University Press.

Negarestani, R. (2008), *Cyclonopedia: Complicity with Anonymous Materials*, Melbourne: Re.press.

Neimanis, A. (2017), *Bodies of Water: Posthuman Feminist Phenomenology*, London and New York: Bloomsbury.

Newell, J. (2020), *A Century of Weird Fiction, 1832–1937: Disgust, Metaphysics and the Aesthetics of Cosmic Horror*, Cardiff: University of Wales Press.

Nixon, R. (2011), *Slow Violence and the Environmentalism of the Poor*, Cambridge, MA: Harvard University Press.

Okorafor, N. (2009), 'Organic Fantasy', *African Identities*, 7 (2): 275–86.

Okorafor, N. (2017) [2011], *Akata Witch*, New York: Speak.

Okorafor, N. (2019), 'Africanfuturism Defined', *Nnedi's Wahala Zone Blog* (blog). 19 October. Available online: http://nnedi.blogspot.com/2019/10/africanfuturism-defined.html (accessed 19 September 2022).

Ongley, J. and R. Carey (2013), *Russell. A Guide for the Perplexed*, London: Bloomsbury.

Onishi, B. (2020), 'Weird Ecologies and the Uncanny in The Happening', in J. Beever (ed.), *Philosophy, Film and the Dark Side of Interdependence*, 157–74, Lanham, MD: Lexington Books.

Palmer-Patel, C. and K. Dodd (2016), 'About Us', *Fantastika Journal*. Website. Available online: https://www.fantastikajournal.com/about-us (accessed 18 January 2022).

Parisi, L. (2017), 'After Nature: The Dynamic Automation of Technical Objects', in J. Weinstein and C. Colebrook (eds), *Posthumous Life: Theorizing Beyond the Posthuman*, 155–78, New York: Columbia University Press.

Pereira, A. and D. Lehmann (eds) (2013), *The Unity of Mind, Brain and World. Current Perspectives on a Science of Consciousness*, Cambridge: Cambridge University Press.

Pickard, S., B. Bowman and D. Arya (2020), '"We Are Radical In Our Kindness": The Political Socialisation, Motivations, Demands and Protest Actions of Young Environmental Activists in Britain', *Youth and Globalization*, 2 (2): 251–80.

Pollan, M. (2013), 'The Intelligent Plant: Scientists Debate a New Way of Understanding Flora', *The New Yorker*. 15 December. Available online: https://www.newyorker.com/magazine/2013/12/23/the-intelligent-plant#main-content (accessed 19 September 2022).

Powell, M. and A. Garner (2010), 'Alan Garner: How I Came to Write a Children's Classic', *The Times*. 1 October. Available online: https://www.thetimes.co.uk/article/alan-garner-how-i-came-to-write-a-childrens-classic-qqspz9d09pz (accessed 20 March 2023).

Prout, A. (2005), *The Future of Childhood: Towards the Interdisciplinary Study of Children*, New York and London: Routledge.

Puig de la Bellacasa, M. (2017), *Matters of Care: Speculative Ethics in More than Human Worlds*, Minneapolis, MN: University of Minnesota Press.

Pullman, P. (2010), *Four Tales*, London: Penguin Random House.

Randall, L. (2017), *Dark Matter and the Dinosaurs: The Astounding Interconnectedness of the Universe*, London: Vintage.

Roske-Martinez, X. and Earth Guardians (2014), 'Speak for the Trees', United Nations Climate Change. 8 July. Available online: https://unfccc.int/news/8-july-2015-this-week-climate-song-for-paris-cop21 (accessed 21 March 2023).

Rovelli, C. (2017), *Reality is Not What it Seems: The Journey to Quantum Gravity*, London: Penguin.

Rovelli, C. (2018), 'Meaning and Intentionality = Information + Evolution', in A. Aguirre, B. Foster and Z. Merali (eds), *Wandering Towards a Goal: How Can Mindless Mathematical Laws Give Rise to Aims and Intention?*, 17–27, New York: Springer.

Russell, B. (1992), *The Analysis of Matter*, London: Routledge.

Ryle, G. (2000), *The Concept of Mind*, London: Penguin.

Sainsbury, L. (2013), *Ethics in British Children's Literature: Unexamined Life*, London: Bloomsbury.

Sainsbury, L. (2021), *Metaphysics of Children's Literature: Climbing Fuzzy Mountains*, London: Bloomsbury.

Schopenhauer, A. (1969), *The World as Will and Representation. Vol 1*, translated by E. F. J. Payne, New York: Dover Press.

Scovell, A. (2015), 'Short Film – Weirdstone (For Alan Garner)', *Celluloid Wicker Man* (blog). 2 February. Available online: https://celluloidwickerman.com/2015/02/02/short-film-weirdstone-for-alan-garner/ (accessed 19 September 2022).

Scovell, A. (2017), *Folk Horror: Hours Dreadful and Things Strange*, Leighton Buzzard: Auteur Press.

Seager, W. E. (2006), 'The "Intrinsic Nature" Argument for Panpsychism', *Journal of Consciousness Studies*, 13 (10–11): 129–45.

Seager, W. E. (2020), 'Introduction: A Panpsychist Manifesto', in W. E. Seager (ed.), *The Routledge Handbook of Panpsychism*, 1–12, Abingdon and New York: Routledge.

Seymour, N. (2013), *Strange Natures. Futurity, Empathy, and the Queer Ecological Imagination*, Urbana, IL: University of Illinois Press.

Seymour, N. (2018), *Bad Environmentalism. Irony and Irreverence in the Ecological Age*, Minneapolis, MN: University of Minnesota Press.

Shakespeare, W. (1939), *The Merry Wives of Windsor 1602* (Shakespeare Quarto Facsimiles No 3), London: The Shakespeare Association & Sedgwick and Jackson.

Sheldon, R. (2016), *The Child to Come: Life After the Human Catastrophe*, Minneapolis, MN: University of Minnesota Press.

Sheldrake, M. (2020), *Entangled Life: How Fungi Make Our Worlds, Change Our Minds & Shape Our Futures*, London: Penguin Random House.

Silverstein, S. (1964), *The Giving Tree*, New York: Harper and Row.

Simard, S. (2021), *Finding the Mother Tree: Uncovering the Wisdom and Intelligence of the Forest*, New York and London: Penguin.

Simard, S. and D. M. Durall (2004), 'Mycorrhizal Networks: A Review of their Extent, Function, and Importance', *Canadian Journal of Botany*, 82: 1140–65.

Song, M. H. (2011), 'Becoming Planetary', *American Literary History*, 23 (3): 555–73.

Sparrow, T. (2014), *End of Phenomenology: Metaphysics and the New Realism*, Edinburgh: Edinburgh University Press.

Spivak, G. C. (1999), *A Critique of Postcolonial Reason: Toward a History of the Vanishing Present*, Cambridge, MA: Harvard University Press.

Spivak, G. C. (2003), *Death of a Discipline*, New York: Columbia University Press.

Spivak, G. C. (2015), '"Planetarity" (Box 4, WELT)', *Paragraph*, 38 (2): 290–2.

Stevenson, K. (2021), 'The Death of Birdsong, the Birdsong of Death: Algernon Charles Swinburne and the Horror of Erosion', in C. Tidwell and C. Soles (eds), *Fear and Nature: Ecohorror Studies in the Anthropocene*, 91–109, University Park, PA: Pennsylvania State University Press.

Strassburg, B. B. N., A. Iribarrem and H. L. Beyer (2020), 'Global Priority Areas for Ecosystem Restoration', *Nature*, 586: 724–9.

Strawson, G. (2016), 'Consciousness Isn't a Mystery. It's Matter', *The New York Times*. 16 May. Available online: https://www.nytimes.com/2016/05/16/opinion/consciousness-isnt-a-mystery-its-matter.html (accessed 31 March 2020).

Taylor, A. (2013), *Reconfiguring the Natures of Childhood*, London: Routledge.

Thacker, E. (2011), *In the Dust of This Planet: Horror of Philosophy Vol. 1*, Winchester: Zero Books.

Thacker, E. (2015), *Starry Speculative Corpse: Horror of Philosophy Vol. 2*, Winchester: Zero Books.

Thew, H., L. Middlemiss and J. Paavola (2020), '"Youth Is Not a Political Position": Exploring Justice Claims-Making in the UN Climate Change Negotiations', *Global Environmental Change*, 61 (March): 102036.

Thomas, E. E. (2019), *The Dark Fantastic: Race and the Imagination from Harry Potter to the Hunger Games*, New York: NYU Press.

Thomas, E. E. (2020), 'Young Adult Literature for Black Lives: Critical and Storytelling Traditions from the African Diaspora', *The International Journal of Young Adult Literature*, 1 (1): 1–15.

Toadvine, T. (2007), 'How Not to Be a Jellyfish', in C. Painter and C. Lotz (eds), *Phenomenology and The Non-Human Animal: At the Limits of Experience*, 39–55, Dordrecht: Springer Netherlands.

Toadvine, T. (2012), 'Enjoyment and Its Discontents. On Separation from Nature in Levinas', in W. Edelglass, J. Hatley and C. Diehm (eds), *Facing Nature. Levinas and Environmental Thought*, 161–89, Pittsburgh, PA: Duquesne University Press.

Tononi, G., M. Boly, M. Massimini and C. Koch (2016), 'Integrated Information Theory: From Consciousness to Its Physical Substrate', *Nature Reviews Neuroscience*, 17 (7): 450–61.

Tsing, A. (2015), *The Mushroom at the End of the World: On the Possibility of Life in Capitalist Ruins*, Princeton, NJ: Princeton University Press.

van der Tuin, I. and R. Dolphijn (2012), '"There Is Contingent Being Independent of Us, and This Contingent Being Has No Reason to Be of a Subjective Nature" – Interview with Quentin Meillassoux', in I. van der Tuin and R. Dolphijn (eds), *New Materialism: Interviews & Cartographies*, Ann Arbor, MI: Open Humanities Press.

van der Tuin, I., R. Dolphijn and K. Barad (2010), '"Matter Feels, Converses, Suffers, Desires, Yearns and Remembers" – Interview with Karen Barad', in I. van der Tuin and R. Dolphijn (eds), *New Materialism: Interviews & Cartographies*, Ann Arbor, MI: Open Humanities Press.

Turnbull, J. (2021), 'Weird', *Environmental Humanities*, 13 (1): 275–80.

Tylor, E. B. (1873), *Primitive Culture. Researches into the Development of Mythology, Philosophy, Religion, Language, Art and Custom in Two Volumes. Second Edition. Vol. 2*, London: John Murray.

Velmans, M. (2012), 'Reflexive Monism Psychophysical Relations Among Mind, Matter, and Consciousness', *Journal of Consciousness Studies*, 19 (9–10): 143–65.

Vetlesen, A. J. (2019), *Cosmologies of the Anthropocene. Panpsychism, Animism and the Limits of Posthumanism*, Oxon and New York: Routledge.

Voigt, A. (2010), 'The Rise of Systems Theory in Ecology', in A. Schwarz and K. Jax (eds), *Ecology Revisited: Reflecting on Concepts, Advancing Science*, 183–94, New York: Springer.

Wagner, A. (2007), 'From Bit to It: How a Complex Metabolic Network Transforms Information into Living Matter', *BMC Systems Biology*, 1 (1): 33.

Wake, P. (2009), 'Waiting in the Hundred Acre Wood: Childhood, Narrative and Time in A. A. Milne's Works for Children', *The Lion and the Unicorn*, 33 (1): 26–43.

Walker, S. I. (2018), 'Bio from Bit', in A. Aguirre, B. Foster and Z. Merali (eds), *Wandering Towards a Goal: How Can Mindless Mathematical Laws Give Rise to Aims and Intention?*, 77–87, New York: Springer.

Walker, S. I., P. Davies and G. Ellis (eds) (2017), *From Matter to Life: Information and Causality*, Cambridge: Cambridge University Press.

Wall Kimmerer, R. (2013), *Braiding Sweetgrass. Indigenous Wisdom, Scientific Knowledge and the Teachings of Plants*, London: Penguin.

Weinstein, J. and C. Colebrook (2017a), 'Preface: Postscript on the Posthuman', in J. Weinstein and C. Colebrook (eds), *Posthumous Life: Theorizing Beyond the Posthuman*, ix–xxix, New York: Columbia University Press.

Weinstein, J. and C. Colebrook (2017b), 'Introduction: Critical Life Studies and the Problems of Inhuman Rites and Posthumous Life', in J. Weinstein and C. Colebrook (eds), *Posthumous Life: Theorizing Beyond the Posthuman*, 1–16, New York: Columbia University Press.

Woodward, W. and E. Lemmer (2019), 'Introduction: Critical Plant Studies', *Journal of Literary Studies*, 35 (4): 23–7.

Wheeler, J. A. (1989), 'Information, Physics, Quantum: The Search for Links', *Proceedings of the Third International Symposium on Foundations of Quantum Mechanics*: 354–8.

Whitehead, A. N. (1967), *Science and the Modern World*, New York: The Free Press.

Whitfield, J. (2007), 'Fungal Roles in Soil Ecology: Underground Networking', *Nature*, 449: 136–8.

Wiener, N. (1965), *Cybernetics, or Control and Communication in the Animal and the Machine*, Cambridge, MA: The MIT Press.

Willerslev, R. (2007), *Soul Hunters: Hunting, Animism, and Personhood among the Siberian Yukaghirs*, Oakland, CA: University of California Press.

Williams, D. (2020), 'Witches, Monsters, and Questions of Nation: Humans and Non-Humans in *Akata Witch* and Trail of Lightning', *International Journal of Young Adult Literature*, 1 (1): 1–19.

Wohlleben, P. (2016), *The Hidden Life of Trees*, translated by Jane Billinghurst, Vancouver, BC: Greystone Books.

Wohlleben, P. (2021), *The Heartbeat of Trees*, translated by Jane Billinghurst, London: William Collins.

Wolf-Meyer, M. J. (2019), *Theory for the World to Come: Speculative Fiction and Apocalyptic Anthropology*, Minneapolis, MN: University of Minnesota Press.

Ziarek, E. P. (2001), *An Ethics of Dissensus: Postmodernity, Feminism, and the Politics of Radical Democracy*, Stanford, CA: Stanford University Press.

Index

www.ingramcontent.com/pod-product-compliance
Lightning Source LLC
Chambersburg PA
CBHW070529100726
47907CB00004B/1037

* 9 7 8 1 3 5 0 4 1 7 2 7 4 *